THE CRITMAKER™ GUIDE TO DICE CRAFT
A.J. WEATHERALL

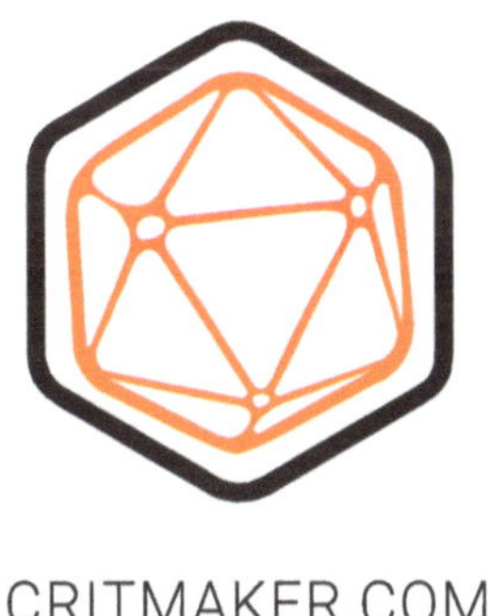

CRITMAKER.COM

The Critmaker Guide to Dice Craft by A.J. Weatherall

2nd Edition 2024

Critmaker.com

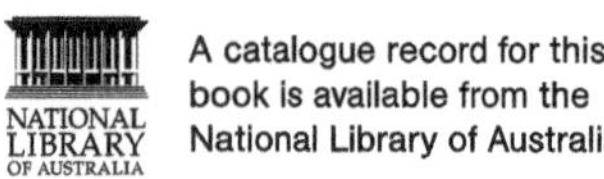

A catalogue record for this book is available from the National Library of Australia

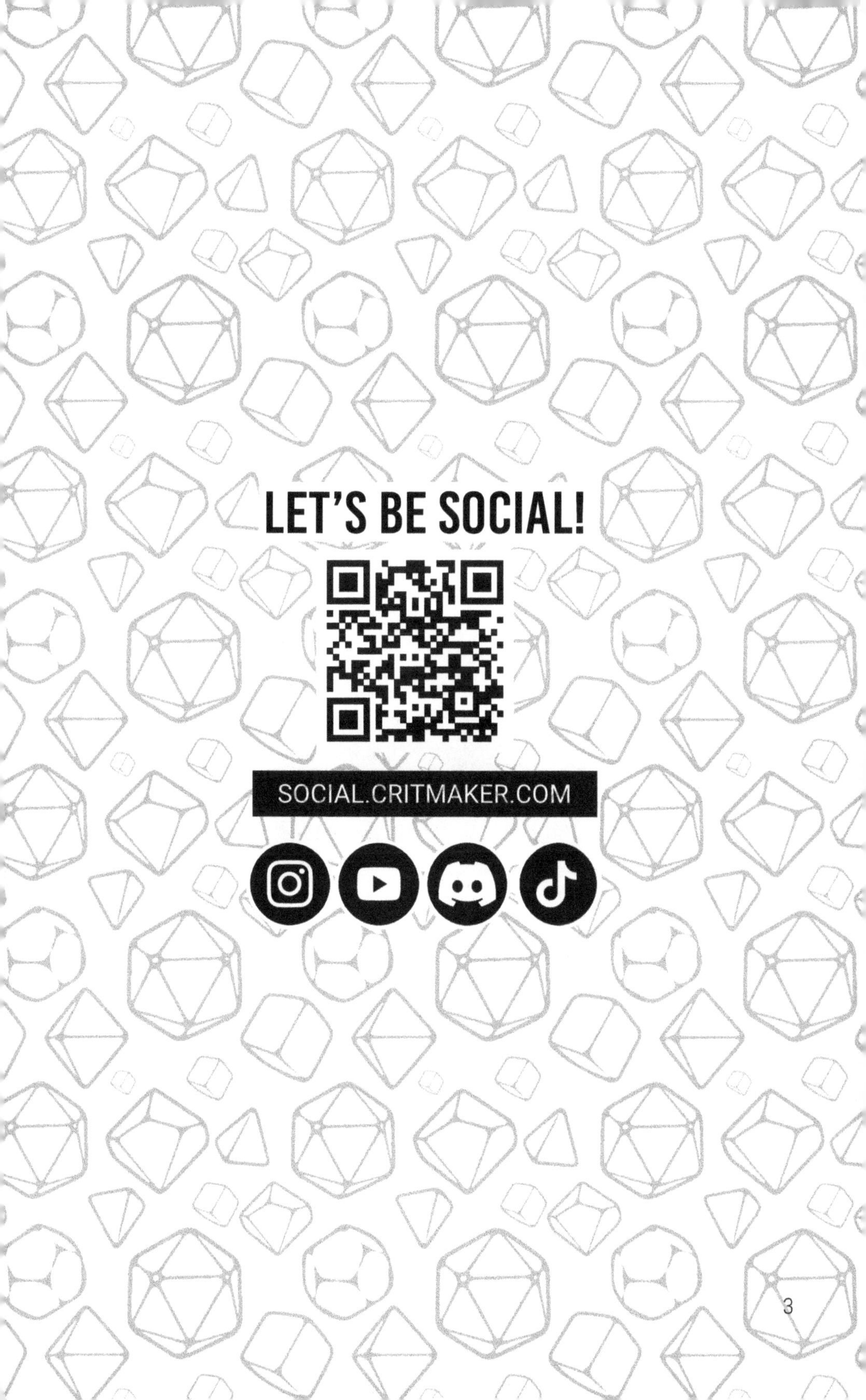

LET'S BE SOCIAL!
SOCIAL.CRITMAKER.COM

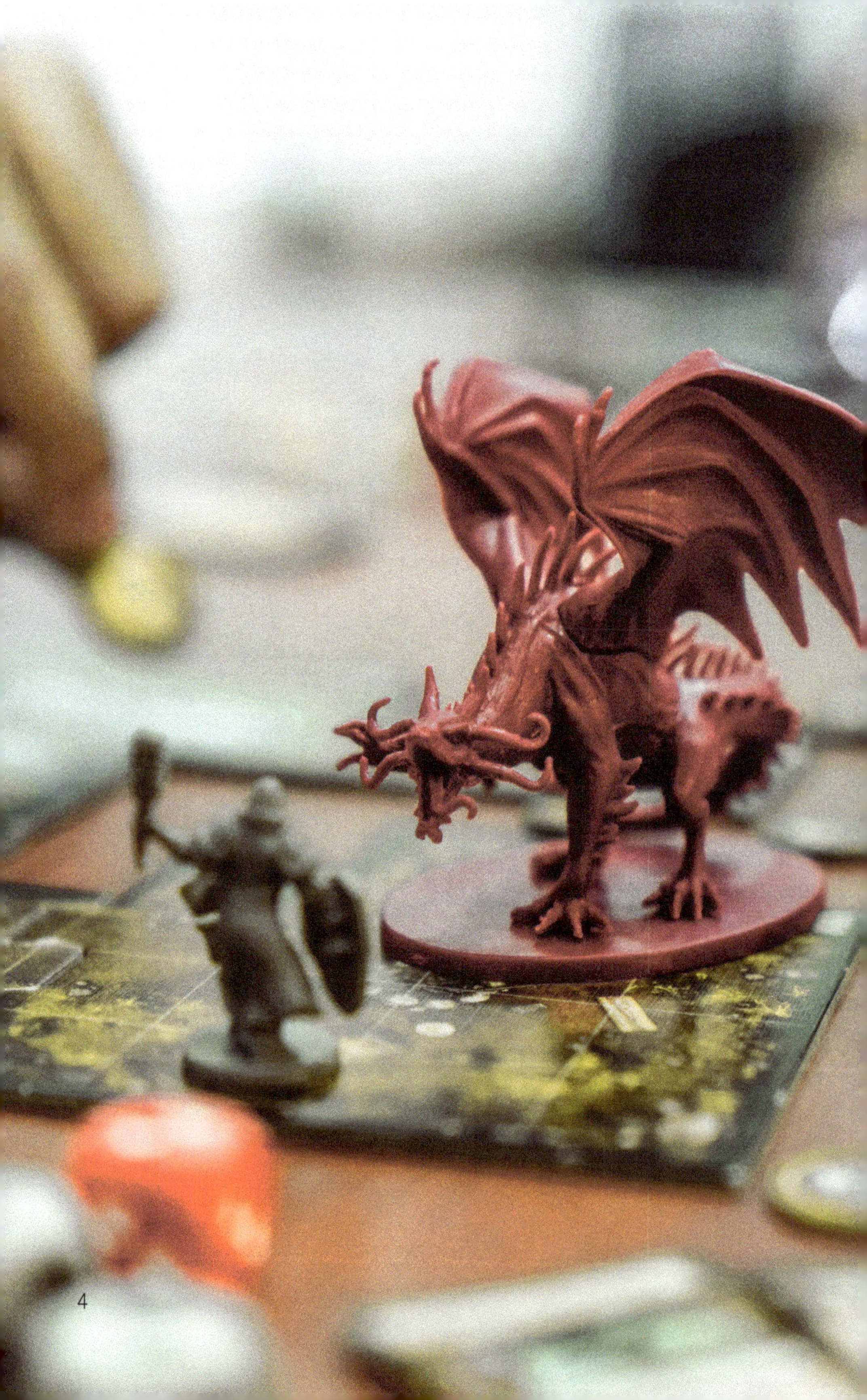

INTRODUCTION

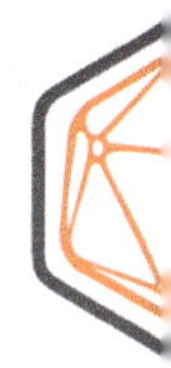

The best ideas don't just materialise, they're more often the result of an overlap in a life-sized Venn diagram. This concept is often referred to as the cross-pollination of ideas – when two or more things overlap, something new is born. Like many others living with ADHD, I've found the "hobby trap" is a very real thing. You find something interesting, obsess over it, research it, try it, get bored of it and move on. The constant cycle of interest and expertise can be incredibly frustrating to those around us (and ourselves). However, the constant flow of hobbies and interests does make for some interesting ideas!

When I left my job in 2023, I set out to find something that could combine all my passions into one. Making, writing, educating, social marketing, web development and design. Combined with my countless hobbies over the years, Critmaker™ was born. A brand that can help people to do the things they love. Help new people find the excitement that comes from a new hobby. Help express their passion to others. And to help grow an already incredible, close-knit community of exceptional makers.

When I sat down to write this, it was originally going to be a four-page booklet to include in our dice-making kits. But, as I reflected on all the things that I'd learned, I realised I couldn't compress it down into so few pages. This book covers the basics of dice craft and more advanced topics to help you perfect your dice and even scale your hobby into a business.

WHAT INSPIRED THIS GUIDE?

Like many others, I was heavily into role-playing and war gaming during high school. My friends and I would play D&D on Saturday mornings, followed by lengthy campaigns of Warhammer 40k and Magic: The Gathering.

I collected many dice over the years, but as time progressed, my dice moved from pride of place down into the "drawers of random objects and cables" before finally settling under a layer of dust.

Thanks to the global pandemic as well as Critical Role and Stranger Things, D&D hit new heights – an activity that could connect people even when they couldn't physically be with each other.

For those outside of Australia, Melbourne had one of the longest and most strict lock-downs in the world – over *262 days* of being unable to leave the house except for a few specific reasons. Many gaming groups and communities sprang up, and thanks to the forced evolution of video platforms and tools like DnDBeyond, virtual gaming became more accessible than ever.

Friends of mine had started a campaign remotely and invited my wife and me to play a couple of one-shot adventures – and we're still playing with the same group every Wednesday night! Returning to the swing of D&D rekindled my love for dice, and it turns out I'm not alone in this renaissance. Thousands of makers proudly show their creations, make tutorials, sell their wares at conventions and push the boundaries of what's possible with resin art.

A guide like this is only possible with the incredible community of dice makers who have pioneered this hobby. Thanks for coming on this journey with me, and I hope you enjoy this guide!

Aaron!

ABOUT CRITMAKER

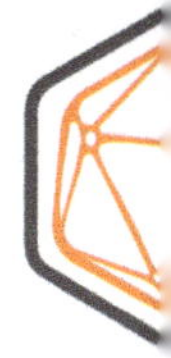

Critmaker.com is an online store, label and publisher. We specialise in education, supplies for dice and mould-making, dice-making kits, apparel and merchandise.

WE'RE NOT THE CRITMAKER, <u>YOU ARE</u>!

A Critmaker is someone passionate about dice craft and bringing new handmade creations into the world. As the back of the book says, a Critmaker is someone who wields the hand of fate and whose creations change any mundane encounter into an adventure!

Our only goal is to see more dice fans become makers and to keep the learning curve as easy as possible to help grow the community.

To help support makers, we've also built an amazing dice-making community on Discord. Come join us!
(Scan QR code or <u>bit.ly/critmaker</u>).

To the dice makers reading this: I am in awe of the incredible, creative images that fill my social feeds. You are the real heroes, the real Critmakers! Our only job is to support your passion.

If we can do anything to make your lives easier or inspire new and upcoming dice makers, we're here to help.

CRITMAKER.COM

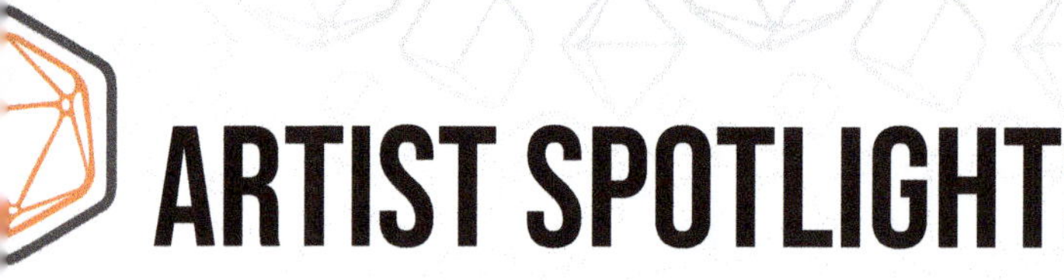

ARTIST SPOTLIGHTS

Throughout this book, I've showcased dice by talented artists. These pieces are inspirational and something we can all aspire to.

As a new dice-maker, it's easy to look at images like these and feel a bit disheartened (I know I have!). The fact is that these makers have (in most cases) been at it for years and have honed their art to amazing levels. Instead of feeling discouraged, try to take them as aspirational, learn from their techniques and develop your own over time!

No one starts with perfect dice, just as no one starts anything and is naturally an expert! It's easy to go down the rabbit hole of self-doubt when as you scroll through your Instagram feed. Be mindful of the fact that people don't generally post their failures or imperfect art there either!

I guarantee that every dice maker featured here has a box of dice that just weren't good enough for their Instagram account!

ALL ARTWORK USED IN THIS GUIDE HAS BEEN INCLUDED WITH THE PERMISSION OF THE ORIGINAL ARTISTS, *PLEASE FOLLOW THEM* ON SOCIALS AND BUY THEIR DICE!

OTHER MEDIUMS

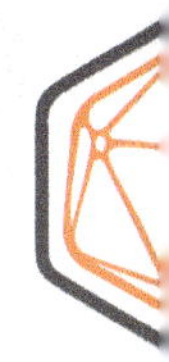

While this book is about the creation of resin dice, it's important to call out that it's not the only way to make them! Well before the "resin revolution", dice were made of wood, stone, glass, bone, semi-precious stones and a large number of other materials.

- Wood, with its natural grains and textures, serves as a rich canvas for woodworkers and resin artists seeking to meld different mediums.

- Semi-precious stones and crystals bring luxury to the table. Talented artisans highlight the innate, natural beauty of these materials using traditional lapidary faceting techniques.

- Bone stands out as a traditional and highly sought-after medium for crafting dice, appealing to collectors and connoisseurs alike. Artists use traditional bone carving and scrimshaw techniques which can set a collector back a huge sum of money. Note: please check that your supplier uses ethically sourced materials.

- Ceramic is another beautiful medium that brings a sense of fragility and old-world beauty to dice. We have a spotlight from one of my favourite artists, FightingChanceStudio on page 142. Their dice are moulded and fired using traditional ceramic techniques.

- Jesmonite and Polymer clay are both incredible mediums for making dice too. Both can be moulded in standard silicone moulds but produce rich colours and textures that cannot be achieved with resin.

While many artists specialise in one thing, it can be exciting to break free from the limitations of a single medium. Experimenting with textures, colours and forms can bring depth and complexity to your creations.

Different materials require different equipment, specialised skills and a level of artistry beyond what I'm capable of.

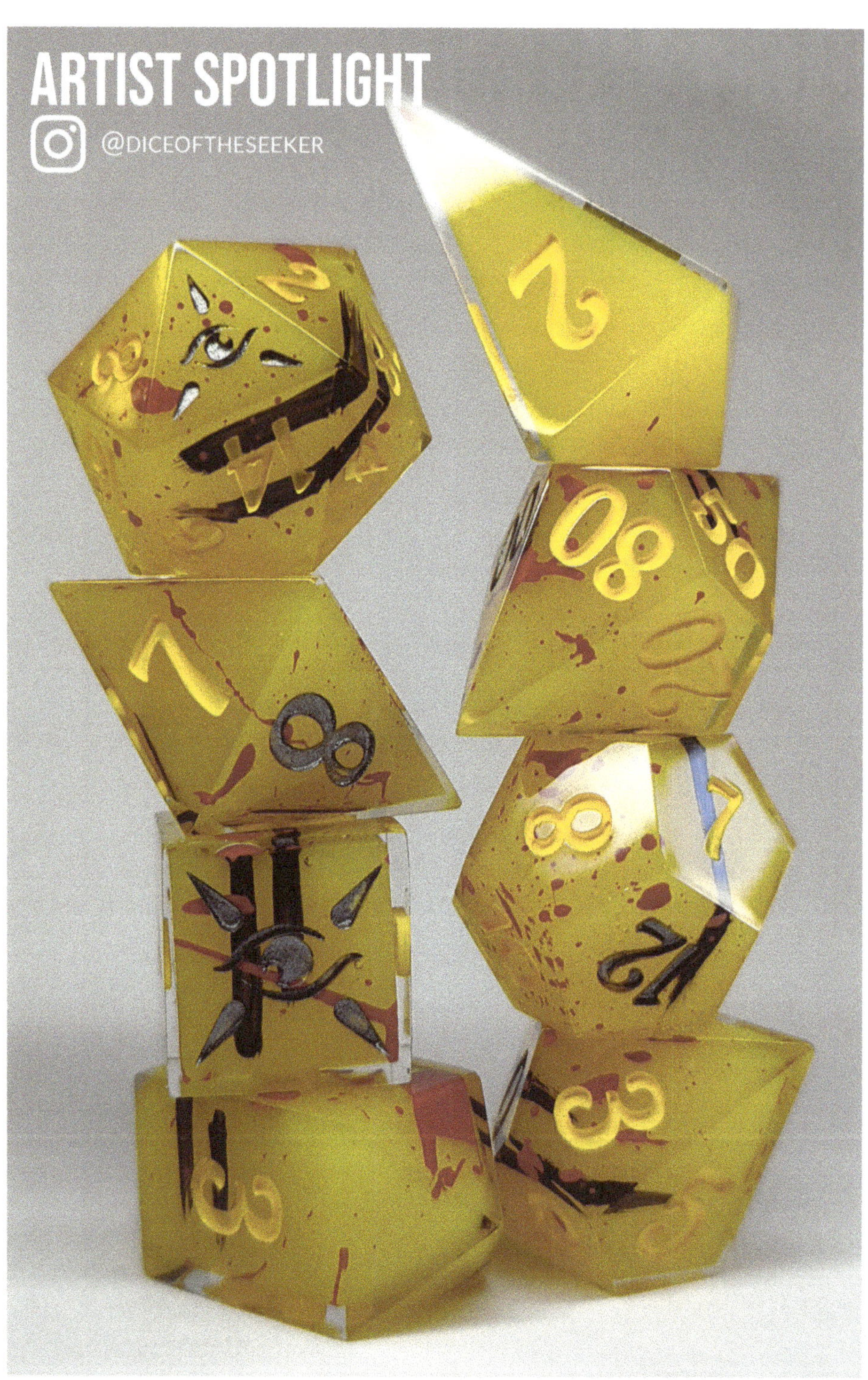

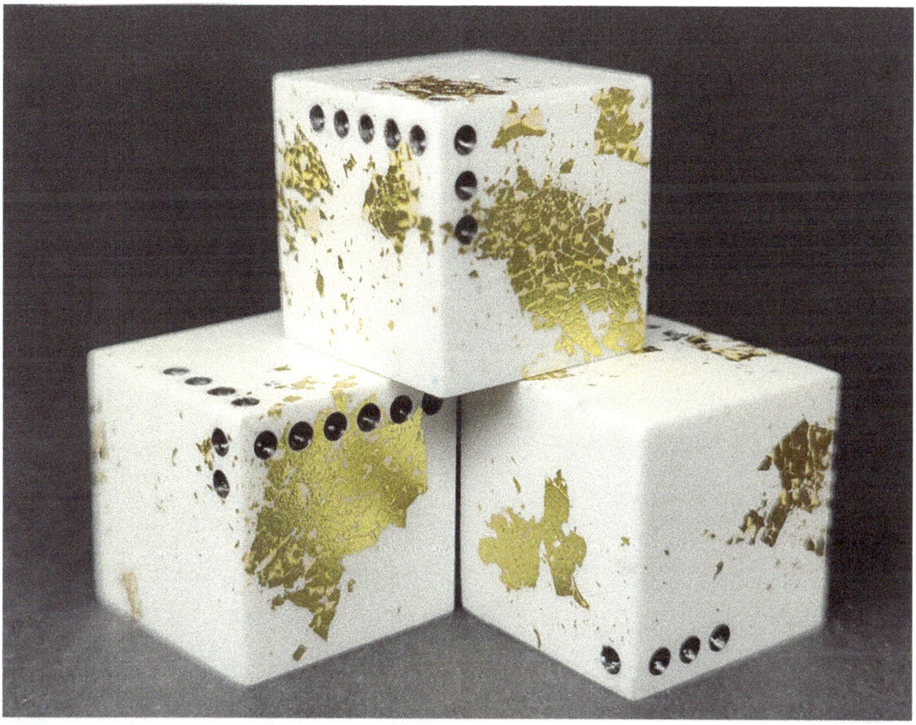

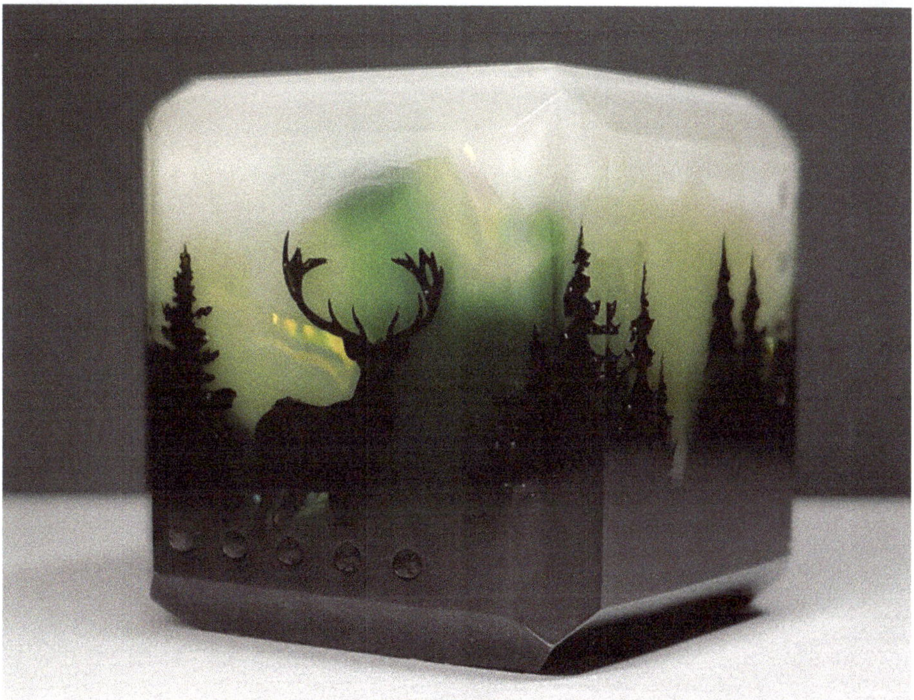

CONTENTS

USING THIS GUIDE

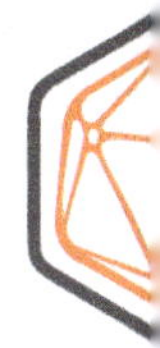

In this guide, we use symbols at the top of each page to show the topic's difficulty level. We also show any recommended Personal Protective Equipment (PPE).

LEVEL RECOMMENDATIONS

LEVEL: (1) 2 3 4

For everyone, from beginners to the most advanced.

LEVEL: 1 (2) 3 4

For intermediate dice-makers who want to improve their craft.

LEVEL: 1 2 (3) 4

For advanced makers who want to create their own moulds.

LEVEL: 1 2 3 (4)

For professional dice-makers who want to make production easier and make their own dice masters.

SAFETY RECOMMENDATIONS

Pages containing PPE symbols show what safety gear we recommend. Topics without a recommendation are either informational or do not involve hazardous items. Items in black we deem essential, and grey are optional unless specified in the Safety Data Sheet (SDS).

PPE:

THESE *RECOMMENDATIONS* <u>DO NOT</u> REPLACE ANY *REQUIREMENTS* MADE IN THE SDS FOR YOUR MATERIALS.

ARTIST SPOTLIGHT

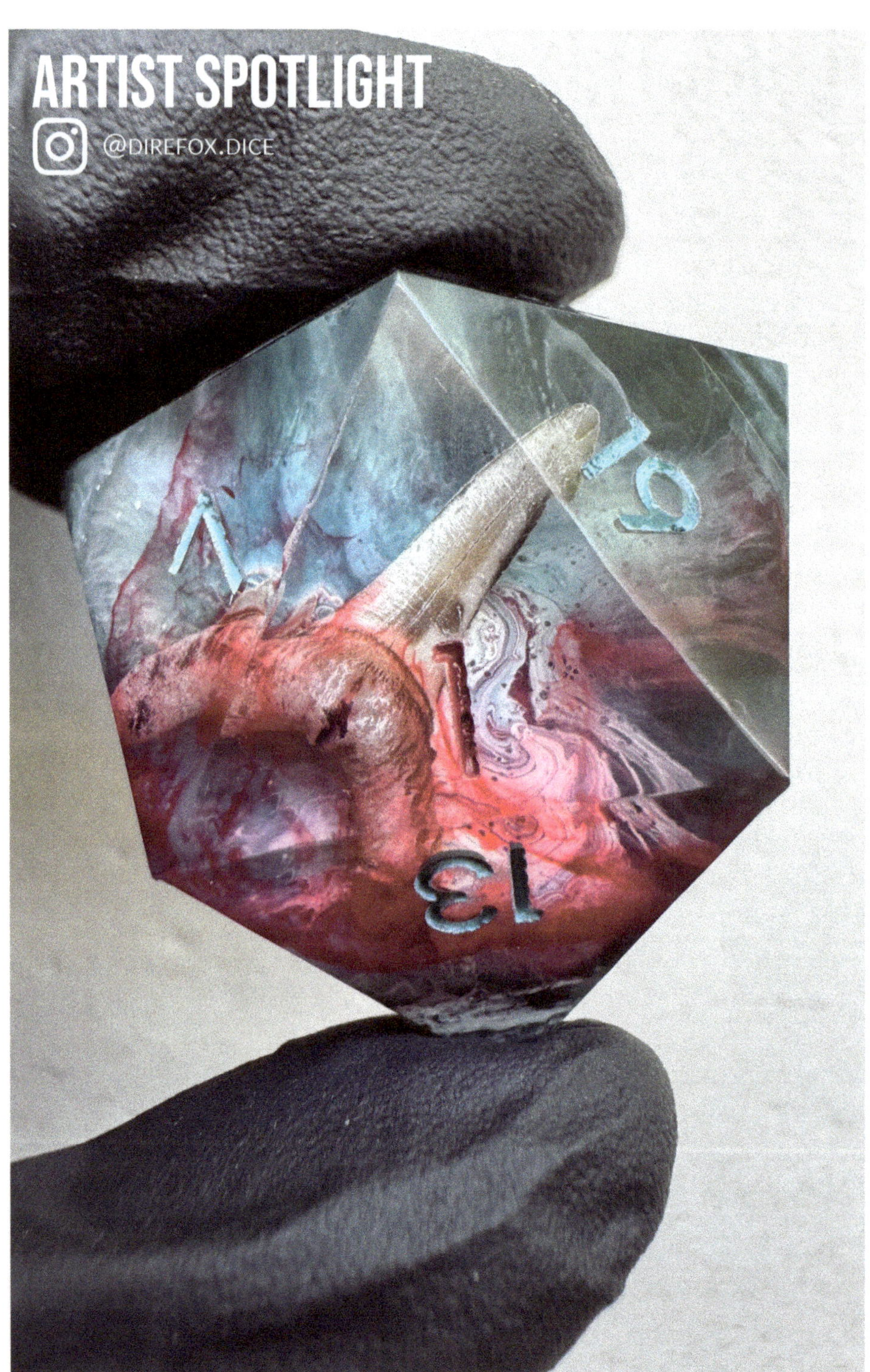

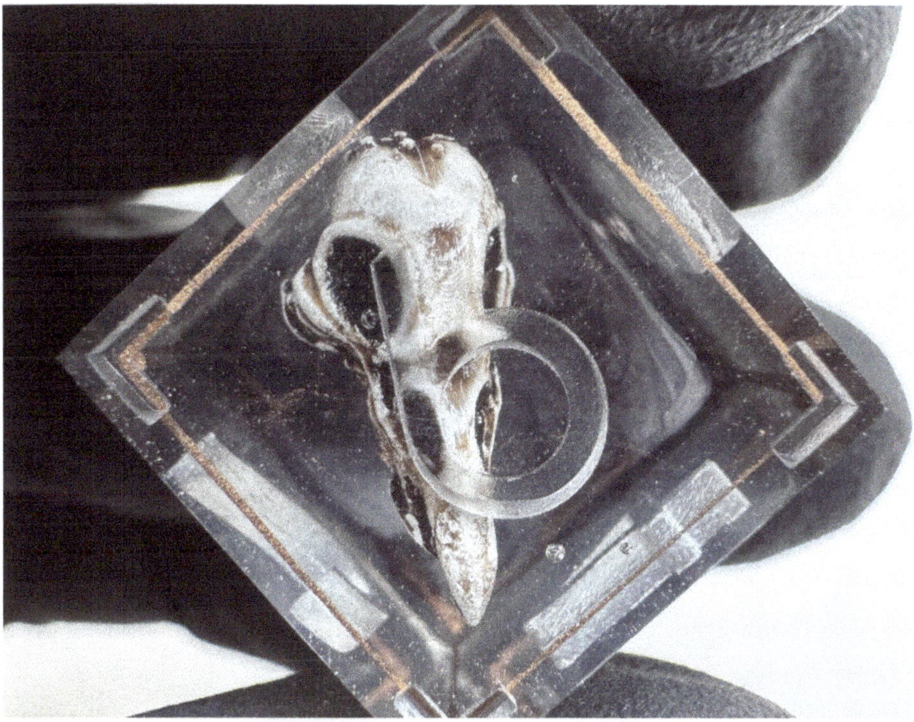

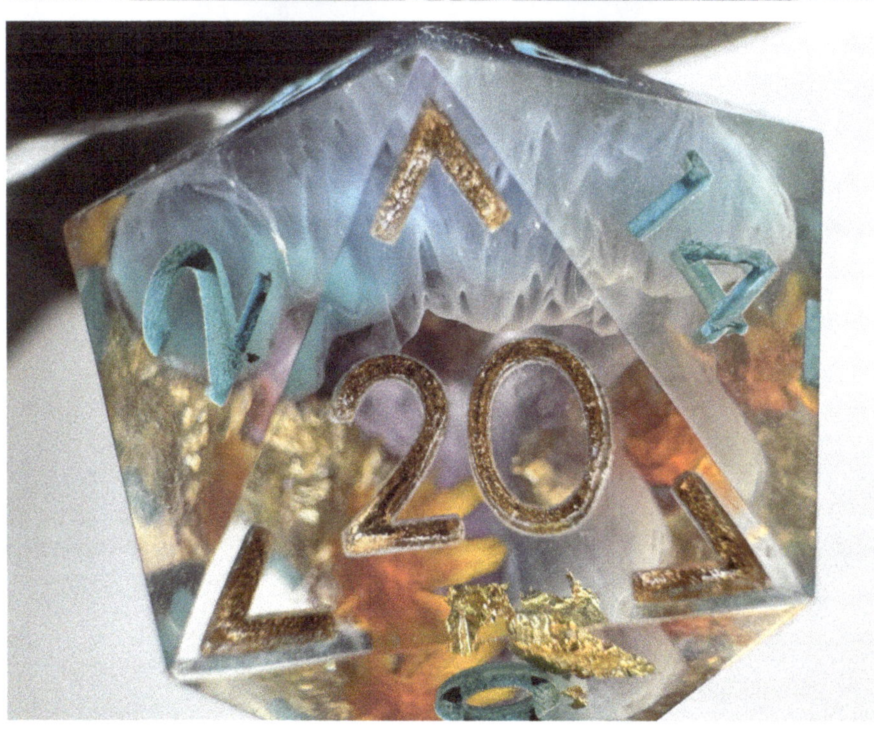

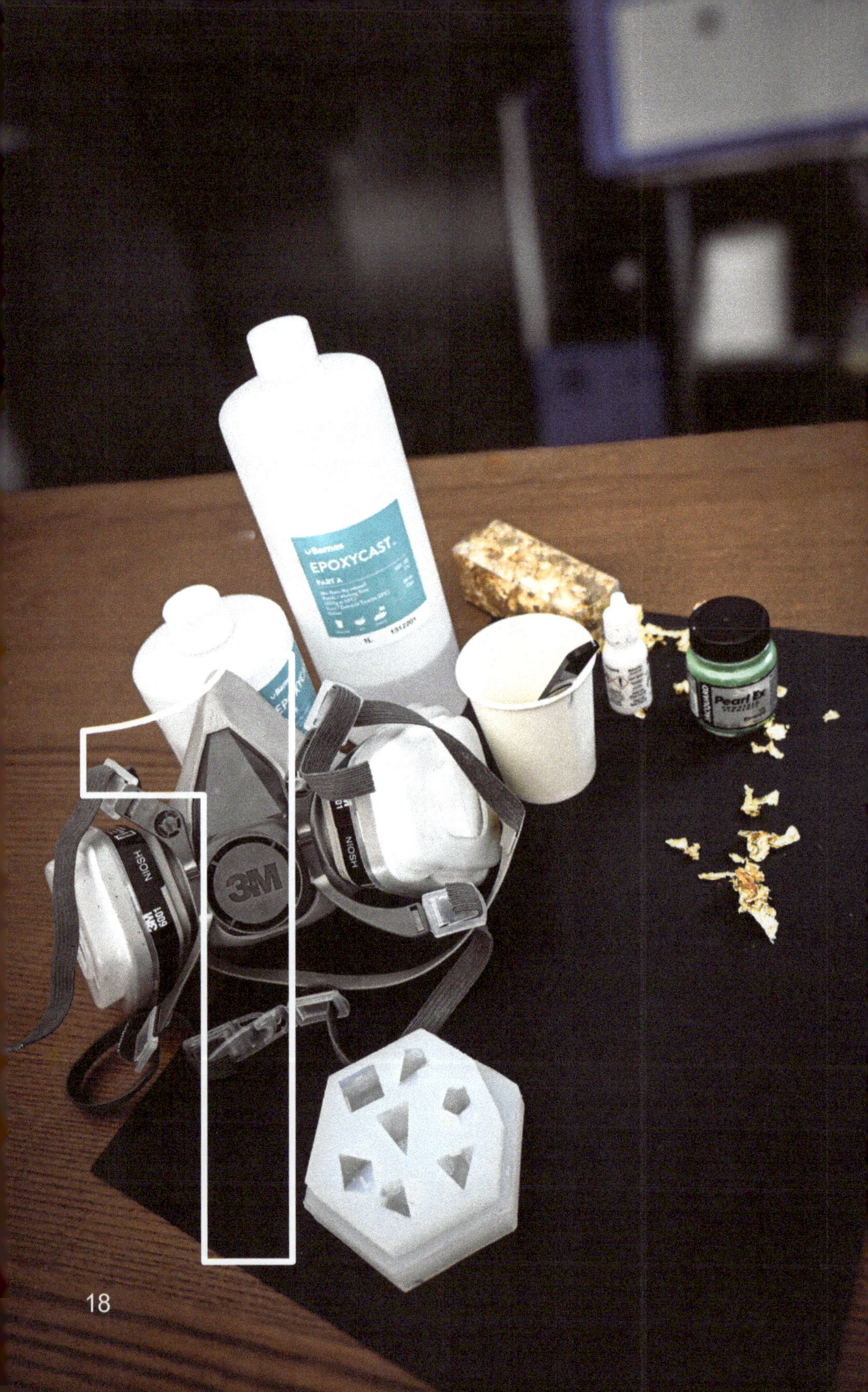
EPOXYCAST
PART A
Pearl Ex

GETTING STARTED

In this section, we'll cover the basic requirements for each stage of your dice-making journey including the correct safety equipment. We've also included a handy shopping list for those getting started!

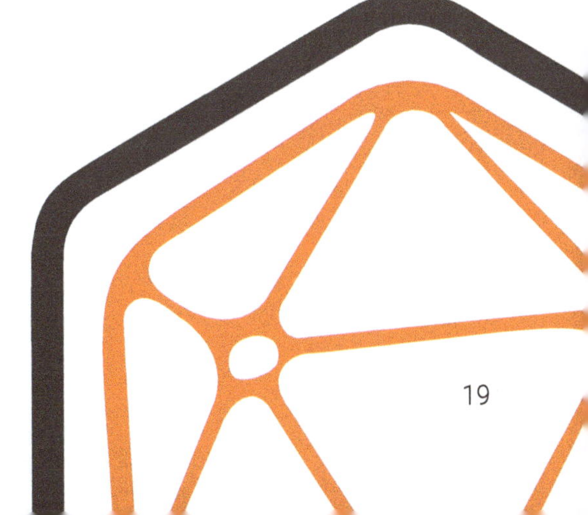

PART ONE

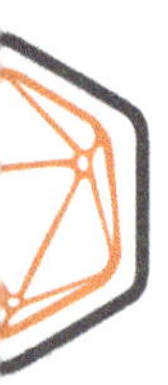

RESIN SAFETY

LEVEL:  **1**   2   3   4

Working with resin can be enjoyable, but, it's essential to take necessary precautions to protect yourself. While cured resin is typically non-toxic, uncured resin can be dangerous if improperly handled. Exposure to hardening agents before and during the curing process can result in poisoning and other health issues. When using resin, *children must be supervised at all times* and resin products must be locked out of reach.

There are *four ways* uncured resin can be dangerous but not limited to:

Toxic Fumes
Inhaling excessive amounts of epoxy vapour can cause nose, eye, and throat irritation. It can also lead to respiratory problems like asthma.

Ingestion
Extensive damage to the mouth, throat, eyes, lungs, oesophagus, nose, and stomach are possible. The outcome depends on the extent of this damage.

Direct Contact
Direct contact with unmixed and uncured resin can lead to skin allergies and irritation, such as redness, swelling, and itching.

Dust During Sanding
Sanding resin can release dust. This dust can cause issues similar to fumes.

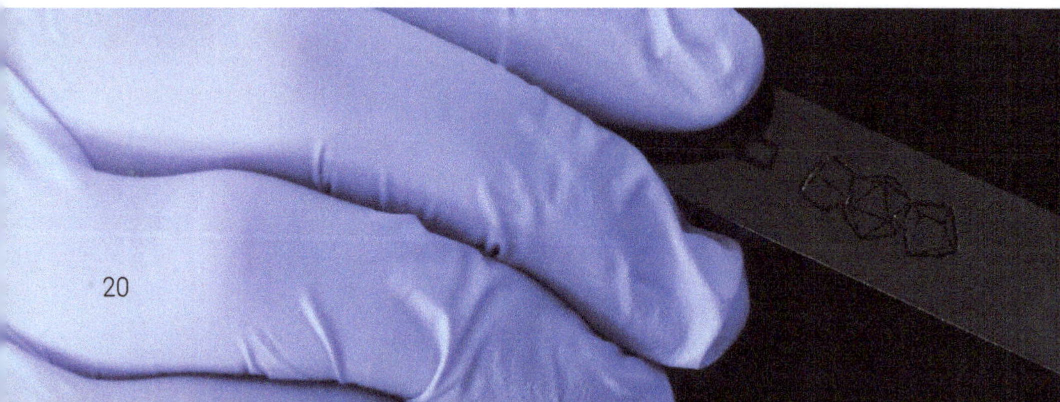

READ THE SAFETY DATA SHEET (SDS)

You *must* read the SDS for both parts A and B of your resin to ensure safe handling and instructions in an emergency. The SDS will be different for each new resin product you buy meaning the requirements for one may not be sufficient for another. Most manufacturers recommend gloves, goggles, and a respirator suited to organic vapour. *Note: an N95 mask is not sufficient to protect you from resin vapour.*

Additionally, it's *crucial* to work in a well-ventilated area.

By taking a few simple precautions, you can safely enjoy working with resin while protecting you, your family, and the environment.

EVERY RESIN SHOULD COME WITH AN SDS SHEET. IF THERE ISN'T ONE, ASK THE SUPPLIER FOR IT. IF THEY DON'T HAVE ONE, CHOOSE A DIFFERENT SUPPLIER.

RECOMMENDED PPE

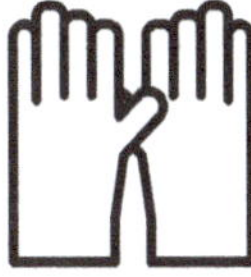 Nitrile Gloves

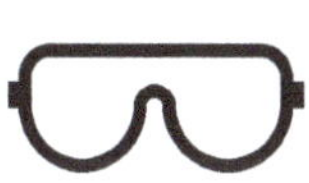 Protective Goggles

 Respirator suited to organic vapours

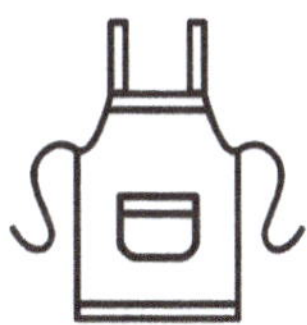 Apron to protect your clothes

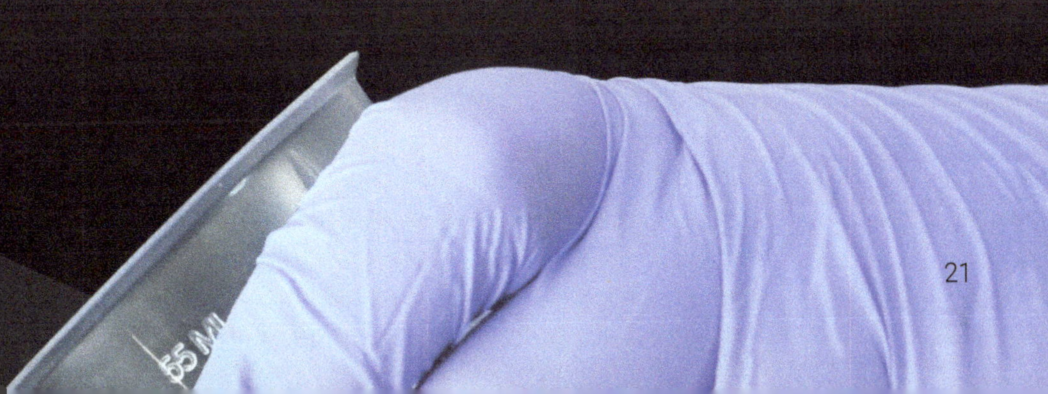

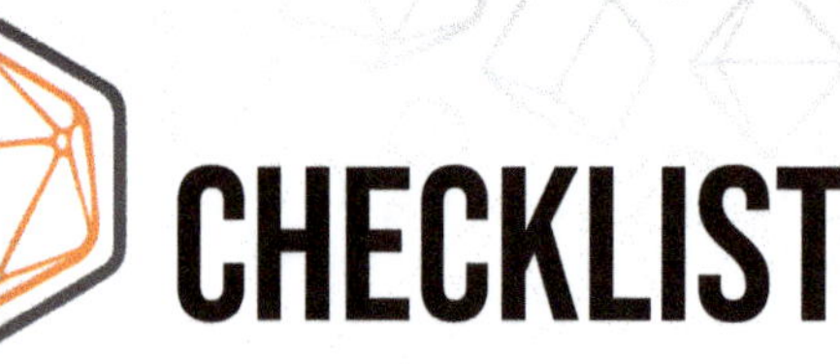

CHECKLIST

LEVEL: ① 2 3 4

SHOPPING LIST

For those starting out, you'll need the following items. We cover each of these in more detail in the coming chapters.

If you purchased one of our kits (available at critmaker.com), you'll need PPE, epoxy resin and a long neck lighter!

- [ ] Half face respirator – suited to organic vapour
- [ ] Nitrile gloves (not silicone or latex)
- [ ] Safety glasses
- [ ] An apron to cover your clothing
- [ ] A dice mould
- [ ] Epoxy resin
- [ ] Mix-ins (mica powder, glitter, etc.)
- [ ] Polishing papers
- [ ] Stirrers
- [ ] 60mL / 2oz measuring cups
- [ ] Acrylic paint & brush
- [ ] Long neck lighter
- [ ] Silicone mat – to keep your workspace clean

EQUIPMENT BY LEVEL

LEVEL: **1**   2   3   4

LEVEL ONE *You're just getting started, and some bubbles are okay!*

Personal Protective Equipment (PPE)

Always read the Safety Data Sheet (SDS) for your resin and obey any recommendations. You'll need a respirator suited to organic vapour. Also, wear nitrile gloves, safety glasses, and an apron to protect your clothes. See "Resin Safety" on page 20.

Dice Mould

The mould has imprints of the dice. Hundreds of makers are selling great-looking moulds (or make one yourself - see "Mould Making" on page 118).

Epoxy Resin

We cover this in "Which Resin?" on page 29.

Measuring Cups

Most resins are measured by volume, so you'll need disposable measuring cups. Small 60mL / 2oz cups are great for dice making as well as cardboard cups for mixing.

Mix-Ins

Dice-making uses four main mix-ins: mica powder, resin pigment, alcohol ink and glitter. ALL. THE. GLITTER. See "Choosing Mix-Ins" on page 32.

Polishing Papers

3M/Zona polishing papers are the gold standard in dice polishing. You'll need them all from 30 to 1 micron. See "Polishing Paper" on page 31.

Stirrers

Simple wooden sticks or tongue depressors are great. Some resin casters avoid using them because they can transfer air trapped in the wood into the resin. Grab some decent stirrers from Amazon or the Critmaker store.

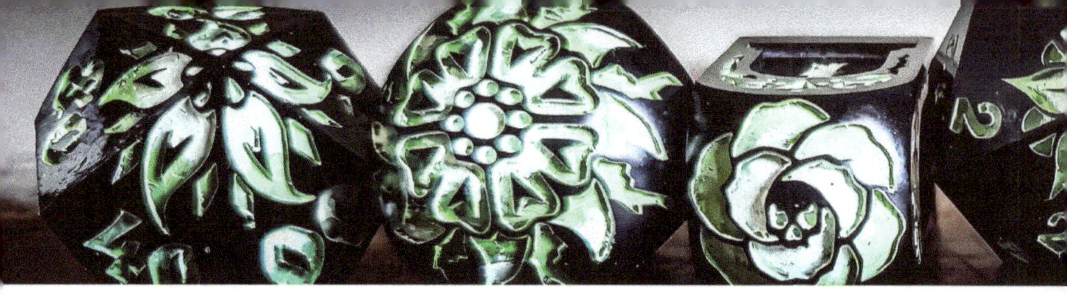

Acrylic Paint + Brush

You will be using acrylic paint to ink your dice (fill in the numbers). Golds and silvers are best for your first dice!

Long Neck Lighter

A long neck lighter is helpful for popping surface bubbles. Avoid using a butane lighter, as the high heat can burn your silicone moulds.

Silicone Mat

Any baking-style mat is fine; resin won't stick to silicone, so it's easy to clean even if cured.

Isopropyl Alcohol (IPA)

This is great to keep on hand to clean up any spills and cleanse your work surfaces after your pouring session. Be mindful of fumes and refer to the SDS.

Plastic Storage Containers

The longer you work with dice, the more mix-ins you'll collect. We keep these in handy clear plastic storage containers.

LEVEL TWO *You want more consistent results and bubbles gone forever.*

This level requires some investment, including an air compressor and pressure pot. This equipment will improve your dice *dramatically*. But, it won't help you get better at the artistic side of dice craft!

Air Compressor

Any compressor with at least 10L (2½ gal) capacity will work best. We recommend a "silent" or "quiet" compressor if working indoors.

Pressure Pot

A pressure pot compresses bubbles in resin and silicone, giving crystal-clear castings every time. See "Pressure Casting" on page 62.

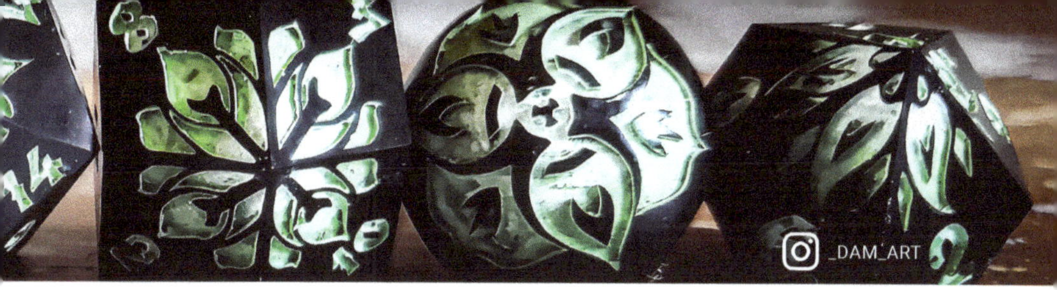

Pressure Pot Insert

You'll want a flat surface in your pressure pot and, most likely, shelves to produce more dice. We sell these in kit form for most pressure pots.

Mini Pottery Wheel

This can save hours in sanding. See "Mini Pottery Wheel" on page 76.

Rotary Tool

A rotary tool like a Dremel is not only great for polishing, but some great effects too such as "geodes" or "kintsugi" style dice. See "Rotary Tool" on page 77.

Polishing Compound

We recommend 3M Perfect-It, Meguiar's PlastX or Chemical Guys V34. They're arguably the best polishes in the world – and happen to be incredible for polishing dice. If you find a better brand, be sure to let us know on our Discord!

LEVEL THREE *You want to make your own moulds.*

Mould Frame

You can use almost any container from a simple PVC pipe, Lego bricks, or our own Critmaker mould makers for more consistent results.

Silicone

You'll need silicone. LOTS. OF. SILICONE for mould making. We'll discuss silicone in detail in "Silicone Basics" on page 107.

Scales

Many silicones are measured *by weight* meaning that you will need some accurate digital scales to mix correctly. Grab a decent set from Amazon or your local homewares store.

Cuticle Trimmers

These are the "hands down" the best thing for removing flashing from silicone moulds. Grab a pack of them from our store or Amazon.

LEVEL FOUR *You're ready to increase production and make your own masters.*

Vibratory Tumbler
A vibratory tumbler "vibrates" various media to polish the dice over a long period. The best media type for dice is 3-4mm ceramic beads, which give a perfect shine over 24-48 hours. See "Vibratory Tumbler" on page 78.

Dehydrator
It allows faster curing of dice that contain alcohol inks or during colder weather. You can use any dehydrator, but you cannot use it for food afterwards. See "Dehydrator" on page 80.

Ultrasonic Cleaner
An ultrasonic cleaner makes clean-up after tumbling trivial! Pop the dice in for 10-20 minutes, and they're perfect. See "Ultrasonic Cleaner" on page 79.

Resin Printer
You'll need a quality resin printer to print dice masters. We recommend high-resolution Elegoo Mars or Saturn series printers. See "3D Printers" on page 133.

Dice Models
Most dice makers either use a dedicated dice generating application or design them in a 3D modelling tool. See "Designing Masters" on page 134.

Magnifying Light
This is a must-have tool for preparing your masters. It allows you to see the finest imperfections and micro-scratches. Grab one on Amazon.

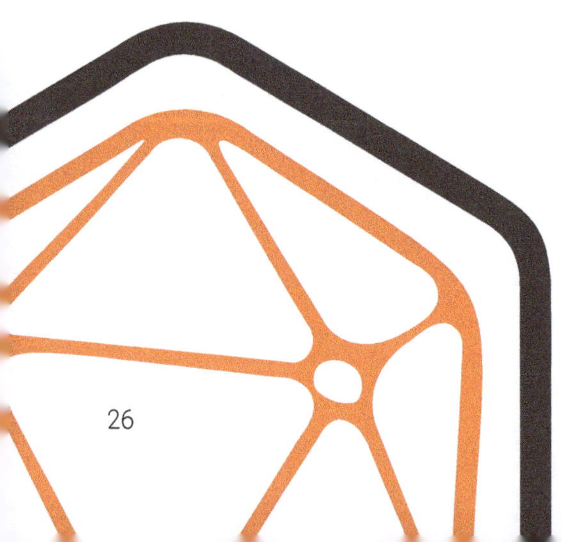

IMPORTANT RESIN TERMS

LEVEL: **1**　2　3　4

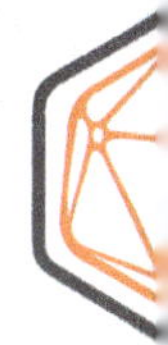

By Weight

A 2:1 ratio by *weight*, means that you must use scales and weigh out the parts of your resin. e.g to mix 30g of resin you need to mix 20g of Part A and 10g of Part B. Most resin is measured by volume unless specified.

By Volume

A 2:1 ratio *by volume* means that you need to use a measuring cup to *measure* out 20mL of Part A to 10mL of Part B to make 30mL of resin.

Casting

Casting is the process of making solid objects by pouring liquid resin into a shaped mould. Once the resin hardens, it becomes a casting! Confusing? Yes.

Catalyst

A chemical compound that causes resin to harden. The catalyst (or hardener) is the Part B in your resin. Each catalyst is designed for a specific resin with a specific ratio.

Cure Time

Cure time refers to the period of time required for resin to fully harden or set.

Demoulding

The process of removing a casting from a mould.

Demould Time

When the resin reaches a solid enough state, we can remove it from the mould for full curing.

Exothermic Reaction

A heat producing reaction that occurs when the resin and hardener are mixed. Incorrectly mixed resin or resin mixed in large batches can sometimes cause exothermic runaway or flash curing which rapidly heats and solidifies the resin.

Flashing
Flashing is excess material outside the mould due to overflow or leakage.

Mix Ratio
The proper proportions (either by *weight* or *volume*) of the two parts of your resin. See *By Weight* and *By Volume.* Try to choose a resin with a simple ratio such as 2:1 or 1:1, more advanced resins such as polyurethane sometimes have more complicated mix ratios such as 100:88 which may be more difficult for new resin users.

Mix-In
Anything you add to the resin to give colour or depth such as mica powder, alcohol ink. glitter, etc.

Mould or Mold
Whether you spell it mold or mould depends on where you live – just like color or colour. A mould is simply an imprint of an object – this creates a cavity that can be filled with resin.

Shore Hardness
A measure of how hard/flexible a material is. See "Shore Hardness" on page 112.

Viscosity
Viscosity refers to how a substance *flows*. Viscosity is measured in cps (centipoise) with a lower number meaning *less viscous* and a higher number meaning *more viscous*. For example water has low viscosity (1cps) and flows easily, whereas honey (2000-3000cps) has high viscoscity and does not flow as easily.

Void
Bubbles caught on the surface or within your casting leave an empty space.

Working Time/Pot Life
Working time is how long you have to work with the resin before it begins to cure.

WHICH RESIN?

When it comes to the "best" resin, opinions are far and wide. Some swear by a particular brand, others by another. At Critmaker, *our rule is simple* – go to a local resin/craft supply shop and ask them about their products. If nothing else, it'll be a great starting point and you'll avoid wading through the thousands of contradictory reviews online.

In Australia, we have an excellent relationship with Barnes (barnes.com.au). Their resins are consistent, affordable, and give us great results. We have that relationship because we talked to the friendly staff about our needs.

TYPES OF RESIN

You'll hear about three main types of resin in dice casting.

Epoxy Resin

We recommend using epoxy resin as it cures crystal clear, has a long working time of 30 to 60 minutes and takes about 24 hours to cure. Epoxy resin is the easiest resin to work with and comes in many varieties depending on the working time and cure time. Most dice makers use epoxy resin for their dice.

Polyurethane Resin

If you're looking to make dice faster with simple mix-ins, polyurethane can be a good option. Some polyurethanes cure in as little as 30-60 minutes though, in our experience, it does require a pressure pot. Unlike epoxy, most polyurethane resins cure opaque, making it unsuitable for many techniques. We don't recommend this for beginners.

UV Resin

Ultraviolet (UV) resin is a one-part resin that needs UV light to cure. It's useful for filling voids and takes colours well. Get a squeeze bottle of UV resin and a 405nm UV torch.

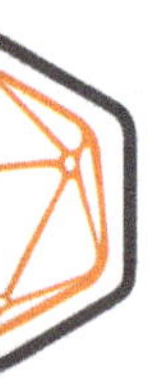

CASTING OR DEEP POUR?

LEVEL: (1) 2 3 4

Technically all casting resin is considered *deep pour*. The reason being is that compared to many resin applications which are brushed onto the surface of an object such as polyester resin used for fibreglass, moulding anything deeper requires a different reaction.

Most resin suppliers have different resins based on the *thickness* of the cast item.

CASTING RESIN

For example, jewellery (or dice) are usually made using a basic casting resin as it's designed for objects under 5cm/2" thick. It has a decent working time of 30-60 mins and a cure time of 24-48 hours. Given the small object size and short curing time, a pressure pot can be used to minimise the bubbles that either form during the reaction or come out from the mixing.

DEEP POUR RESIN

For thicker items such as those incredible river tables you see on Youtube, a "deep pour" or "mass pour" resin is used. Given the size of the objects, a pressure pot is generally out of the question, so the resin remains a liquid *significantly longer* allowing more bubbles to come to the surface to pop naturally. Given the thickness of the resin used in this style of pouring, the cure time is still around 24-48 hours, though the working time is significantly longer.

CAN YOU USE DEEP POUR RESIN FOR DICE?

Maybe. Many "deep pour" resins are designed for layers 5cm/2" or thicker. The thinner the layer, the longer it will take to cure. Most resins will eventually cure, though it's worth checking with the manufacturer. If casting dice without a pressure pot, this style of resin may actually allow you to cast with less bubbles, though it may take 48-72 hours (or longer) to cure.

Speak to your local resin supplier before you decide!

POLISHING PAPER

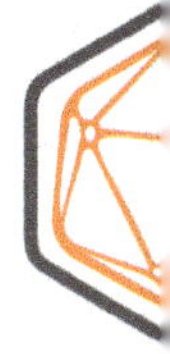

LEVEL: (1)   2   3   4

For many dice makers, the gold standard of dice polishing is 3M WetorDry Tri-M-Ite paper. You can find it at many jewellery supply stores or via online retailers. It's sold by Zona Tools in the U.S., and most dice makers call it "zona paper".

Polishing paper (or lapping paper as it's also known) is more expensive than sandpaper, but it lasts *much* longer. Polishing paper is covered in graded particles of Aluminium Oxide or Silicon Carbide. The particles are much finer than sandpaper and are bonded to a backing sheet of mylar or polyester. Jewellers, knife-makers and machinists use it to polish their wares to a mirror finish.

30 Micron	15 Micron	9 Micron	3 Micron	2 Micron	1 Micron
Green	Grey	Blue	Pink	Light Blue	White

WHAT IF YOU CAN'T GET 3M PAPER?

In many countries, 3M polishing paper is simply not available. Thankfully, there are alternatives.

Sandpaper and a Rotary Tool (preferred by many dice makers) – Most hardware or automotive repair stores will sell sandpaper up to 800 or even 2000 grit. Gently sand your dice using 800 grit and then progress to your finest. To get that final shine, the best tool for the job is a rotary tool or Dremel (see "Rotary Tool" on page 77). Using a combination of soft polishing pads and a quality plastic polish, you should be able to get the dice shining in no time!! You can also consider a vibratory tumbler, see "Advanced Finishing" on page 75.

MicroMesh – are small polishing pads that come in kits from 1500 to 12000 grit. Be careful if you're using the padded ones sold at craft stores as you can take the edges off your dice if you press down too hard. Like 3M paper, MicroMesh lasts a very long time!

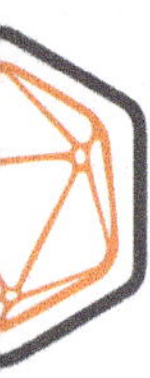

CHOOSING MIX-INS

LEVEL:  **1** 2 3 4

Mix-ins, such as pigments, inks, glitter, and natural materials, are added to resin to give colour or depth. Mix-ins can be added before or after pouring resin into the mould and can be layered to create amazing visual effects. With creativity and experimentation, mix-ins can yield genuinely unique and beautiful pieces.

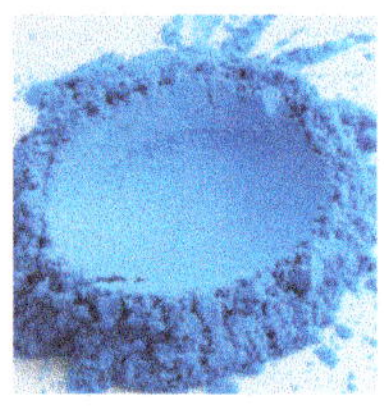

Mica Powder

Mica is a natural stone mineral containing shiny flakes which have been ground down to form a fine powder. This shimmery pigment looks like a fine glitter and is available in many vibrant colours. Go for a great brand like Pearl Ex by Jacquard or other high quality mica powder.

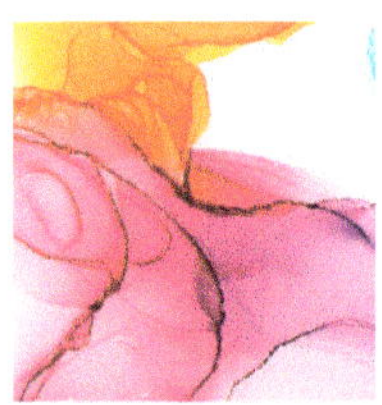

Alcohol Inks

Unlike acrylic inks, alcohol inks won't stop resin from curing. They come in many colours and can create stunning results. Piñata and Ranger Ink are both excellent. Note: some colours, such as blues and purples, may turn brown in resin. Not all brands have this issue – you may need to experiment or try resin pigments instead.

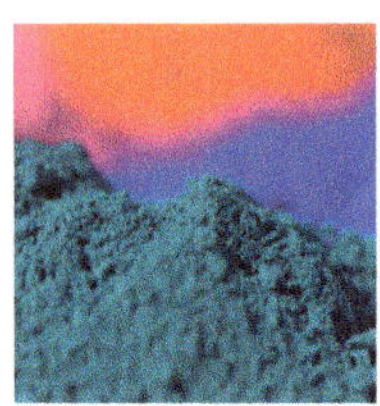

Resin Pigments

Resin pigments are intended to blend seamlessly into your resin. They come in powder, liquid and paste form. Pigments can produce an opaque colour or a transparent look, depending on how much you add. A little goes a long way! JustResin sell great pigments.

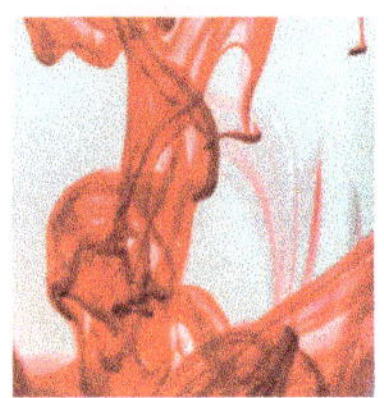

Sinker Ink

Though still an alcohol ink, "Piñata Blanco Blanco", is a dense, white pigment that helps pull ink down into the resin. It creates those beautiful strands we see in petri dice. See "Petri" on page 90.

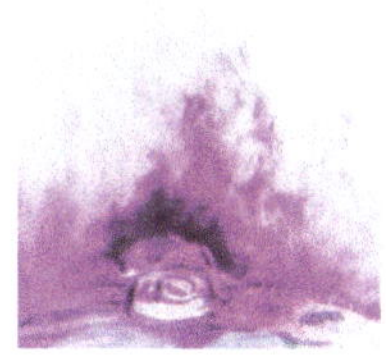

Food Dyes

We don't recommend these as some resins are sensitive to the water content. Your results may vary and many dice makers have had great success with them. We recommend sticking to dedicated resin pigments or alcohol inks where possible.

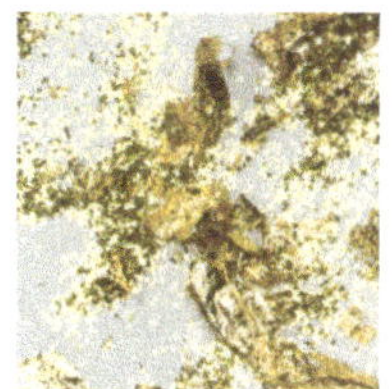

Foils, Fibres and Mylar Flakes

From 24k gold leaf to rainbow holographic – foils are a great way to add metallic flashes of colour to your dice. Shiny fibres such as Angelina fibres as well as mylar flakes can also add incredible depth and inner shine.

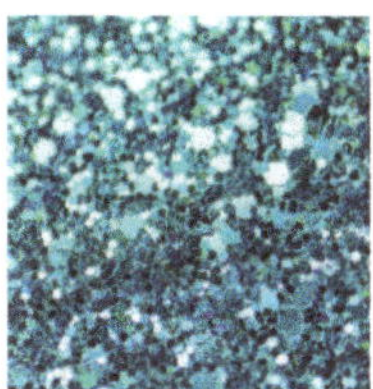

Glitter

Glitter comes in many shapes, sizes and colours, from ultra-fine pearl to chunky holographic chunks; glitter is the icing on the cake for dice making.

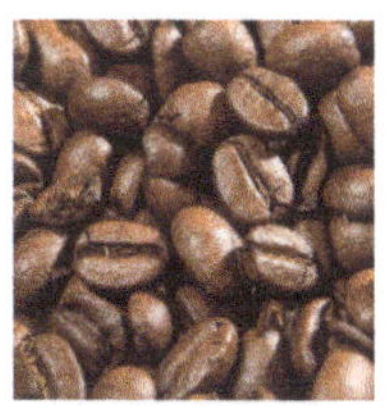

Natural Objects

Think coffee beans, feathers, seeds, dried flowers, shells, dried insects. Lots of natural objects make for incredible, unique dice!

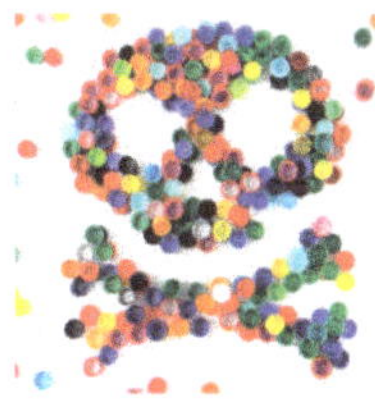

Other Objects

You can mix *almost anything* into your dice but be mindful of heavier items such as glass or metal. Heavy items can throw out the balance, making them "unfair". It's best to use items made of resin; if you have a resin 3D printer, be creative!

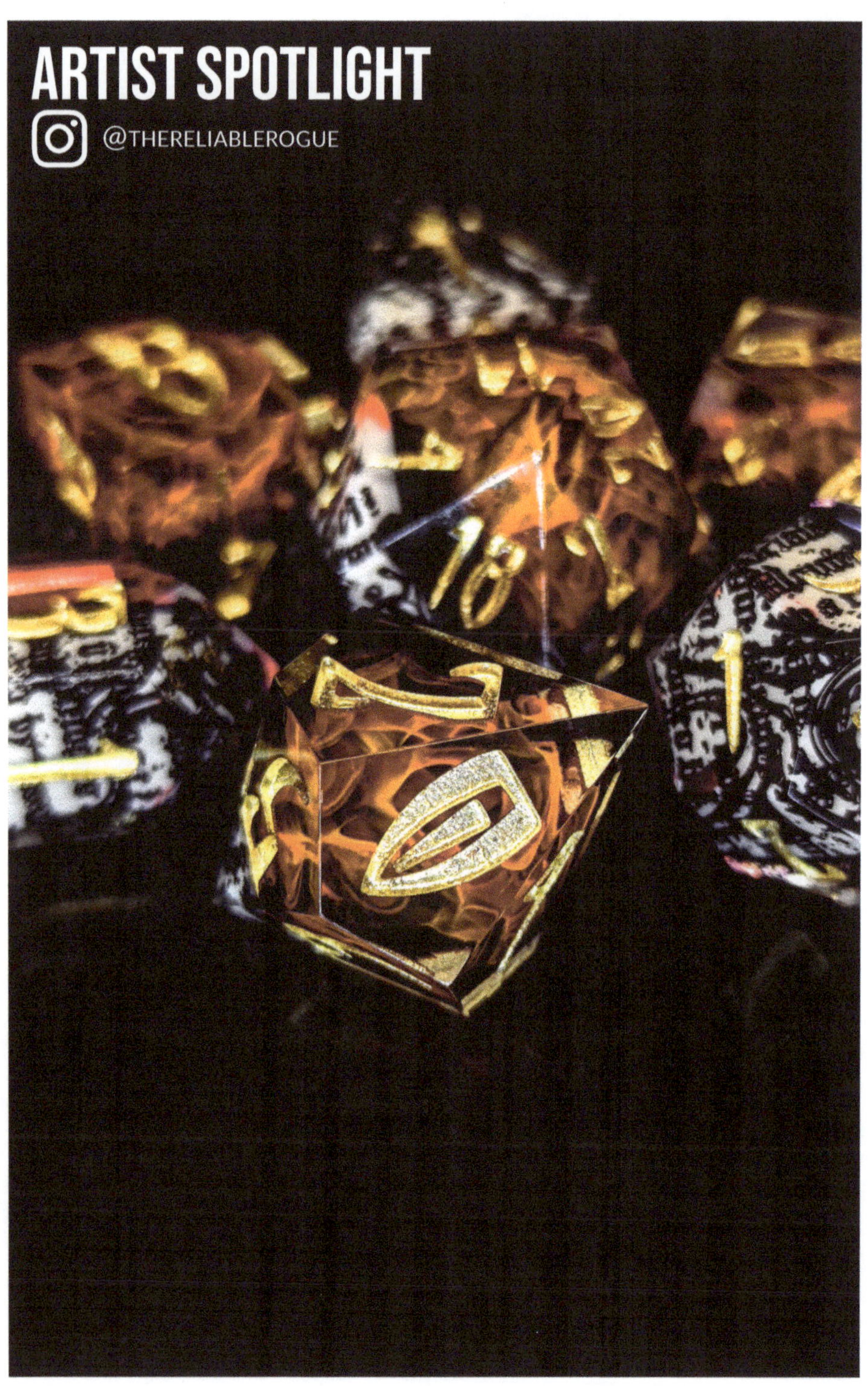

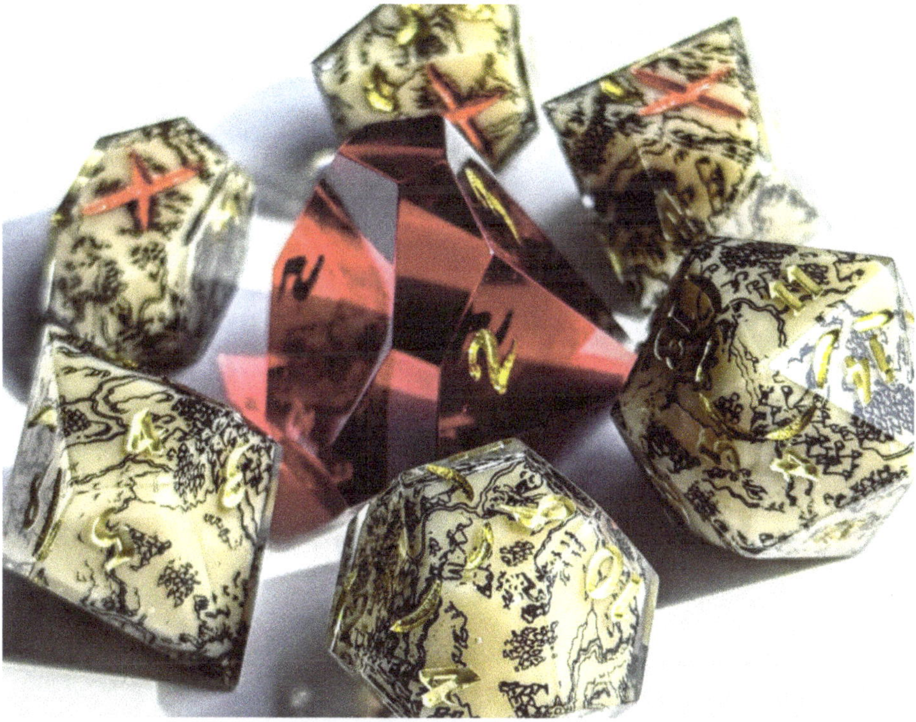

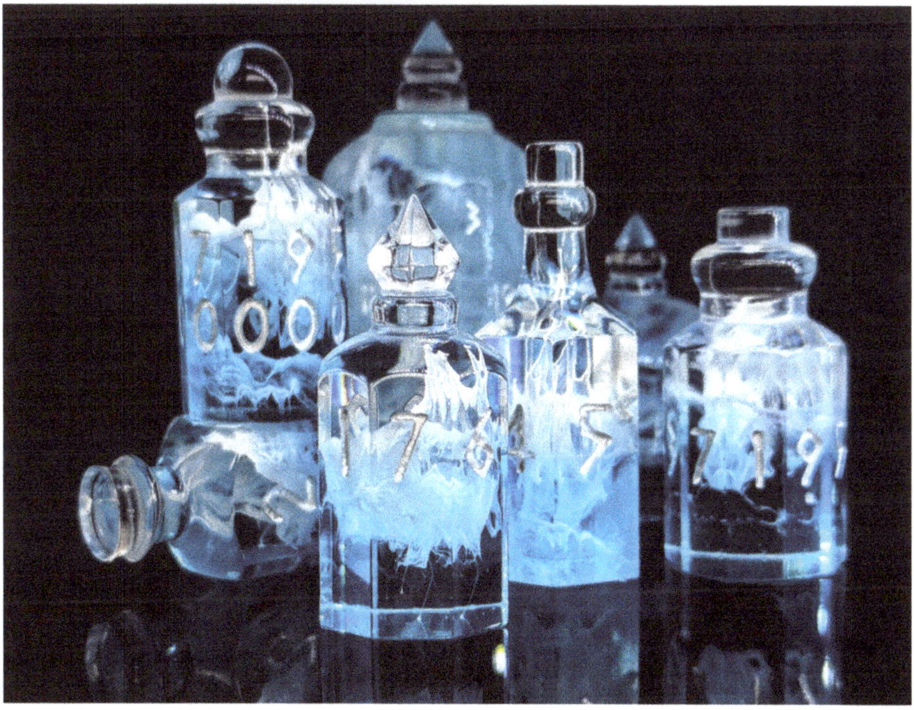

THE BASICS

In this section, we'll explore if dice craft requires a pressure pot, how to organise your workspace and dig into some tips and tricks for avoiding bubbles and raised faces.

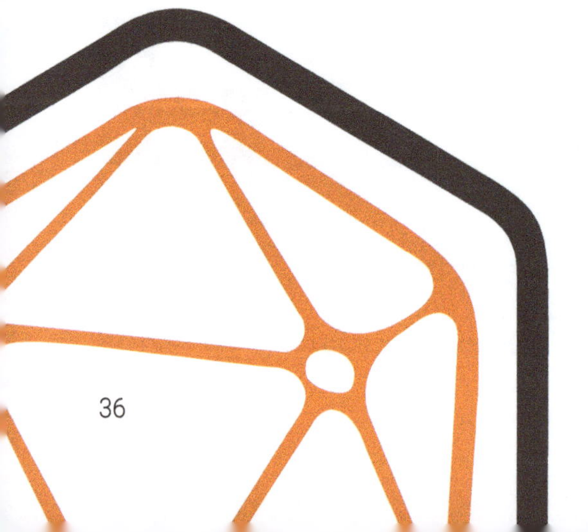

PART TWO

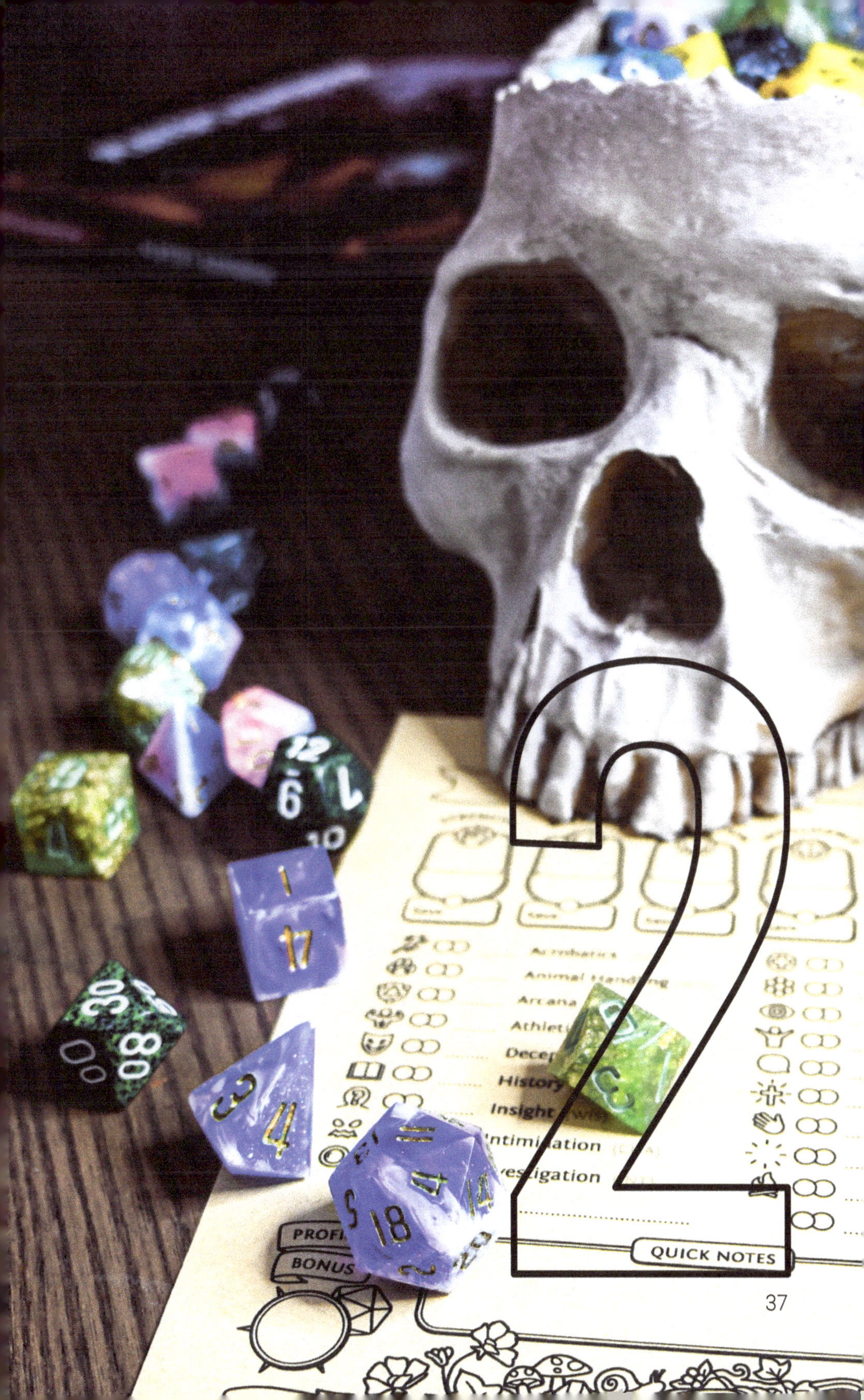
QUICK NOTES

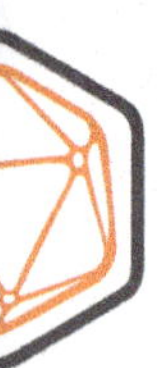

DO I NEED A PRESSURE POT?

LEVEL:  (1) 2 3 4

If you're okay with some bubbles in your dice, then the answer is no – you can go to the next topic and pick this one up again later! You can get some great results without a pressure pot, but it can be much more challenging to get it right. It's going to be almost impossible to cast without any bubbles at all.

There are two ways that bubbles get into resin. Firstly, during mixing – as we swish it around, we introduce excess air into the mixture. The second way is during the chemical reaction between the resin and the hardener/catalyst as it cures. This is why a vacuum chamber isn't ideal for resin casting as bubbles can form *after* pouring.

WHAT DOES A PRESSURE POT DO?

A pressure pot is simply an airtight steel chamber that has air pushed into it with an air compressor.

Instead of eliminating them, bubbles are compressed until they are too small to be seen by the naked eye. The pressure also assists in pushing the resin into every corner and crevice of the mould. This means a flawless casting without any air pockets or bubbles. See "Pressure Casting" on page 62.

WHILE YOU CAN EASILY MAKE YOUR OWN DICE WITHOUT A PRESSURE POT, IT TAKES MORE WORK AND IS FAR LESS RELIABLE THAN USING ONE. THE FACT IS THAT ALL PROFESSIONAL DICE MAKERS USE PRESSURE POTS - IT'S THE EASIEST WAY TO TAKE YOUR DICE FROM GOOD TO INCREDIBLE!

MINIMISING BUBBLES

PPE:   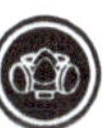 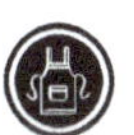

If you want to make dice without a pressure pot, you may need to experiment to figure out what works best for your resin.

Heat the resin in a warm water bath.
Putting the sealed bottles in a warm water bath for 10 or 15 minutes can help make the resin thinner and help any bubbles rise faster. This is important if it's below 20–23°C (70–75°F) which most resin needs to cure. But, be warned, *heating the resin can lower the working time.*

Mix slower
Less vigorous mixing means you will introduce fewer bubbles – take your time and move slowly.

Wait 10-15 minutes before pouring.
You'll want to wait anyway, but giving the resin time to settle after mixing will allow any bubbles to rise to the surface. Pop them with your long neck lighter.

Spread some resin around inside the mould before pouring.
Get the resin right into the corners and numbers with a soft brush. By pushing resin into these areas, it may prevent bubbles from catching and wrecking your casting. Don't use a sharp object like a toothpick!

Dip any inclusions in resin.
Items such as dried flowers often have plenty of spots for air pockets to form. Soak in resin for a few minutes and stir slowly to dislodge any bubbles.

Squeeze the mould a few times while pouring.
This can help dislodge some bubbles caught around the corners and numbers.

Embrace the bubbles.
Turn them into a *feature*; bubbles and glitter can look awesome!

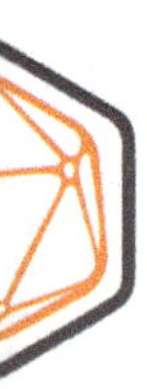

RESTING THE RESIN

 PPE:   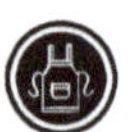

Resting your resin might be the most frustrating step for a new dice-maker, especially if this is your first pour. However, this is one of the most important!

As the resin comes to the end of its working time (or pot life), the reaction starts to speed up. At this point, the resin starts to move from a *liquid* state to a *gel* state before becoming a *solid*.

Somewhere between the *liquid* and *gel* state is the goldilocks zone where the resin starts to resemble the consistency of honey. This is the perfect time for most pouring techniques.

WHY WAIT?

If you don't, you'll generally find that your mix-ins sink to the bottom of the dice. For many moulds, the bottom is the crit face, the highest number on the dice! If you've mixed in glitter, this means you won't have it nice and uniform throughout your dice. You'll have it ALL on one face in a thick layer.

As you progress to more advanced techniques, such as petri or layering, this step is even more crucial. You'll want to rest your resin even more for perfect results.

HOW LONG SHOULD I WAIT?

There's no right answer to this. It depends on your resin, its working time and the ambient temperature. The main thing to consider is what you're trying to achieve and what consistency you need to get the desired effect.

As a starting point, you will need to wait $3/4$ of your working time. For a new resin (or a new dice maker), check it every 10 minutes until you get the consistency you want.

THE HONEY ZONE

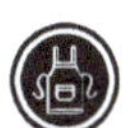

As your resin starts to cure, look for a nice honey consistency. At the start, it may be like water or syrup, but the honey stage is best to keep those mix-ins suspended throughout the dice (and not just on the bottom!).

The resin we use has a working time of 60 minutes. From about 30 minutes onwards, it's suitable for petri effects that don't sink all the way to the bottom. At the 55-minute mark, it's perfect for layering. For a dirty pour, we generally give it 40-45 minutes. As you can see, the right time depends on the resin and what you're trying to do with it!

EXPERIMENTATION

The perfect consistency will take some time and experimentation with your resin. It's important to understand how your mix-ins interact at different viscosities.

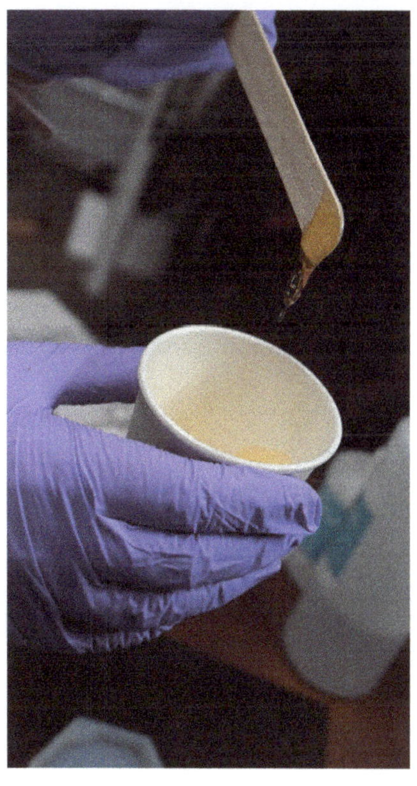

Druid Dice has a *fantastic* video on this subject using candy/chocolate moulds to pour resin at timed intervals.
(Scan QR code or bit.ly/resin-timing)

YOU HAVE SOME TIME TO WAIT, SO WHY NOT WATCH IT NOW?

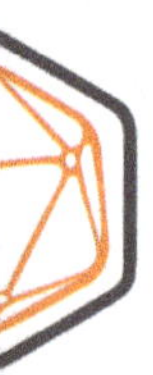

PREVENTING RAISED FACES

In dice-making, raised faces are one of the most common issues you'll encounter when using "cap" or "squish" moulds (used by most dice makers). This occurs when the top of the mould lifts, leaving one face higher than the rest. The numbers on the dice are usually only about 0.9mm deep (0.035") meaning if it's raised too high, you won't be able to fix it. *(See photo to the right)*.

In traditional casting, moulds are often built into a fibreglass or plaster shell (called a mother mould). The two parts are clamped together to prevent the sides from coming apart. Since the cap moulds used for dice rarely have a solid shell, the top and bottom are at the mercy of physics. They can easily be pushed apart by excess resin.

HOW TO PREVENT IT

The most important thing to do is *not overfill the mould*. The more material on top, the more you'll need to "squish" out to get a flat face. All you want to do is "dome" the resin over each dice and then apply a tiny amount of resin on the numbers on the lid. If you overfill the mould, remove it with your stirrer. Now, after putting your cap on, you need to squish it down and "shimmy" it a bit. This will help to force excess resin out of the mould. The less excess resin on top, the less resin you have to clean up later!

CAN A DIFFERENT MOULD PREVENT IT?

The answer is *maybe*. It depends on the type of silicone used, its shore hardness (see "Shore Hardness" on page 112) and the viscosity of the resin. Some mould makers swear by locking or t-shaped keys or making heavy lids. These solutions have merit but sometimes, the keys will stretch or the mould will misshape instead.

MANY DICE-MAKERS ALSO STACK THEIR MOULDS OR APPLY A LIGHT WEIGHT ON TOP - ABOUT THE WEIGHT OF ANOTHER MOULD WORKS WELL. THIS CAN HELP KEEP THE LID DOWN.

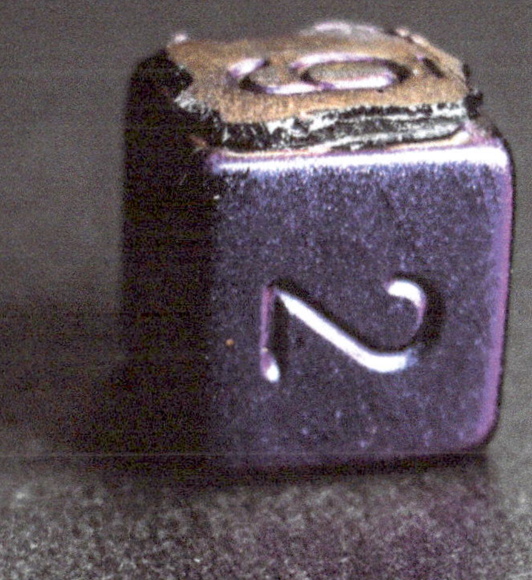

UNFORTUNATELY, NO AMOUNT OF SANDING WILL FIX A FACE THAT'S
RAISED THIS MUCH.

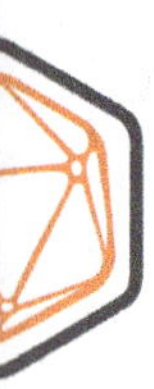

VOID REPAIR

LEVEL: (1) 2 3 4   **PPE:** 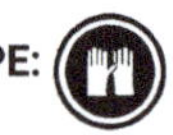  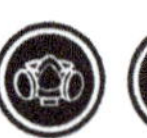

A void is simply an empty cavity in your casting caused by a bubble. Remember when we talked about the different types of resin? This is where UV resin comes in handy. UV resin can be coloured and sanded and looks like epoxy once cured.

Before discussing how to fix voids, it's important to mention that not all voids can be fixed. They can be tough to get right if they're too large or cover parts of the numbers. But you can try this approach if they're in inconspicuous places, such as edges or even corners.

To fix up the voids, you have two choices. Add clear UV resin, or attempt to colour match the void using the same mix-ins.

FIXING VOIDS

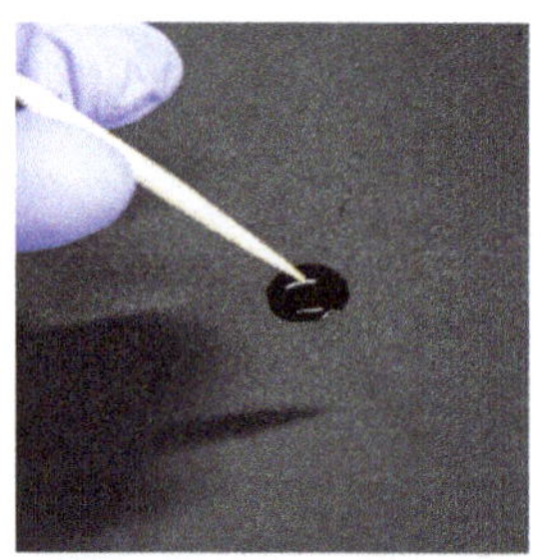

1 To start, pour a drop of UV resin onto a piece of paper or scrap. Don't put it directly onto your dice; you'll have more to clean up. If you're colour-matching, dip a toothpick or matchstick into the mica powder/mix-in. Then mix it through the drop.

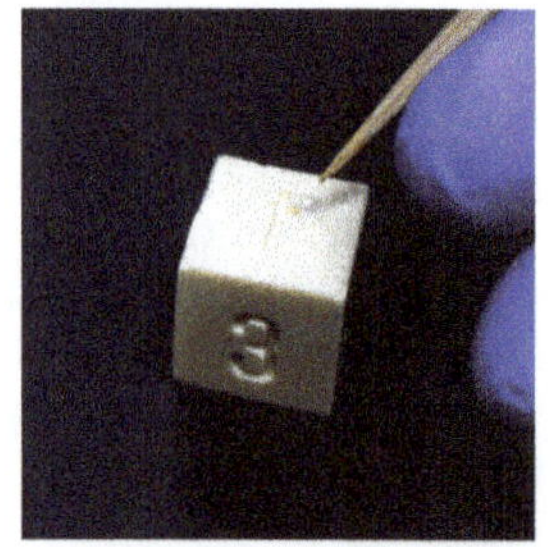

2 When you're happy with the colour, dip your toothpick in the drop and apply it to the void. You want it to be domed slightly (higher than the surface).

3 Now, use your UV light to cure the resin in place. After 10-15 seconds, it should be as hard as glass.

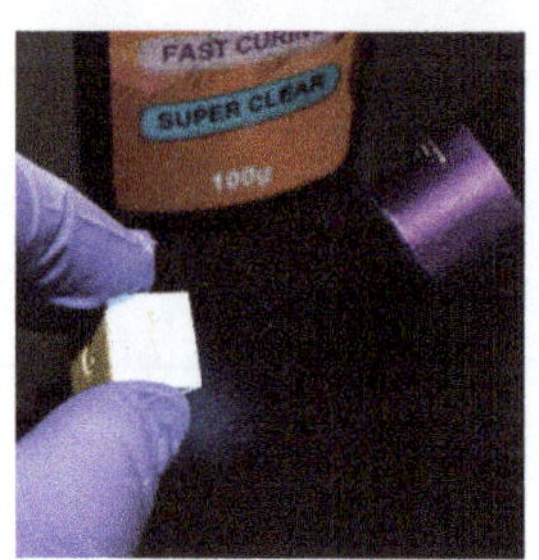

4 With the repair done, you can now move on to sanding and polishing.

WORKSPACE TIPS

LEVEL: (1)   2   3   4

If possible, it's good to have a dedicated workspace for your resin with a large silicone mat. Silicone won't bond with resin, meaning that it can just be wiped off. If the resin is left to cure on the mat, you can easily peel it off – not so for your table as resin will bond to most surfaces permanently.

ORGANISING MIX-INS

Organising your workspace can be a challenge – the longer you make dice, the more stuff you'll collect (I'm looking at you, mix-ins!). More mica powder, more glitter, more bits and pieces left over from those one-off projects. I find organising these is best with clear plastic storage boxes. You can see what's in them, and the handy dividers make organising easy!

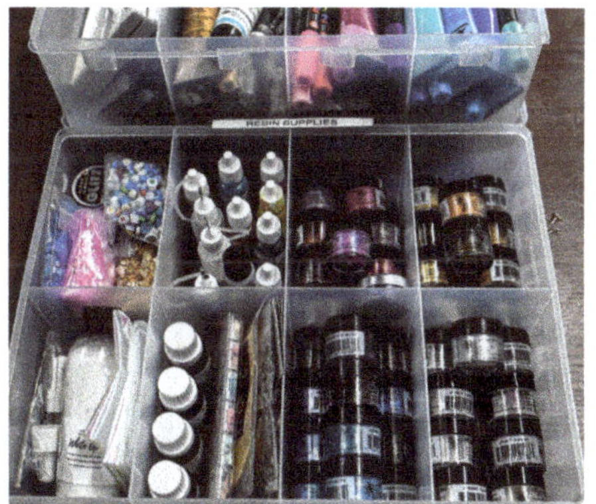

CLEANING

It's important to clean your workspace after every dice-making session. No, I don't do it all the time, but it's important that I say it. It will prevent glitter from covering your entire house (and cat). It will also help keep you inspired next time you sit down to pour some dice! I buy isopropyl alcohol in 4L /1 gal bottles for this purpose – after I'm done, I wipe the surfaces down with alcohol and some paper towel.

DISPOSING OF LIQUIDS

Dice making generates quite a bit of liquid waste including dirty isopropyl alcohol, and resin-saturated cleaning fluids. Don't pour this stuff down the drain. Instead, collect it in a large 20L/5.5gal chemical bottle and dispose of it at your local chemical drop-off.

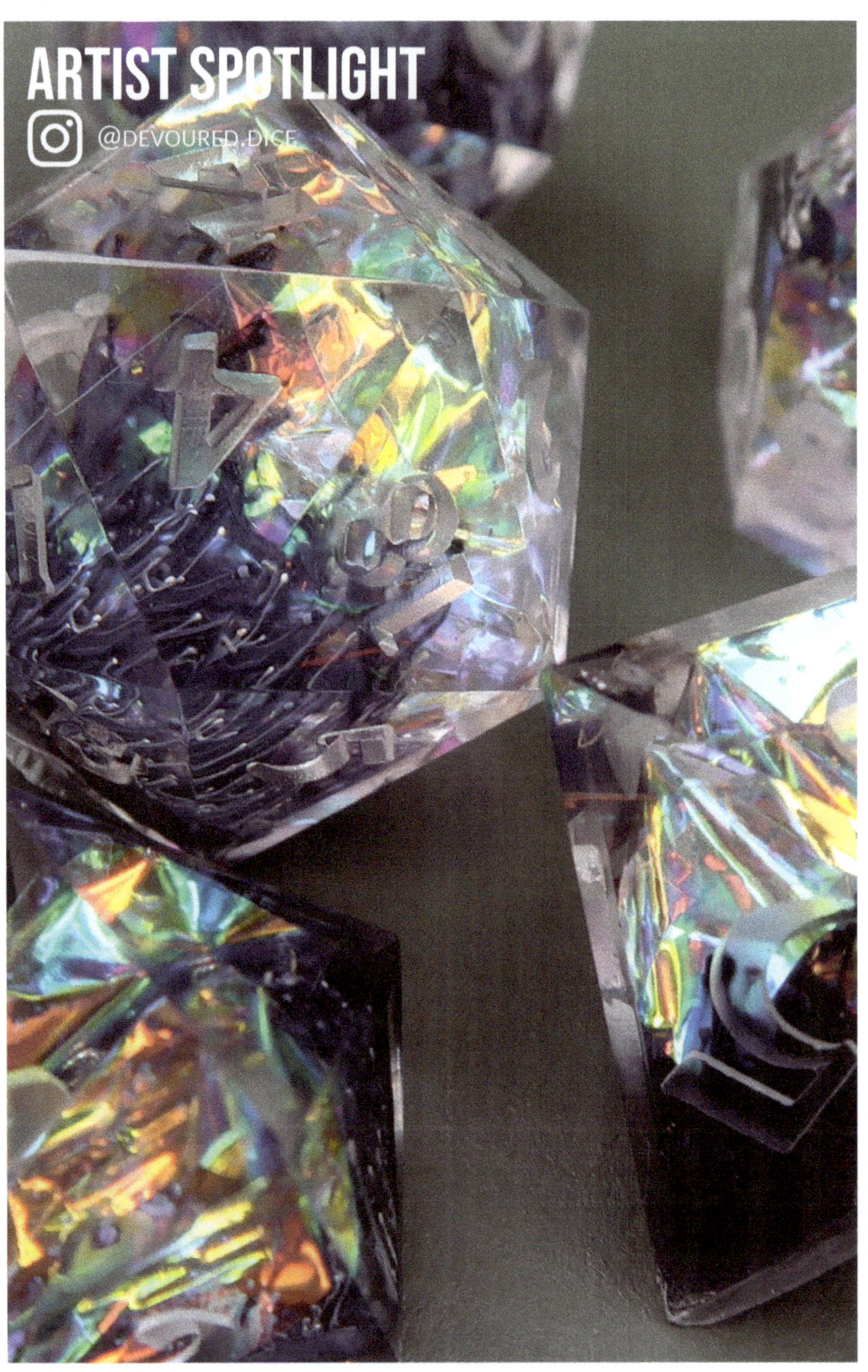

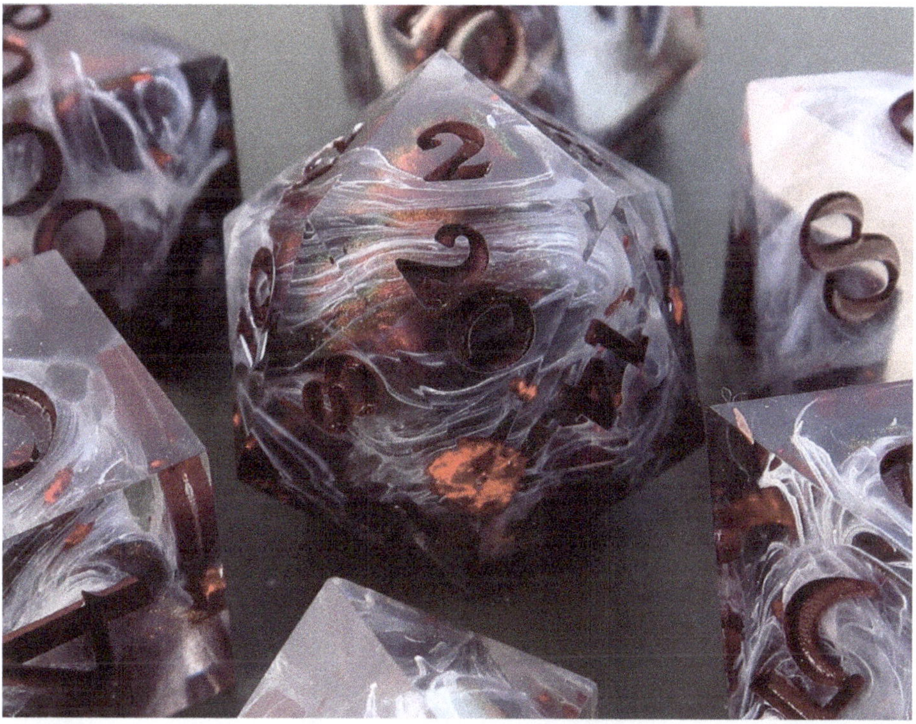

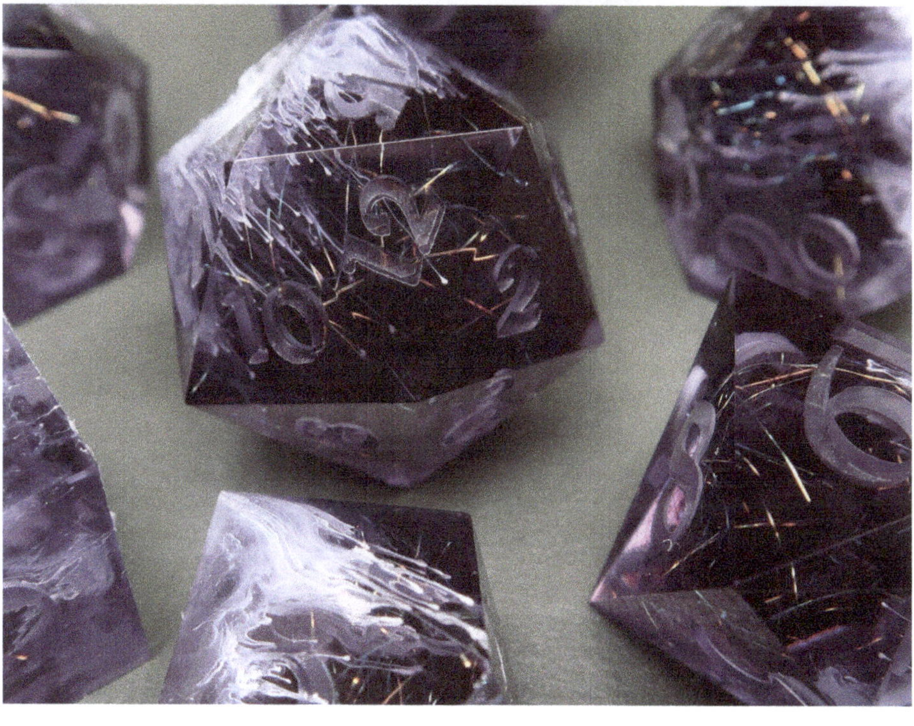

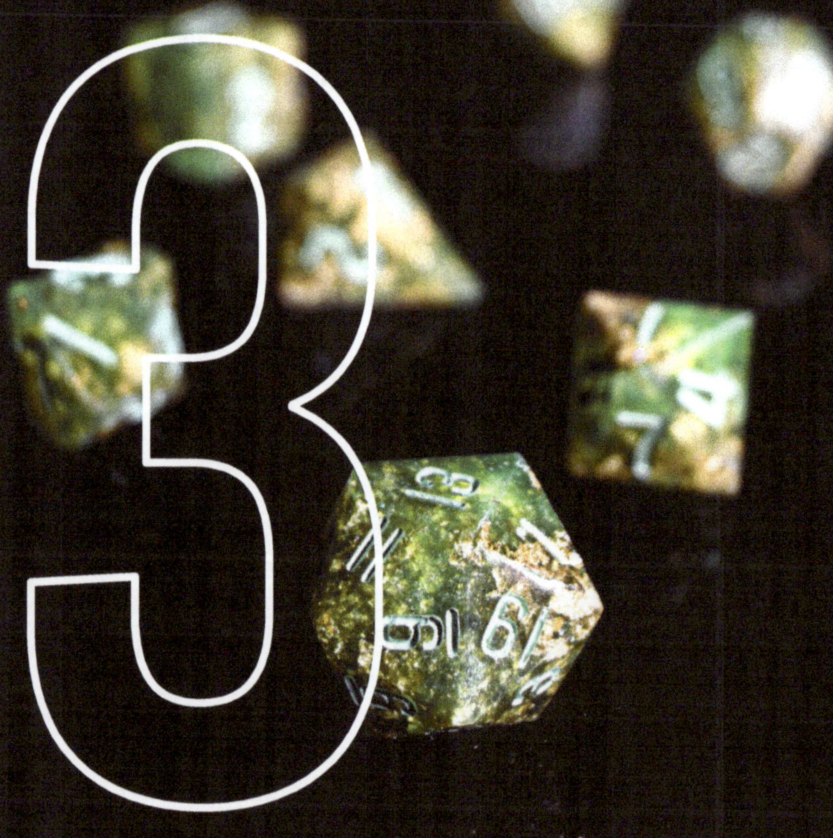

3

YOUR FIRST DICE

In this chapter, we'll follow my wife, Zoe, as she makes her first dice *(pictured to the left)*. We'll cover basic dice-making step by step. From finding inspiration to pouring, demoulding, inking, and cleanup.

Note: We'll be using a pressure pot to cure our dice as it'll be better for our photos. If you don't use one, a theme like this is good for hiding any internal bubbles!

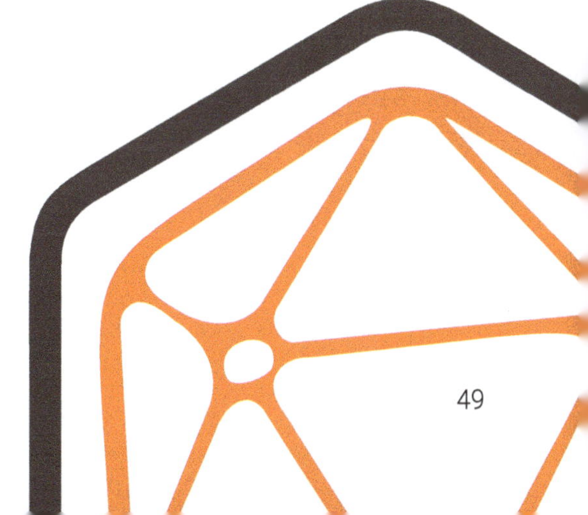

PART THREE

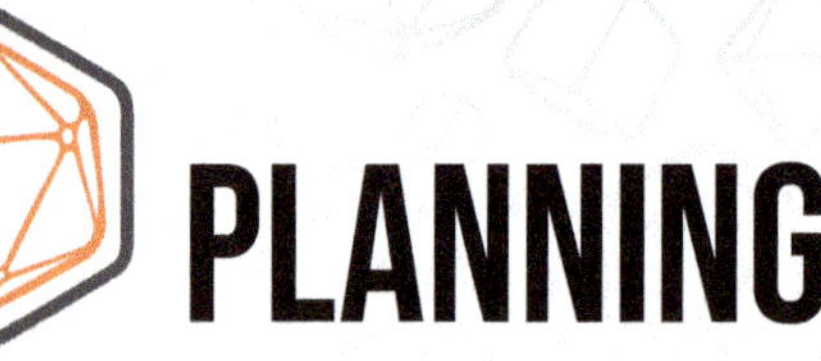

PLANNING

LEVEL: (1) 2 3 4

Before we begin, let's talk about planning your dice.

Jumping in and pouring dice can be fun, but your dice will almost always be better if you start with a plan or some inspiration. Take a minute before pouring your resin, and decide what you hope to achieve.

The example on the following page is from the "Critmaker Journal." It's available from our website or Amazon. It's a great companion to this guide. It helps keep track of your recipes and is also a great place to track your progress!

Here's a run-down of the main fields

 **Inspiration**

Many things can inspire you. It could be a scene in a movie, a painting, a favourite game or your character in D&D. If the dice are a gift, what does the recipient love? Write down the inspiration, even if you don't directly reference it in the materials.

 **Palette**

What colours reflect the inspiration? Is it a night sky or a misty forest? Write down the colours that come to mind or even colour them in.

 **Mix-ins**

Mix-ins are anything you add to your resin, such as mica powders, alcohol inks, glitters, foils, etc.

The second half of the page is what happened during the casting process. It's also great to record in case you want to recreate the same dice again! Keeping a journal is the best way to improve quickly!

Take some time after every ten or so entries to reflect on what's going well and what you can improve.

INSPIRATION

My character, Dhara, has fond memories of walking through the forest in the early morning light. The sun shines through the trees like gold, bathing the trails in beautiful light.

PALETTE

Jade green with lots of gold shining through. I want the gold to catch the light.

MIX-INS

Green mica powder and LOTS of gold foil — and a faint hint of glitter!

TECHNIQUE   Basic

METHOD

RESIN *Barnes EpoxyCast*   REST   *40* MINS

POURING & MIXING DETAILS

I added a single scoop of mica powder and stirred thoroughly. After that I mixed in two large scoops of gold foil followed by a few drops of iridescent glitter ink.

NOTES

I had a tiny void on one face (fixable). I LOVE how these turned out! Next time I'd add less gold foil and more gold glitter instead.

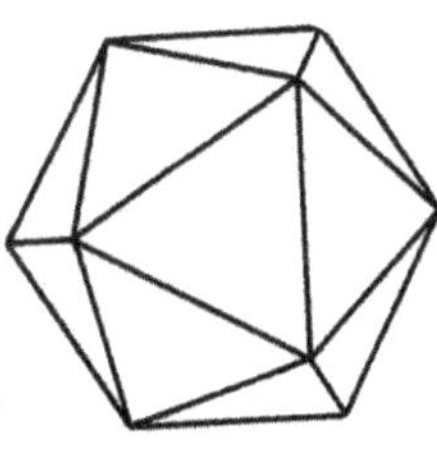

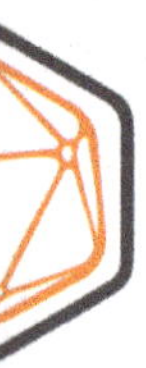

STARTING SIMPLE

LEVEL: **1**   2   3   4

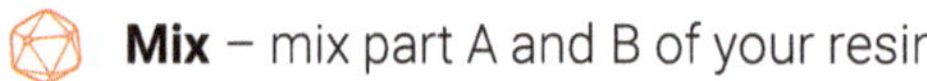

Before we jump into all the exciting techniques you've seen on Instagram or TikTok, let's start simple! For this first pour, we will use resin, mica powder for colouring and something sparkly like glitter or foil. It's simple, and it'll look fantastic!

Almost every technique has the same ten steps:

Mix – mix part A and B of your resin

Rest – wait for the resin to reach the desired consistency

Add – add your mix-ins

Pour – pour your resin into the mould

Cure – let it cure for 24 hours (or the demoulding time of your resin)

Demould – take the dice out of the mould and remove any flashing

Wait – Usually 72 hours (or more depending on the resin) for a full cure

Polish – Sand off any extra flashing and polish with your polishing paper

Ink – Apply acrylic paint to the numbers and wipe of the excess

Admire – the most crucial step!

We've decided on a jade-green theme with lots of gold foil for the dice we're demonstrating in this chapter. The inspiration is the morning sun shining through the leaves of the forest. We'll be using green mica powder as our base colour and some gold leaf, which we've crushed into small pieces.

Feel free to choose your own theme for this set and make it unique!

MIXING RESIN

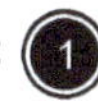
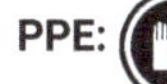

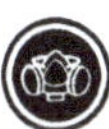

PPE:

WHAT YOU'LL NEED
- Epoxy Resin
- Measuring Cup (60mL/2oz or larger)
- Stirring Stick
- A timer (phone, laptop etc)

1 Double-check the mixing requirements for your resin. The bottle should state the mixing ratio, whether it's *by weight* or *by volume* and the working time. A full set of dice uses around 35mL (0.85 oz), but I'd recommend doing at least 60mL (2 oz) to make sure you have enough.

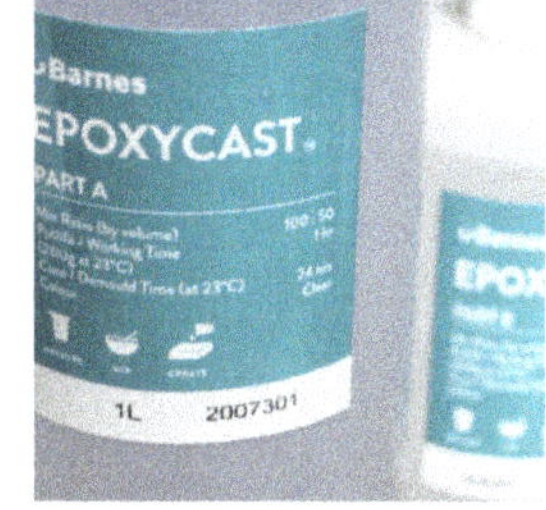

2 Pour the required amount of part A into your measuring cup. The resin used here has a ratio of 100:50 (or 2:1) *by volume* which means we'll add 40mL.

3 Start your timer. The working time for your resin starts from the second you mix the two parts.

4 Pour in the required amount of part B. For this resin, we add 20mL.

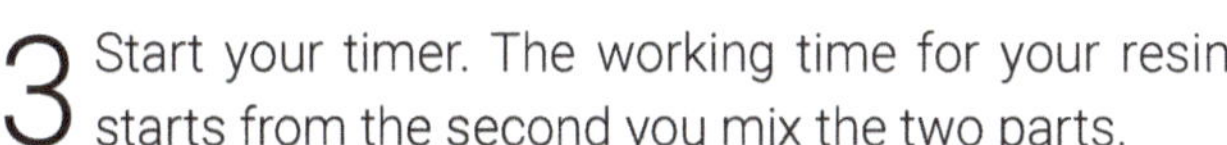
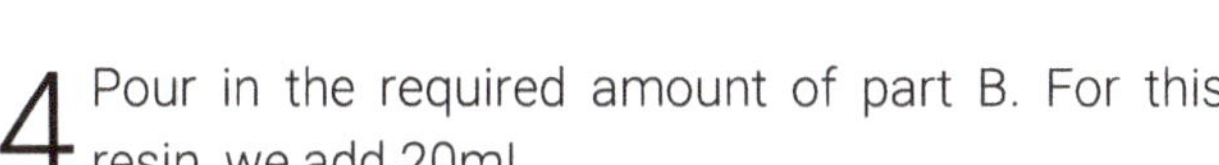
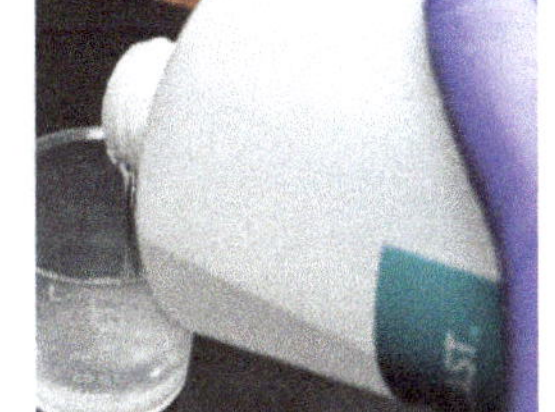

5 Mix for 3-4 minutes, scraping the sides and bottom of the container. Continue until there are no streaks or striations.

6 Transfer the resin to a second container. Mix for another 1-2 minutes until thoroughly blended.

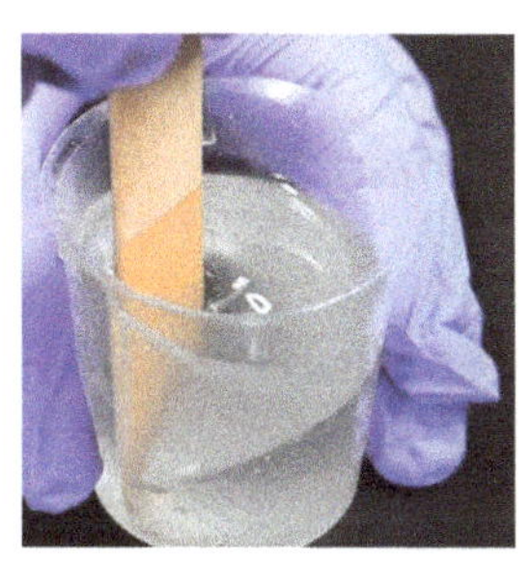

Let your resin rest until it's ready to pour.

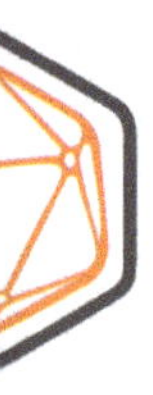

BASIC POUR

LEVEL: (1)   2   3   4    **PPE:** 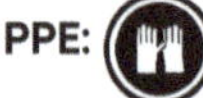   

WHAT YOU'LL NEED

- Your dice mould
- Your mixed resin
- Any mix-ins such as mica, glitter or foil
- A fresh stirring stick

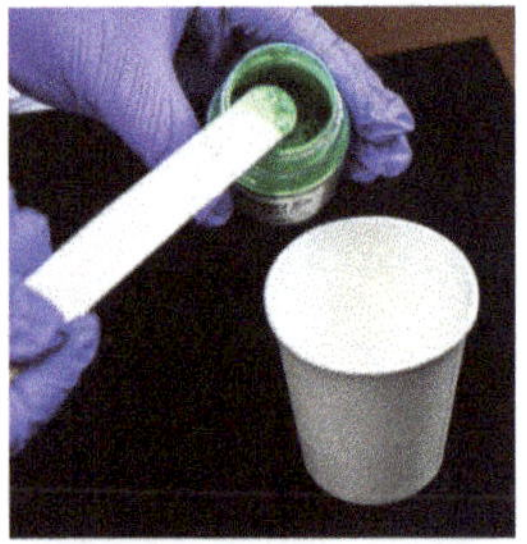

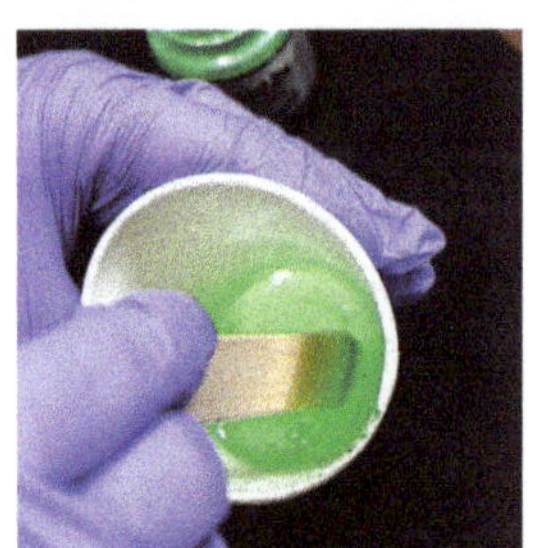

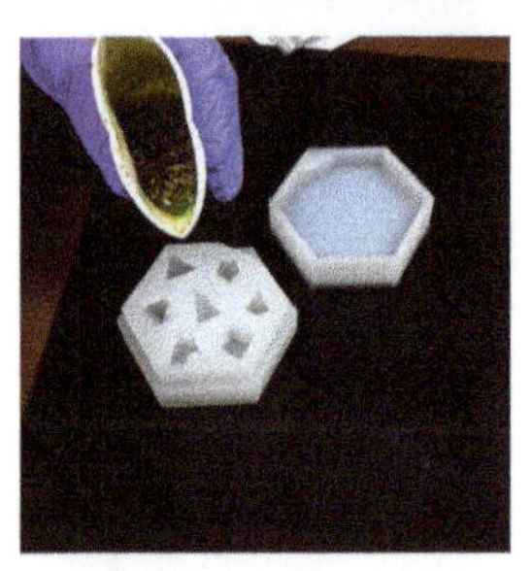

1 When your resin is at the beautiful, honey consistency, it's time to add some mica powder and mix-ins with your fresh stirring stick. For these dice, we wanted to go for a jade tone in the primary colour and a large amount of gold leaf.

2 Slowly pour the mixture into the moulds until it is just above the cavity – it should form a little dome on top. If you poured too much, use a stirrer and remove some.

3 Let it sit for a few minutes for any large bubbles to surface, and pop them with your long neck lighter.

4 Apply a small amount of leftover resin to the mould lid, covering the numbers of the top faces.

5 Put the top of the mould on, align the keys, and gently "squish" it down. This will help to force excess resin out of the mould. The less excess resin on top, the less chance of a raised face!

6 Now, we wait! Note: make sure the mould is out of the way of pets and children (another great reason to use a pressure pot!).

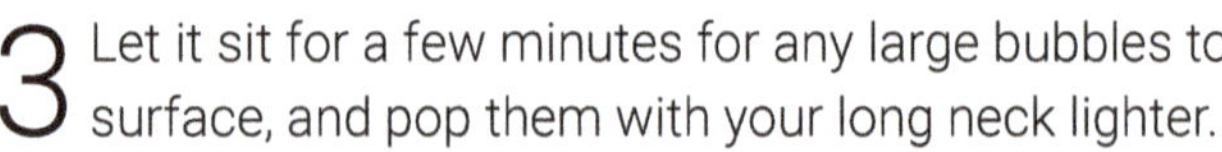
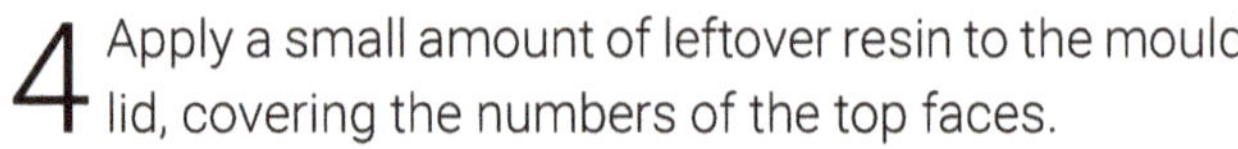

IF USING A PRESSURE POT, PUT THE DICE INSIDE, SEAL IT UP, BRING IT UP TO YOUR PREFERRED PRESSURE AND DISCONNECT THE HOSE.

DEMOULDING

After the recommended demould time (usually 24 hours), it's time to open up those moulds! Take a moment and appreciate how far you've come.

The dice are in a Schrödinger state; they're both perfect and imperfect. You won't know which until you open it!

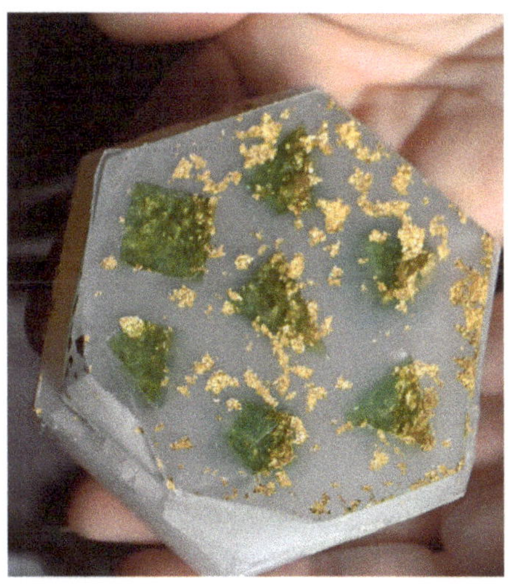

1 Gently pry open the lid of the mould. You may notice some voids or bubbles, but don't despair; we can probably fix that. Look at that gold! (See picture to the left).

2 Give the mould a good squeeze on all sides and crack the flashing, which is the excess resin that has leaked out of the mould. If it's still soft, the dice may need more time. Try not to pull the flashing towards the dice face when removing as it may damage the face; instead pull it away.

3 Over something soft, like a cloth or towel, put your thumb behind the dice and slowly bend the mould backwards with your fingers. The dice should pop right out (hopefully not onto your concrete floor!)

If not, give the mould a bit of a stretch and try again. Doing this gently is essential as the fine numbers in the mould can tear quite easily as the mould ages.

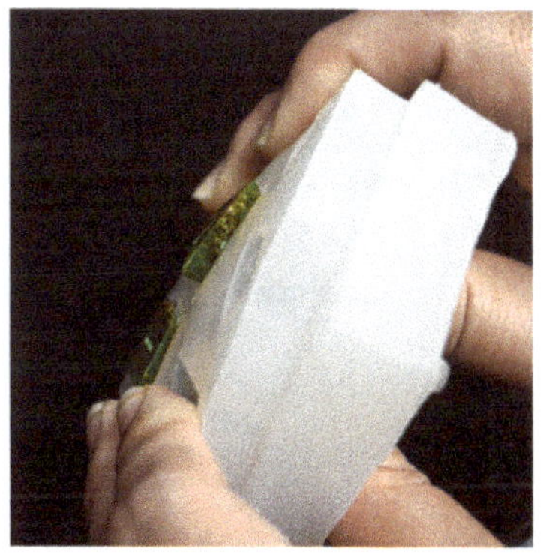

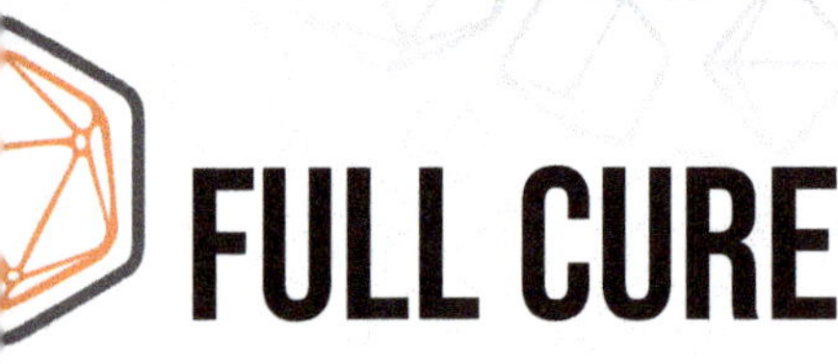

FULL CURE

LEVEL: (1)   2   3   4

As someone who struggles with delayed gratification, I've had issues with this step on more than one *(or several dozen)* occasions. After the excitement of pulling your dice out of their moulds, you may be tempted to jump straight into polishing and inking. However, it's important to mention that most resins don't reach their full hardness for several days. If you start sanding now, you're unlikely to get the shine you're looking for. Semi-cured resin is a surefire recipe for cloudy dice.

Many resins state a full cure time of *72 hours or more*. If you've used a deep-pour resin, alcohol inks, or if the weather is colder, this may take *substantially* longer.

I'M IMPATIENT, WHAT CAN I DO?

The absolute best thing to do is *wait*.

This allows the resin sufficient time to finish its chemical process naturally and reach a full glass-like state.

If, however, you're unable to wait, the alternative is to apply some gentle heat.

Placing the semi-cured resin in a warm room or box can significantly decrease the full cure time, but be careful to keep the temperature constant so as not to cause hazing or other surface issues.

Another alternative is to use a dehydrator (see "Dehydrator" on page 80). A food dehydrator is simply a small, low-temperature oven. It keeps a constant temperature for long periods of time to remove moisture from food (think banana chips or dried apricots).

Note: Please don't use your household dehydrator for curing resin, as the uncured resin vapour can leach into the plastic making it unsuitable for food usage. Buy a dedicated dehydrator or dedicated "resin curing machine".

SAND & POLISH

LEVEL: (1) 2 3 4   **PPE:**   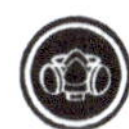 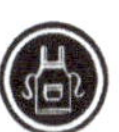

WHAT YOU'LL NEED
- A full set of 3M polishing paper
- A container of water
- 800 grit sandpaper (if needed)
- Polishing Compound (optional)

1 To minimise the amount of dust, you will want to wet-sand your dice. Get a bowl of water and dip the dice – keep the paper (and the dice) nice and wet throughout the process.

2 If any flashing on the faces can't be removed with your fingernail, you may need to use a knife or sand it off with higher grit sandpaper. Be gentle; higher grit paper will remove material faster!

3 For polishing faces, I prefer to work in a circular motion. I usually do 40-50 rotations for each grade of polishing paper (in order) to bring things to a beautiful shine.

For the last two papers (1 and 2 microns), try switching to a quality polishing compound (see "Equipment by Level" on page 23) rather than water to bring out the shine. Your dice will sparkle but will need a quick rinse in water or an ultrasonic cleaner to remove any excess.

> **PRO TIP:** AFTER USING THE POLISHING PAPER, YOU CAN GET *EVEN MORE* SHINE USING A DREMEL OR ROTARY TOOL, SOFT WOOL POLISHING PADS AND MORE POLISHING COMPOUND. THE DIFFERENCE IS *AMAZING*.

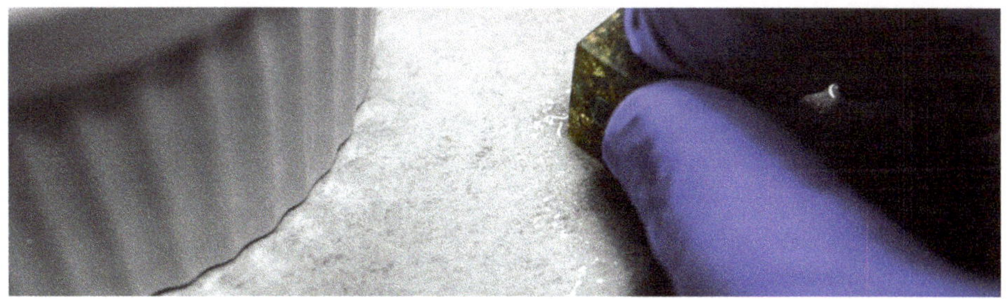

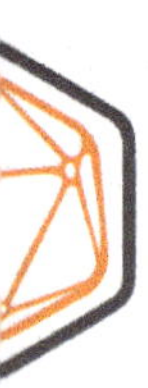

INKING YOUR DICE

LEVEL:  **1** 2 3 4   **PPE:**  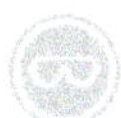  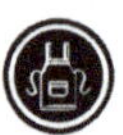

WHAT YOU'LL NEED
- Acrylic paint
- A paint brush
- Paper towel
- Paper or mixing tray

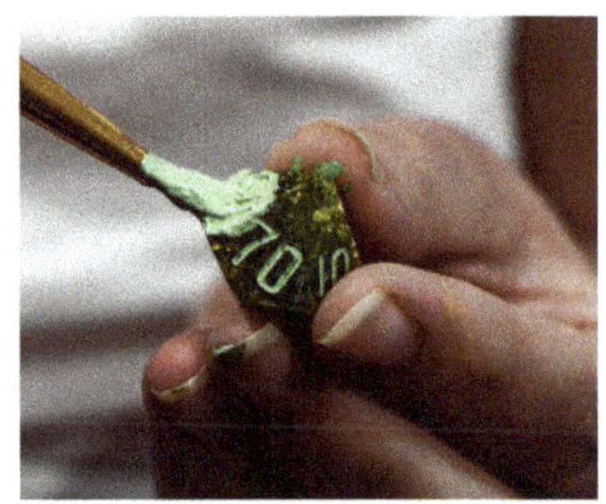

Inking your dice is the term used for filling in the numbers. Don't worry; you don't need a steady hand – we'll be using the "more is better approach". All you do is fill the number with acrylic paint and wipe it off! It's one of the easiest and most rewarding parts of dice-making.

1 Put some acrylic paint on a piece of paper or a mixing tray. If you want to mix a specific colour, now is your chance.

2 Dab your paintbrush in the paint and liberally apply it to the number. Make sure you get it right into the sides of the number as well.

3 Get some paper towel and wipe it across the number. This will remove the excess and leave the number painted. Some people prefer to wipe the dice on the paper instead. Decide what's best for you.

4 If you missed a spot, add more paint and wipe it again. Give the dice a chance to dry, and we can move on to the last step!

STUCK FOR COLOUR IDEAS?

As a general rule: Dark dice, light ink – Light dice, dark ink! Alternately, try a tool like the Adobe colour wheel. The triad mode is great for showing complementary colours! (*Scan QR code or* bit.ly/adobe-colour-wheel).

CLEANUP

The last step – cleanup! For cleaning the dice, it's best to use something gentle like baby wipes or diluted Isopropyl Alcohol (IPA).

If you didn't follow our instructions and wait for the full cure time of your resin (e.g. 72 hours or longer), you may find your dice are dulled by 99% IPA. If so, it's best to use something gentler.

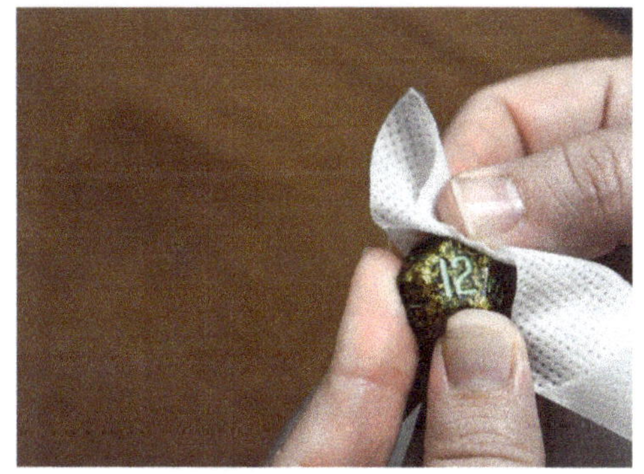

All we want to do here is clean off any paint smudges or leftover polish.

SOME MAKERS LIKE TO TAKE THE DICE BACK OVER THEIR 2 AND 1 MICRON POLISHING PAPERS WITH SOME POLISHING COMPOUND. THIS NOT ONLY REMOVES ANY EXCESS PAINT, BUT BRINGS THEM BACK TO A SUPER SHINE.

CONGRATULATIONS!

LEVEL: (**1**) 2 3 4

Give yourself a pat on the back! Handmade dice are sure to impress most people, even if there are imperfections. If you like to play role-playing games in person, people will soon be asking you to make them some!

If you got this far, you should be proud. You're now a Critmaker, and these dice are a huge first step in the journey. Not everyone who attempts to make dice ever gets this far. But with the help of this book and your tenacity, you did it!

 We've included a "Certificate of Dice Craft" at the end of this book. If you don't want to cut it out, you can download a copy! *(Scan QR code or* <u>critmaker.com/graduate</u>*).*

Print it out and post it on your wall or social media. You deserve it! Come show off your dice in #newbies-corner on our Critmaker Discord!

There's still a lot left in this guide and we hope it will excite you to continue your journey.

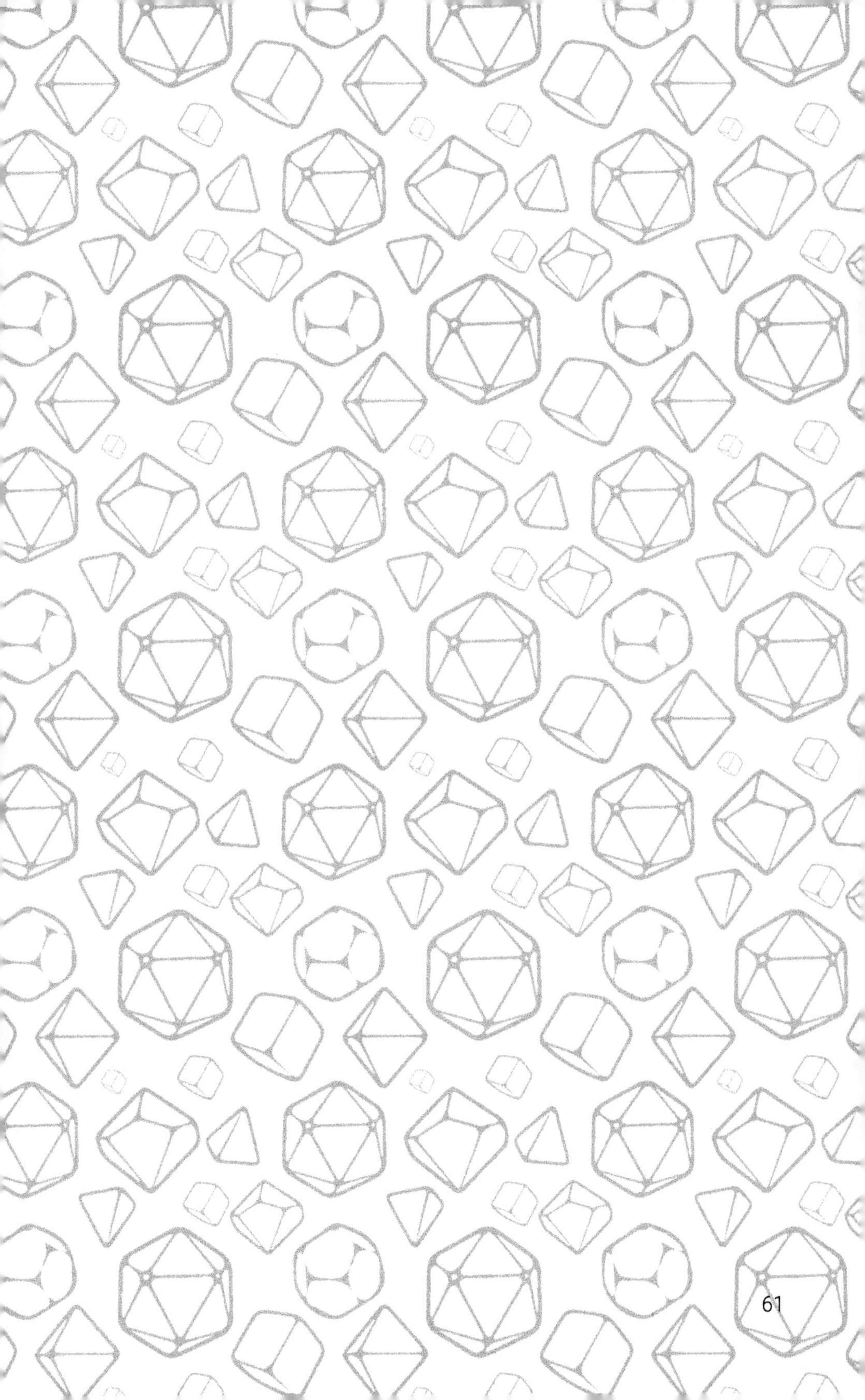

PRESSURE CASTING

In this chapter, we'll be looking at pressure pots. We'll cover what they do, how to make one relatively cheaply using a paint pressure pot and how to test for leaks!

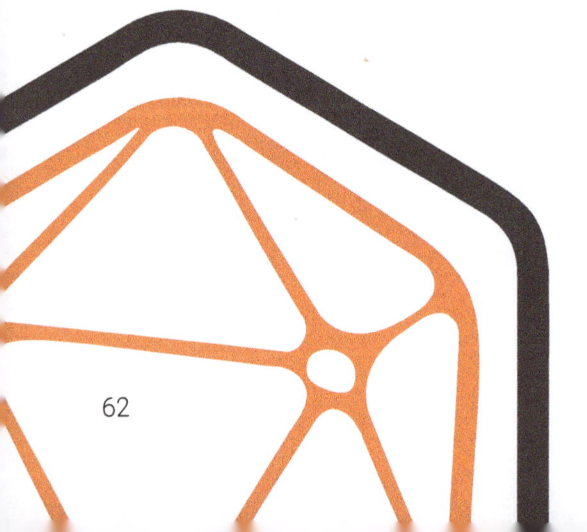

PART FOUR

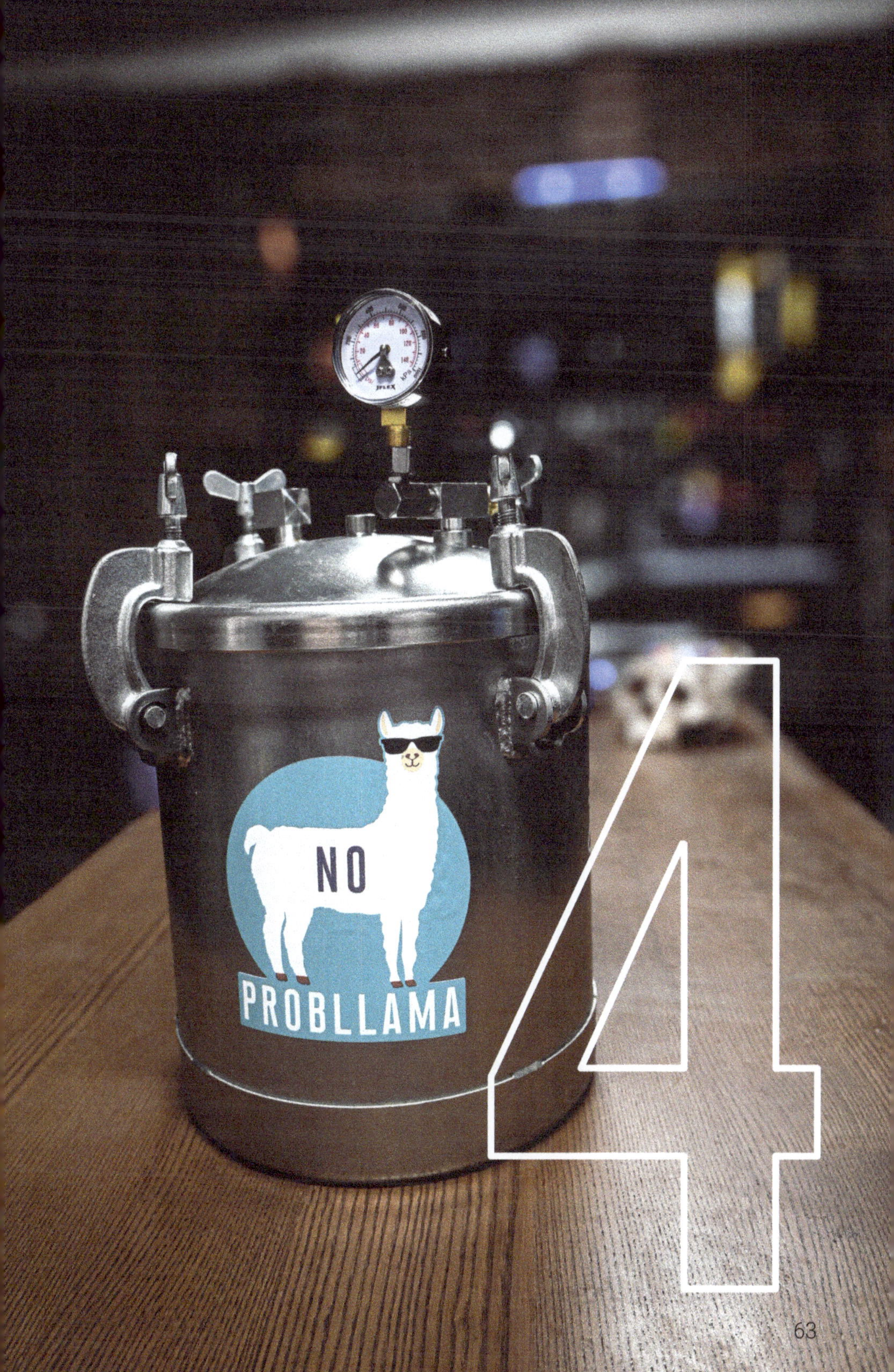

NO
PROBLLAMA
4

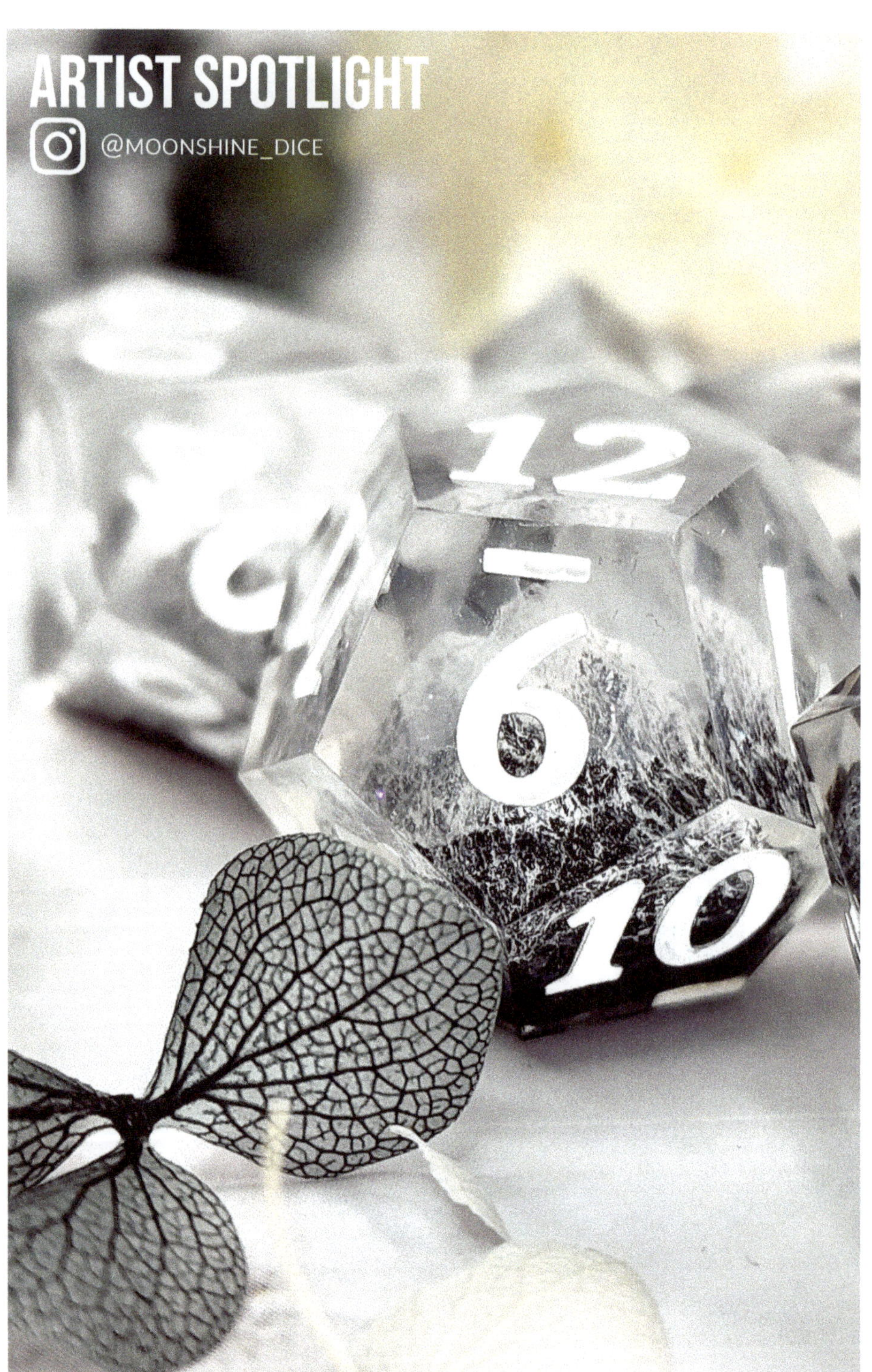

ARTIST SPOTLIGHT
@MOONSHINE_DICE

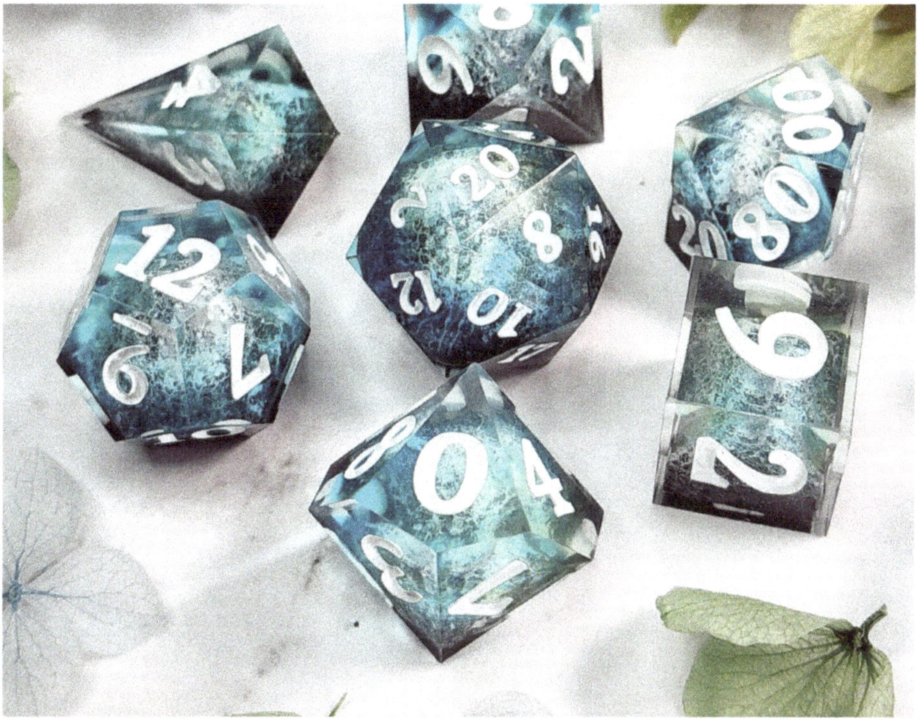

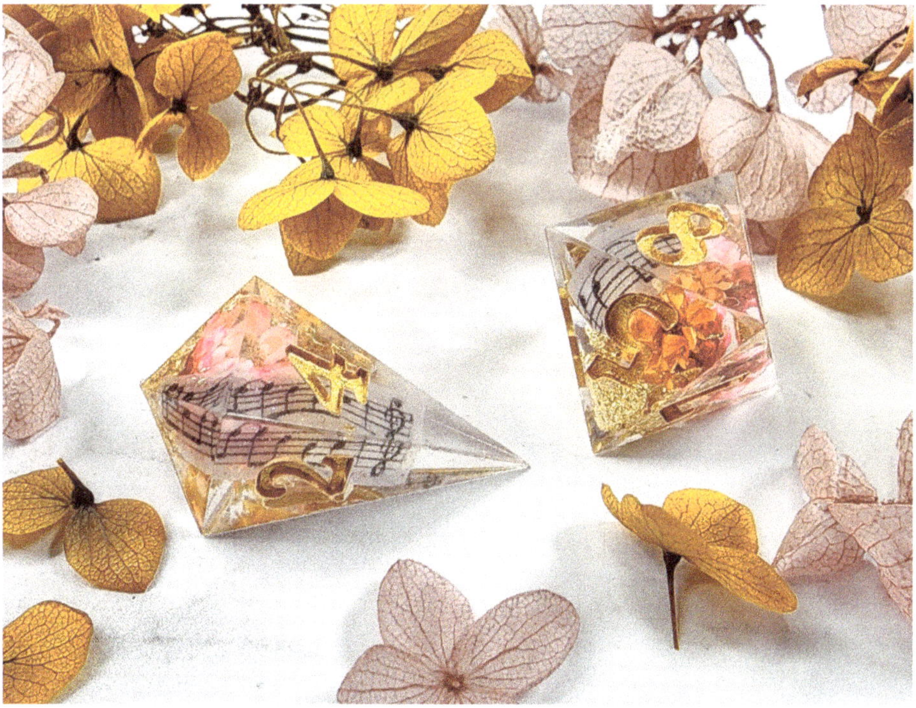

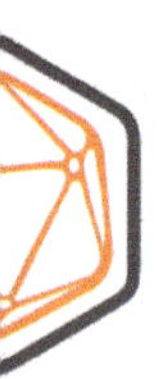

IMPORTANT INFORMATION

LEVEL: 1  2 3 4

HOW BIG A POT DO I NEED?

Most dice-makers use the Harbour Freight, Vevor, California Air Tools, TCP Global or Blackridge pressure pots to cast dice. The basic models are 10L or (2½ gallons). With a decent pressure pot insert, you should be able to fit around 8-12 compact moulds into a single pot.

In Australia, at least, it's cheaper to buy two small pots than one larger one, though a large pot may give you more options for casting larger dice (chonks as they're affectionately known!).

CAN I USE A PRESSURE COOKER?

Under no circumstances should you attempt to use a pressure cooker. While they sound similar, they're two completely different pieces of equipment. A pressure pot is a steel container with air pumped into it – a pressure cooker relies on steam from the liquid in the pot to generate internal pressure.

ARE PRESSURE POTS DANGEROUS?

No more than any other tool – there are many safeguards in place, including:

- They have an emergency release valve that releases all the air if it approaches the limit.

- They're rated for a higher pressure than you'll need – for dice casting, you only need 50 PSI at most. This isn't enough pressure to rupture a steel tank rated for 70+ PSI.

- There's no need to leave it attached to the compressor. Once the pot has come to pressure, you should remove the hose, meaning no more pressure can accumulate.

ARE PRESSURE POTS EXPENSIVE?

Dedicated pressure pots (or chambers) can be expensive as they're designed for professional use. The cheapest way for the home dice maker is with a converted paint pressure pot and an air compressor.

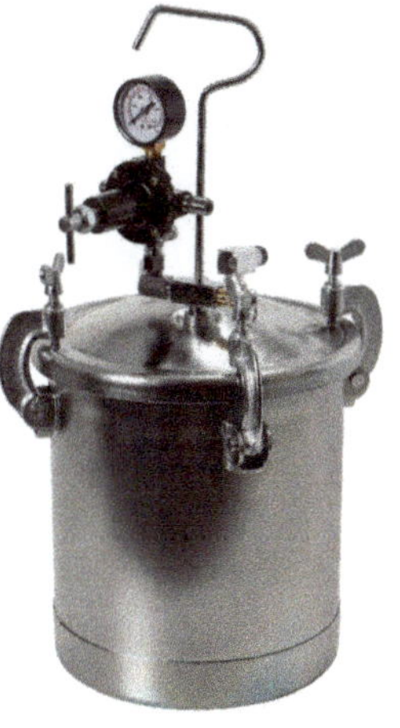

In Australia, 10L paint pressure pots cost between AUD$150-$300 from Vevor or Supercheap Auto. If you're in the U.S., a cheap 2½ gallon pot costs between USD$100–$200 from HarborFreight, California Air Tools or TCP Global (pictured).

Unless you already have one, you'll also need an air compressor. While it's quite an outlay, you'll now have everything you need for crystal-clear dice. Every time.

When selecting a compressor, aim for a tank that is similar in size to your pot or larger. I run a 20L silent compressor for my 10L pressure pots, though you can get away with a smaller capacity or even an airbrush compressor with the correct fittings.

Don't buy the cheapest compressor if you're going to have it indoors, they can be *extremely* loud. Opt for a compressor rated as "silenced" – our silent compressor we use is only 42db compared to our original which was over 90db (louder than my motorcycle).

WHAT PRESSURE DO I NEED?

You'll only need around 20-30 PSI for crystal-clear dice. We often cast as high as 40-50 PSI, though some makers have issues with concave faces. It's often said that dice must be cast at a lower or equal pressure to what the mould was cast at, though, in our tests, we've not seen any significant difference. Experiment to see what works best for your resin and moulds. If the mould was not cast in a pressure pot (which is rare), casting with a pressure pot may cause distortion.

WARNING - ALWAYS RELEASE THE PRESSURE SLOWLY WITH THE VALVE BEFORE YOU OPEN THE POT

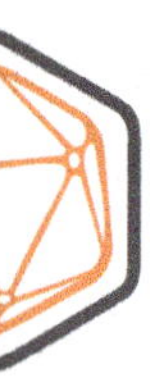

CONVERTING A PAINT POT

LEVEL: 1 **(2)** 3 4

WHAT YOU'LL NEED

- Pressure paint pot
- ¼" inch Pressure Gauge
- ¼" to ¼" Elbow Adapter (if needed)
- ⅜" Ball Valve
- ⅜" Nitto Adapter
- PTFE Tape (or high-pressure thread sealant)
- Large wrench
- Wrench tool that came with the pot

Note: The following articles are for informational purposes only. We take no responsibility for what you do with this knowledge. This kind of modification will void any warranty that may be offered by your pressure pot manufacturer. You must accept that you and you alone are responsible for your safety and the safety of others in any endeavour in which you engage. You are responsible for knowing your limitations of knowledge and experience. Use of these instructions is at your own risk. Critmaker disclaims all responsibility for any resulting damage, injury, or expense. If this is a concern, please buy a dedicated resin-casting pressure pot.

Before getting started, purchase your paint pressure pot to ensure that the sizes above are correct for your model. In Australia, the total cost of the parts mentioned above comes to around AUD$35 (or USD$25).

The hose included with the kit was extremely difficult to connect and disconnect. I'd recommend buying a higher quality one. You only need one hose for all your pressure pots, and it will make you a much happier person in the long run.

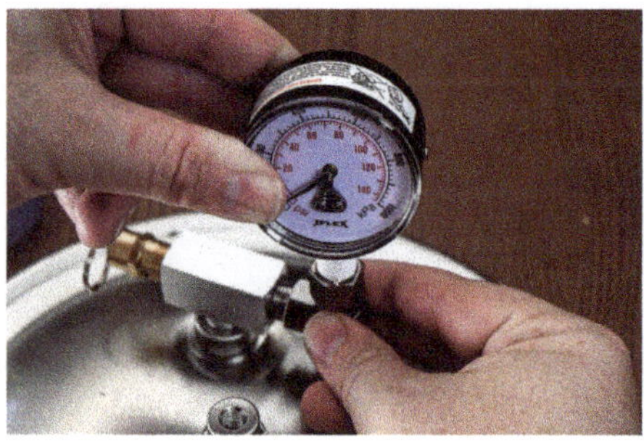

1 Apply PTFE tape to the new gauge, thread it onto the elbow adapter and tighten it with your wrench. The kit I'm using here already has an elbow adapter included; if not, you may need to remove the T-adapter to put it on.

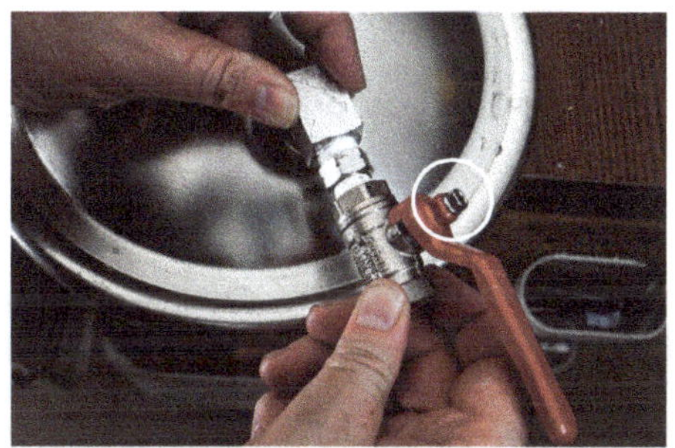

2 To add the ball valve, add PTFE tape to the ⅜" male-to-male adapter and tighten it up. Note: You may need to remove its handle first. A small bolt holds the handle in place (circled).

3 Now, add the ⅜" nitto-style adapter to the other end of the ball valve and tighten it up with the wrench. You may also need the thin wrenches that came with the pressure pot. Use them to twist the locking nuts in separate directions to tighten.

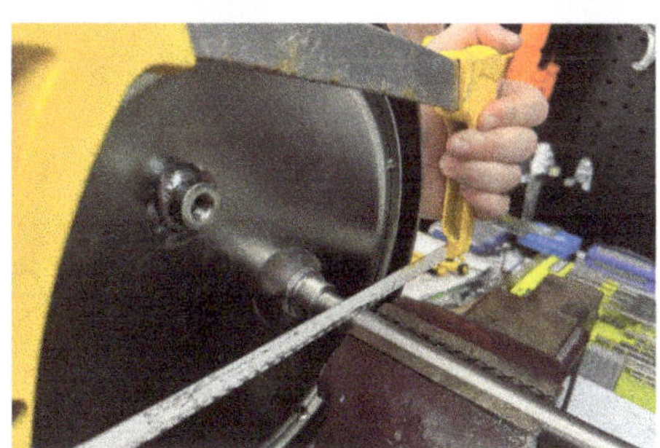

REMOVING THE TUBE

4 The large metal rod down the middle of the pot used to feed air into the tank either needs to be unscrewed or cut off.

If you want to unscrew it, you may need a blowtorch – not only is it tight, but it's most likely been coated in permanent Loctite.

Otherwise, an angle grinder or hacksaw will do the job. Cut it as close to the top as possible. I have done this on three pots without any issue, but the choice of method is up to you.

CONGRATULATIONS, YOU NOW HAVE A PRESSURE POT! NOW LET'S MAKE SURE IT ACTUALLY HOLDS PRESSURE!

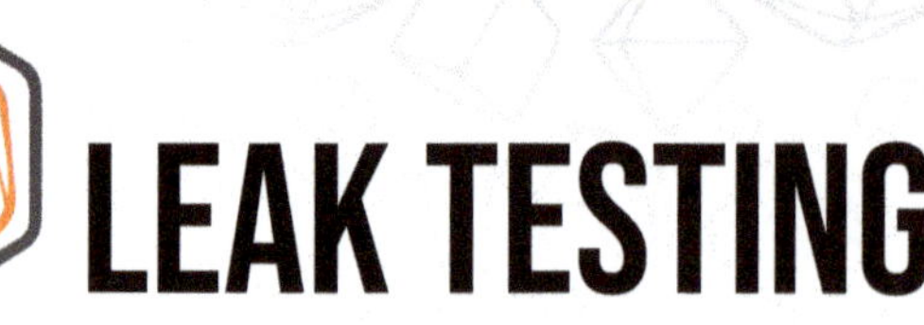

LEAK TESTING

LEVEL: 1   **(2)**   3   4

1 First, check that everything is tightened. Place the lid onto the pot and tighten the locking mechanism all around.

2 Connect your air hose to the pot and slowly allow it to reach a pressure of around 50 PSI, close the valve and remove the hose.

3 If it keeps pressure, great! If the pot is hissing, you've done something wrong and need to recheck all the connections (including the ones that were on there already!). Make sure you've tightened and sealed everything. Then, try again!

4 Get a spray bottle, fill it two-thirds with water and put in a few drops of dishwashing detergent. Give it a shake and spray around every connection – watch closely. If there are any leaks, you'll see the detergent bubbling (see photo on the right).

5 If you find any leaks, gently release the pressure. Undo the part completely, remove any existing sealant, apply new PTFE tape, and re-tighten. Once it's ready, test everything again.

6 When you're confident there are no leaks, take note of the PSI and walk away for a few hours before rechecking. If it's stable, it should be good to use! If not, repeat these steps. If you still can't get it to keep pressure, you may need to consider high-pressure sealant. It takes 24 hours to cure, but will ultimately give a better seal.

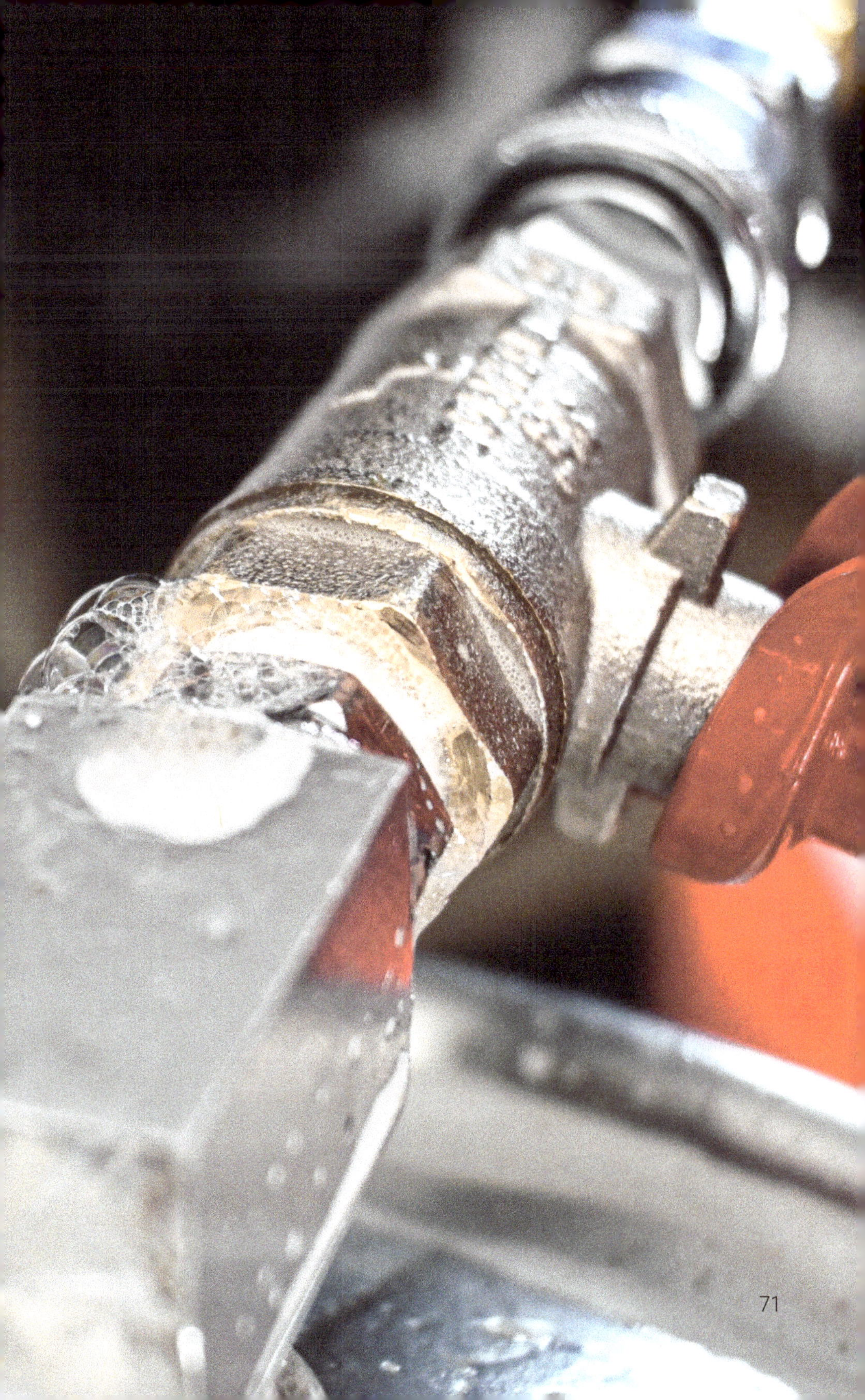

ARTIST SPOTLIGHT

@_YANIIR_

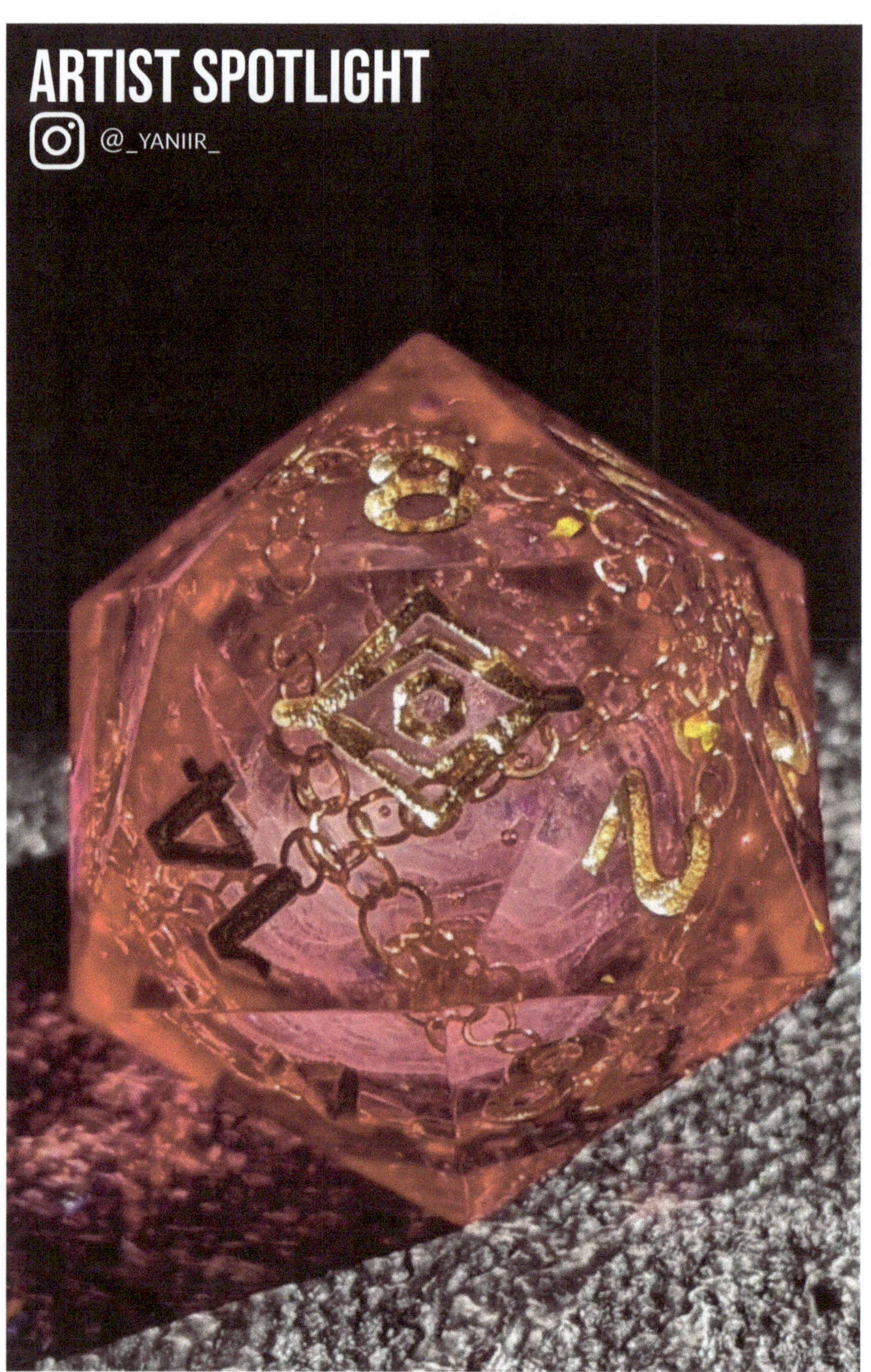

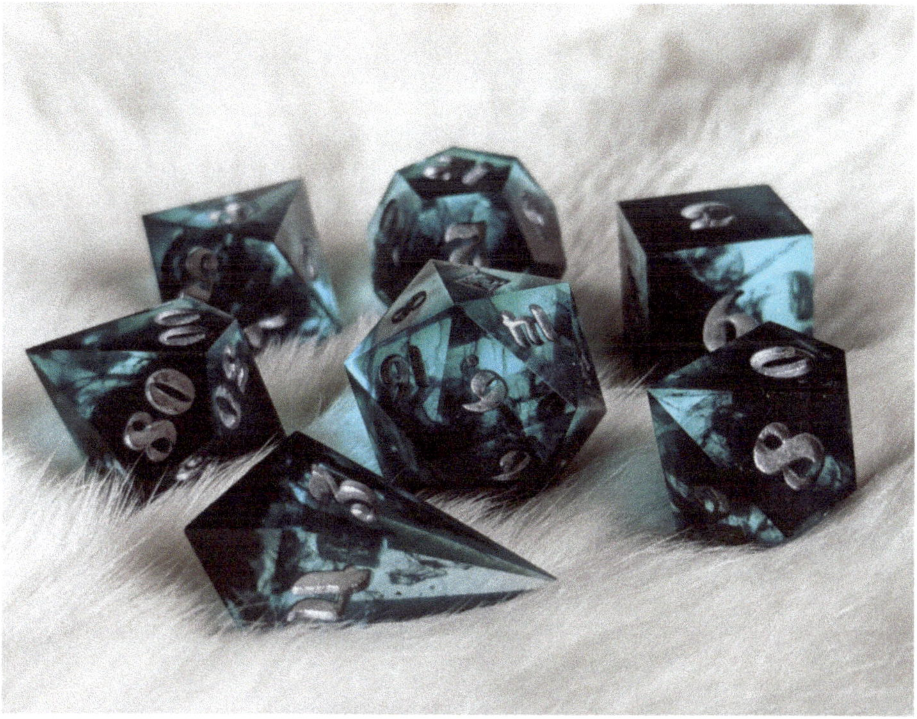

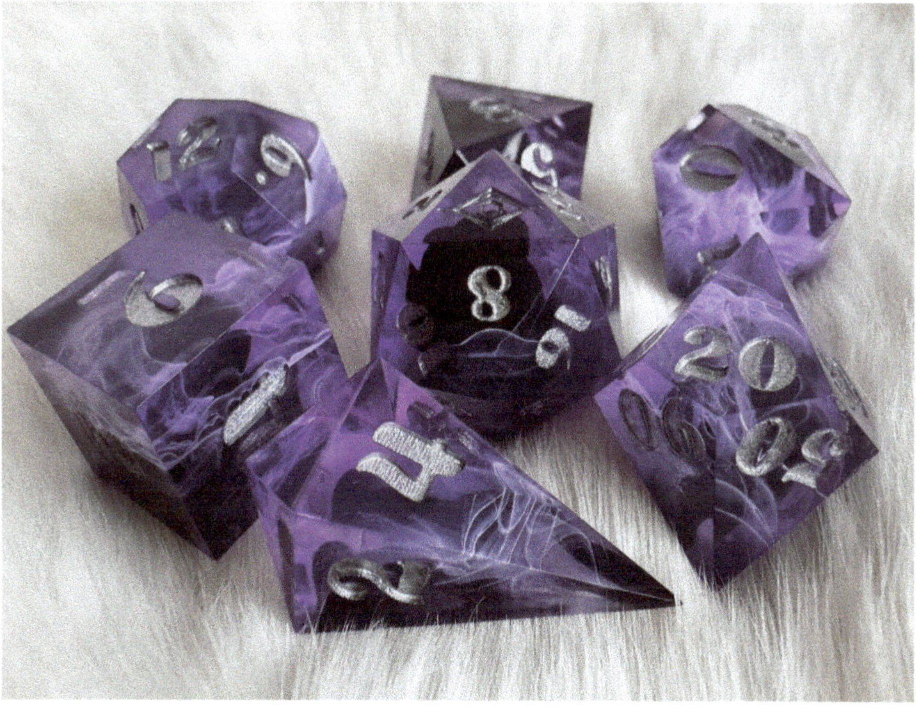

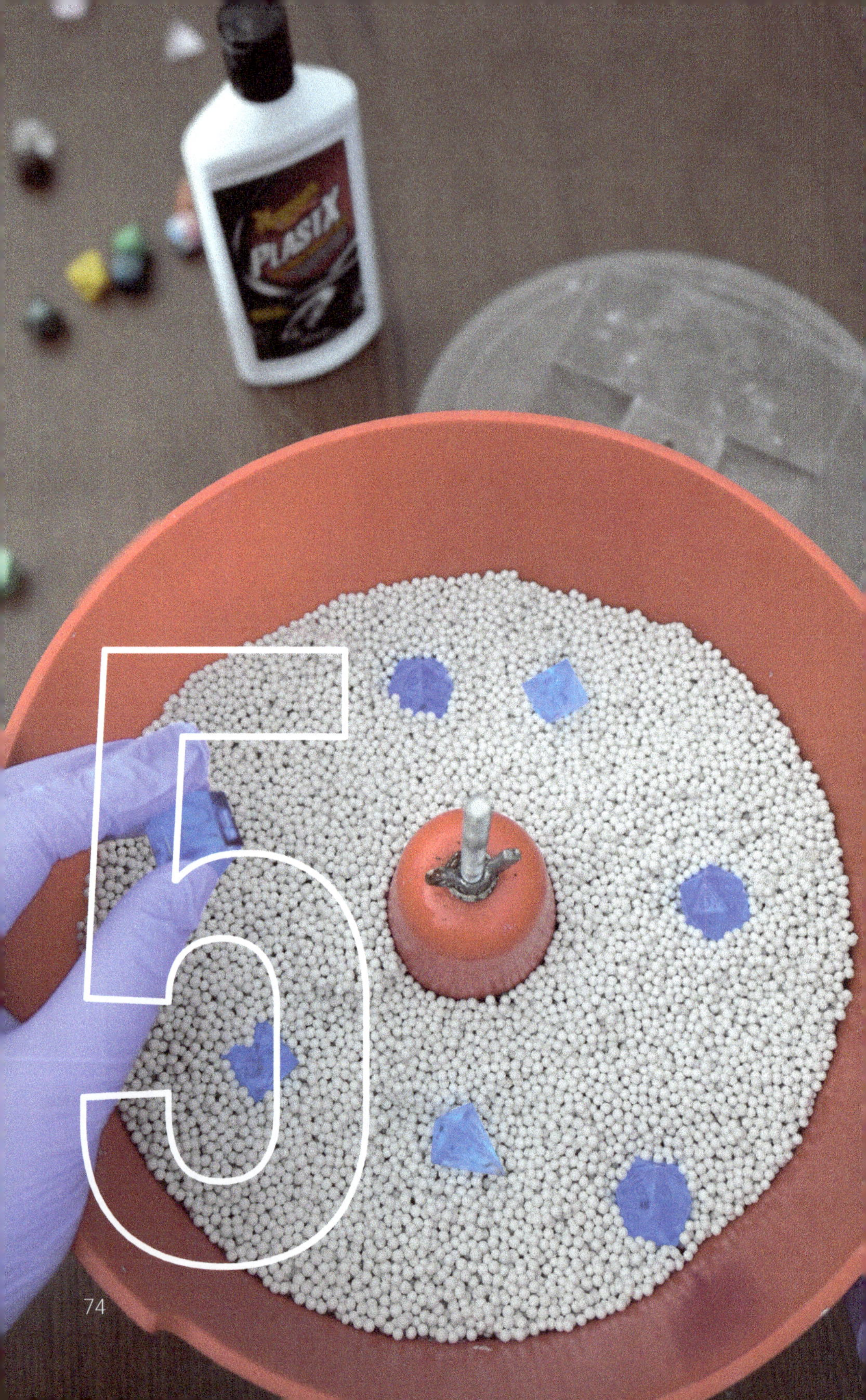

ADVANCED FINISHING

Though we say advanced, there's nothing to stop you from considering these finishing techniques at any stage of your journey! For many, sanding is difficult or even impossible, these machines not only save you hours, but your cramped hands as well!

PART FIVE

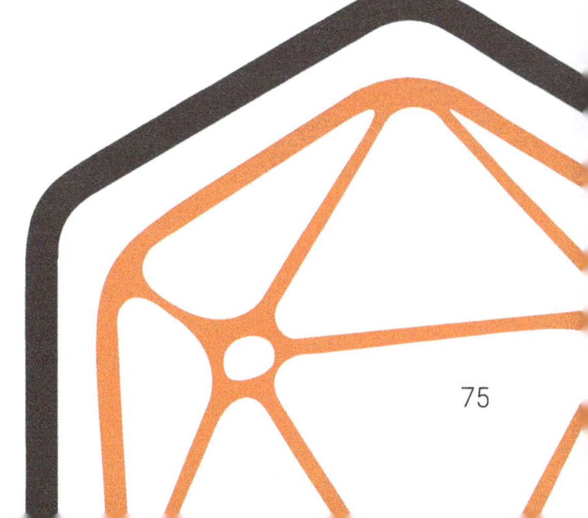

MINI POTTERY WHEEL

PPE: 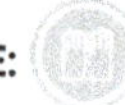 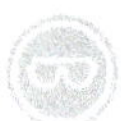 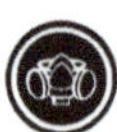 

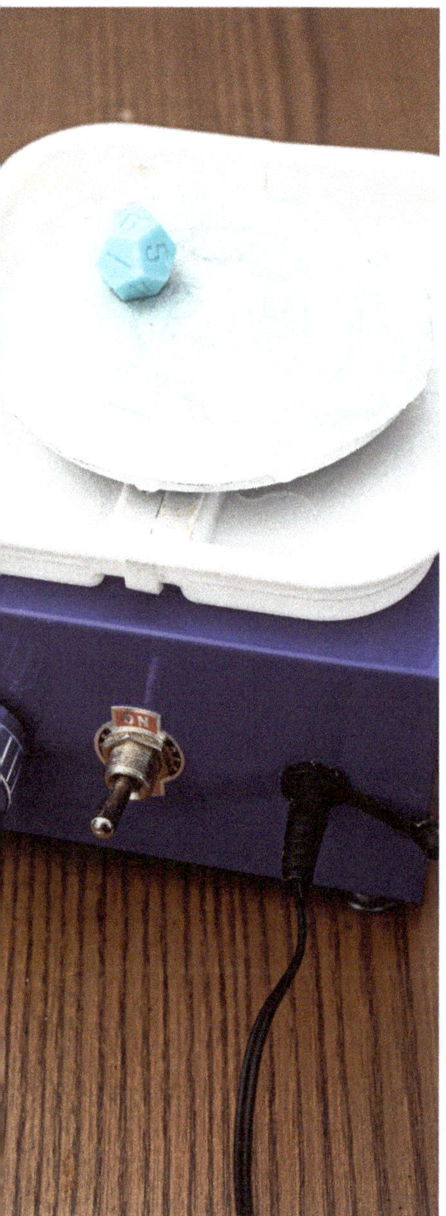

Mini pottery wheels cost about AUD$50 on eBay or Amazon. They might be just what the doctor or physiotherapist ordered! To use a mini pottery wheel, attach your 3M polishing paper with painter's tape, set the speed, and turn it on.

Most standard models (as shown) have a power input, a switch and a dial. The switch has three modes: on (forward), off and on (reverse). The dial controls the speed.

For polishing dice, start on the slowest setting and increase it until you're comfortable. Hold the face flat against the disk and count a few seconds (or rotations).

When you're done with that colour paper, move on to the next.

DON'T GO TOO FAST; YOU CAN RUIN YOUR DICE IN THE BLINK OF AN EYE BY REMOVING ONE OF THE BEAUTIFUL SHARP EDGES!

Larger pottery wheels are great (if you can find one cheaply), as they will wet the paper for you!

We have yet to progress past the mini wheel, but there are many dice makers out there using a full-sized wheel.

ROTARY TOOL

LEVEL: 1 ② 3 4

PPE:   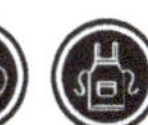

A rotary tool is another great addition to the dice-maker's toolkit. Whether sanding rough edges, hand-carving detailed "geode" blanks, cutting jagged lines for "kintsugi" style dice or polishing to a mirror, the tool has it all!

There are plenty of brands out there (we use a Ryobi rotary tool), but none as well-known as the Dremel brand. Dremel has hundreds of attachments for sanding, polishing, cutting and more – the uses are limited only by your imagination.

Like a pottery wheel, a rotary tool can save you sore hands, a hunched back and hours of time in polishing. Unlike sanding with paper or a wheel, you can use the rotary tool to get right into the numbers and even sand rounded edges and corners.

To use a rotary tool, you need to find the softest polishing attachment you can, wipe some plastic polish onto the dice, choose the lowest settings and start polishing in gentle circles. Take your time and get as many of the marks out as you can. You can increase the speed as you get more comfortable.

If you can, I'd recommend a flexible shaft that's available for most models. It's great for high-precision work.

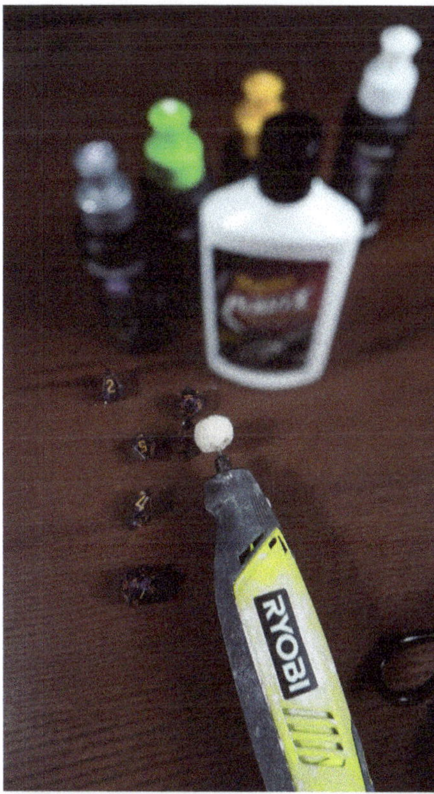

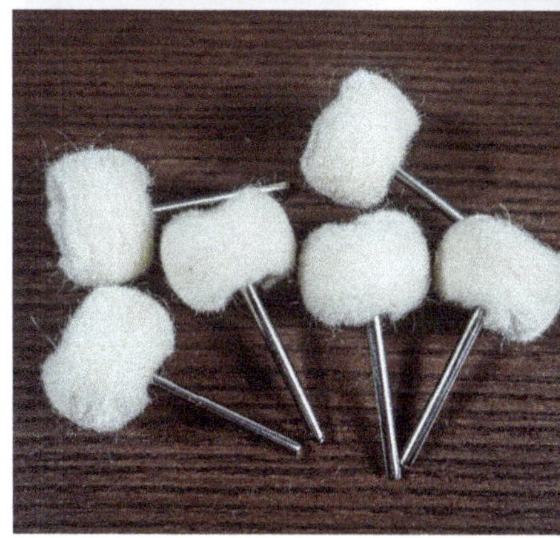

VIBRATORY TUMBLER

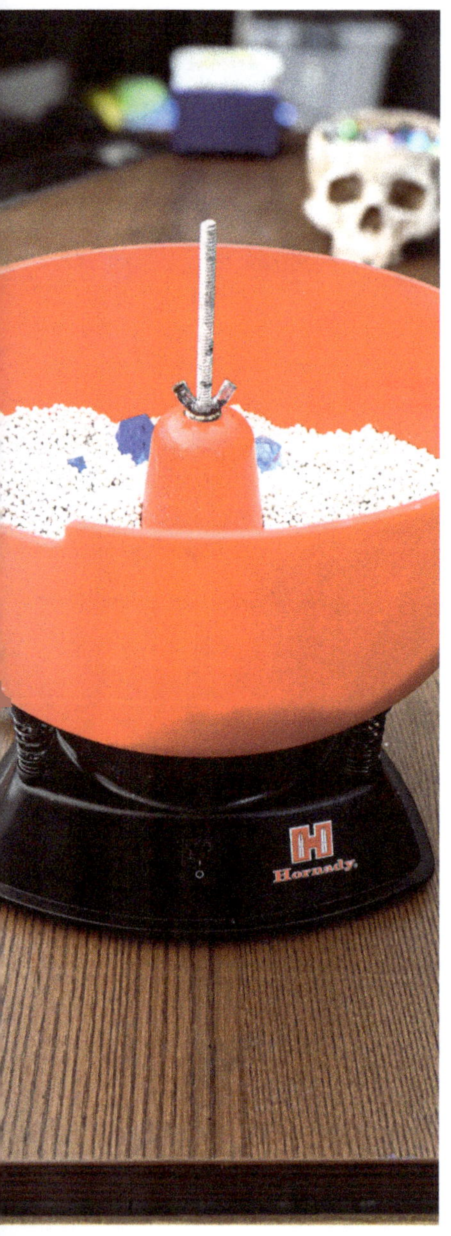

A vibratory tumbler is a finishing tool that uses vibration to polish. The bowl is filled with finishing media, such as wood or ceramic, and a polish. Unlike a rotary tumbler (used for smoothing rocks), the vibratory tumbler won't round the edges of your dice.

For dice making, use 3-4mm ceramic balls (or a combination of the two). Ceramic finishing media is reusable, washable and at that size, they won't get stuck in the numbers on most dice.

As far as the tumbler goes, we use the Hornady M1 Case Tumbler. It's quiet, works well, and is not much more expensive than the generic ones on Amazon.

To use the tumbler, fill it about $2/3$ with finishing media and empty in a bottle of plastic polish. You can add a little dish soap to get more movement from the media. We used 2kg of media (about 4.5lb) to fill the tumbler. If your polishing compound is water-based, you can add a little water when it starts to dry out. Doing this will mean it'll last a long time!

In terms of tumble time, it depends on the finish of your dice. If they've been sanded to 1 micron (white polishing paper), they'll need about 24 hours for perfection. Increase the number of days if you've done less polishing. If using the tumbler for our dice, we generally give them 48 hours or more.

ULTRASONIC CLEANER

LEVEL: 1 2 3 

An ultrasonic cleaner uses sound waves in water to get all the tiny particles out of the grooves in your dice. For those serious about production, few tools are more valuable. When you've finished sanding or polishing your dice (or masters), they will be full of dust and polish. A quick 10-30 minute ultrasonic cleaning will make them pristine again.

For those making moulds, you will also find an ultrasonic cleaner invaluable. After moulding a set of dice, there may be silicone residue, mould release or petroleum jelly left in the numbers and on the faces. Pop them in the cleaner, dry them off, and they're ready for the next moulding.

Note: Make sure you dry the dice off before moulding. The water will repel the silicone, and you'll get voids in your moulds.

For cleaning dice, you need nothing but distilled water as a cleaning fluid. As it gets too saturated, change the water out and discard the leftover fluid in your chemical waste. Please don't put the water down the sink as it contains traces of resin and other chemicals.

There are a lot of great cleaners on the market. We've had success with the Vevor brand. They're cheap, built well, and work great!

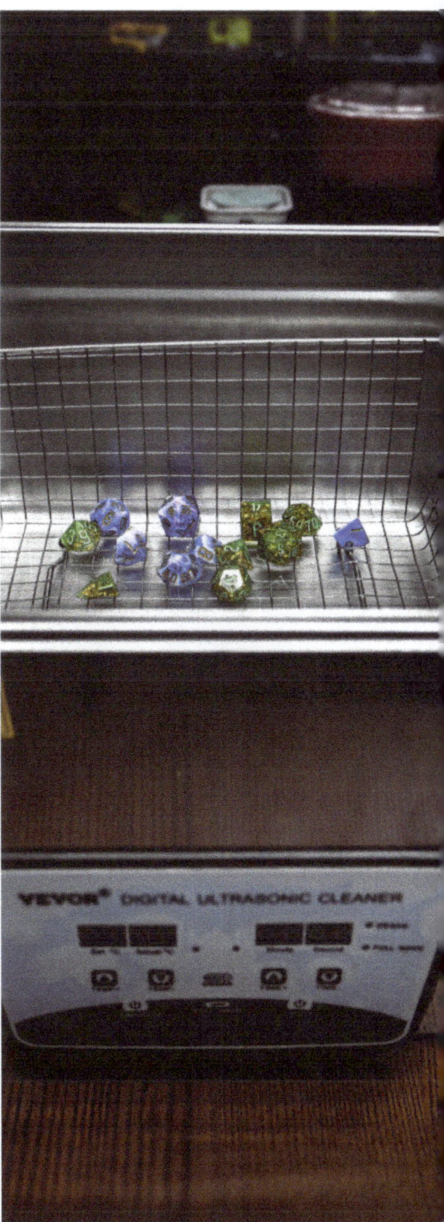

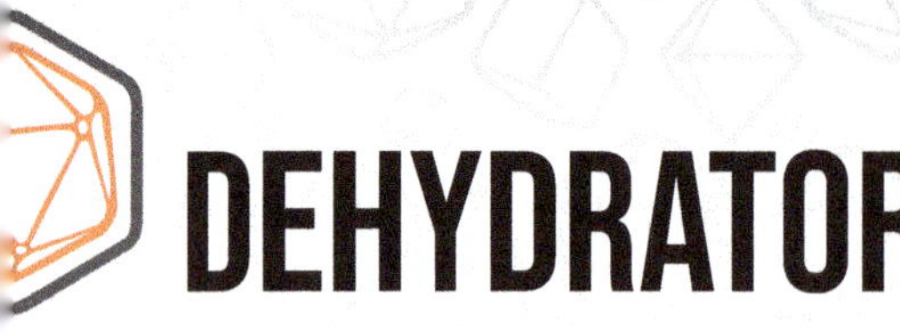

DEHYDRATOR

LEVEL: 1 2 3 (4)

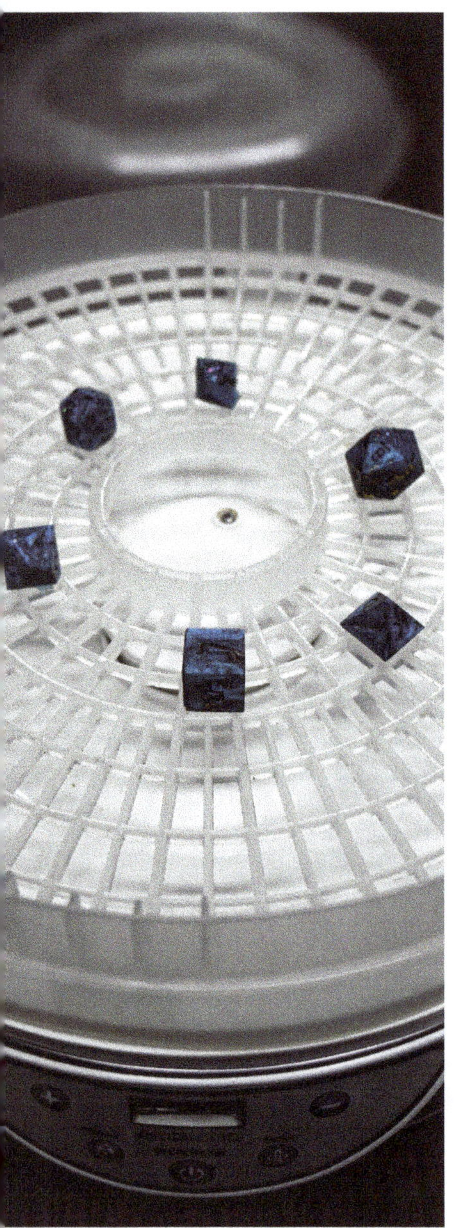

This is an item you don't really need. But, if you have an old one lying around or can pick one up cheaply, you'll wonder why you never did before. We bought ours for only AUD$20 (or about USD$13) from Facebook Marketplace!

When casting dice with alcohol ink, they can take much longer to cure. You can tell by sticking your thumbnail in an inconspicuous spot as it'll leave an indent. The only cure (pun intended) is more time. After a few days, the dice should have hardened completely.

That's where a food dehydrator comes in handy! A dehydrator extracts moisture from food – it's basically a low-temperature oven with a circulating fan. Popping your alcohol ink dice in a dehydrator will harden them up in just 3-4 hours on the lowest setting.

Most "resin curing machines" on Amazon, etc. are just food dehydrators with a higher price tag.

 There's a great video about this on the Evan and Katelyn YouTube channel!

(Scan QR code or bit.ly/resin-curing).

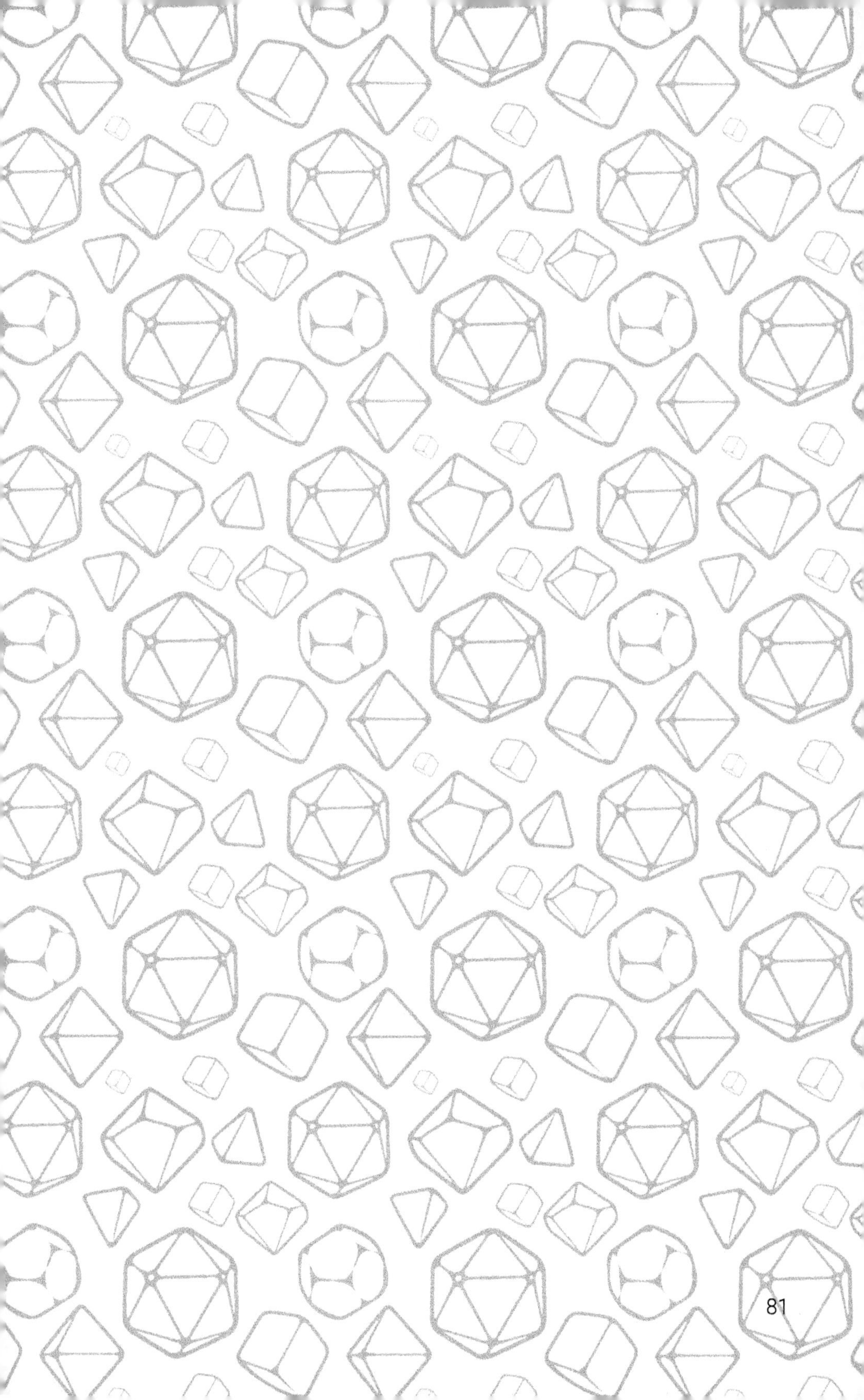

@CHICKENWIZARDDICE

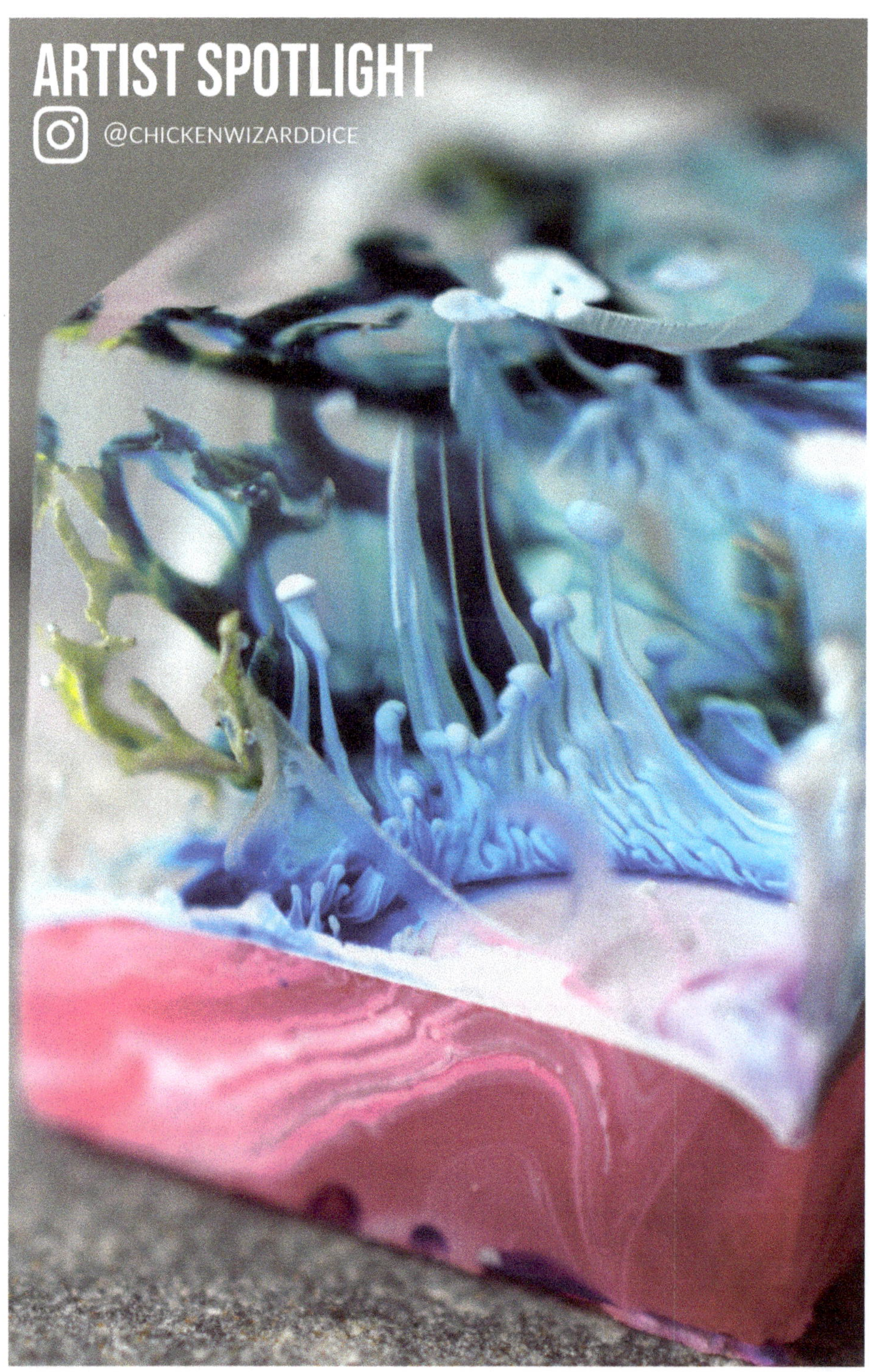

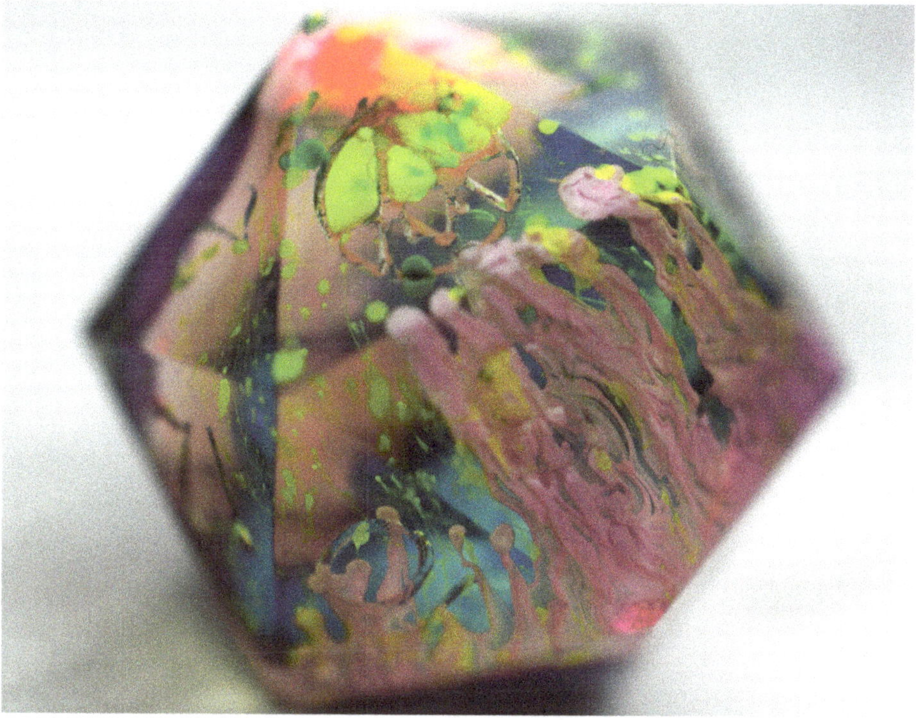

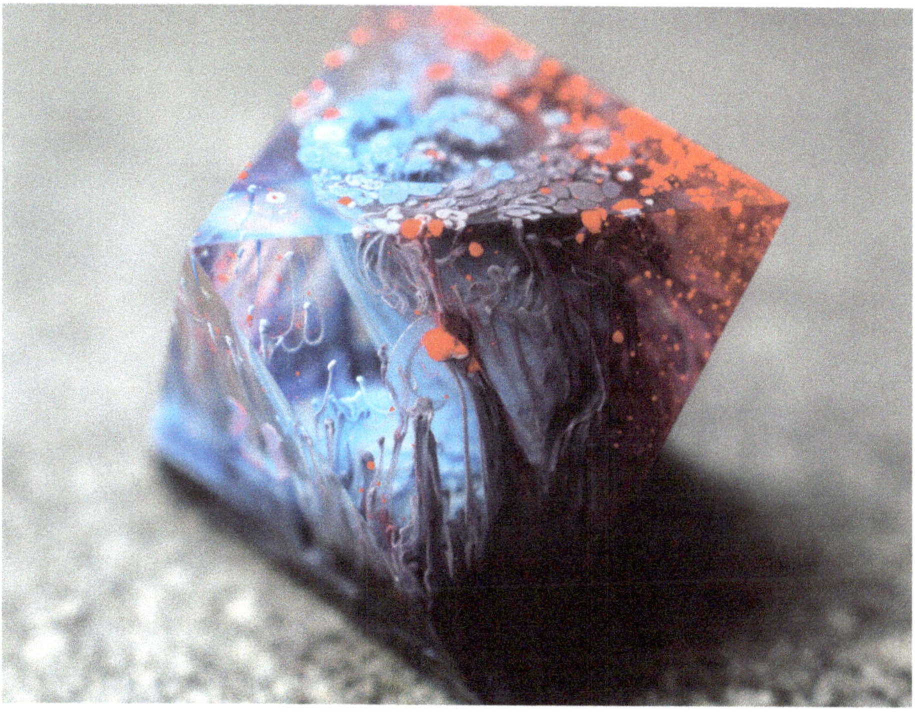

POURING TECHNIQUES

When it comes to dice pouring techniques, there are dozens to choose from! Most techniques come from traditional resin art and casting. They range from the simple to mildly infuriating. We'll be covering several of the most-used techniques in this chapter.

PART SIX

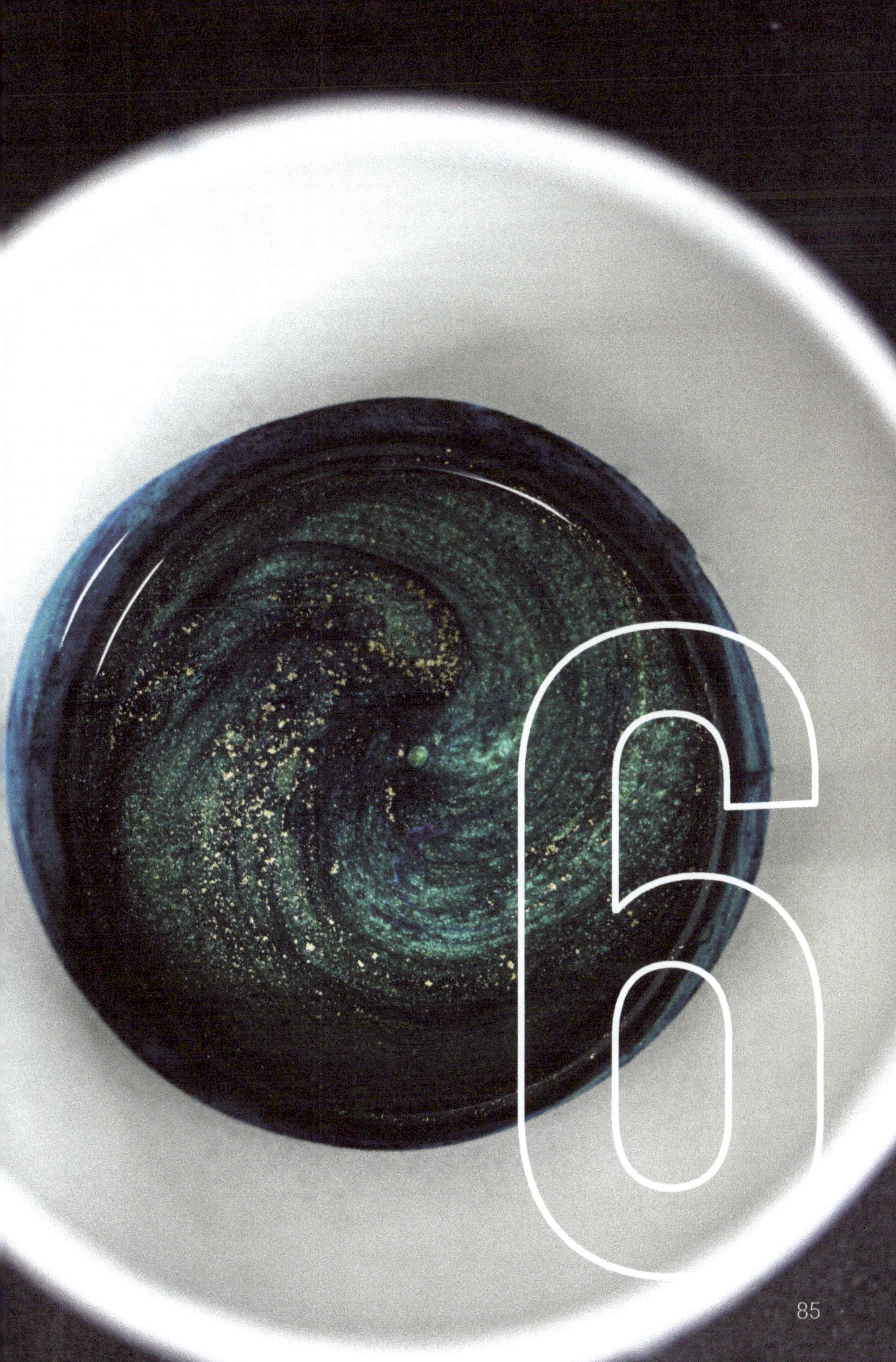

OVERVIEW

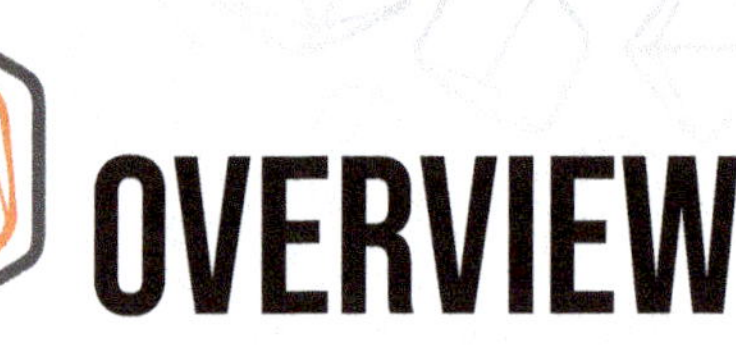

LEVEL: (1)   2   3   4

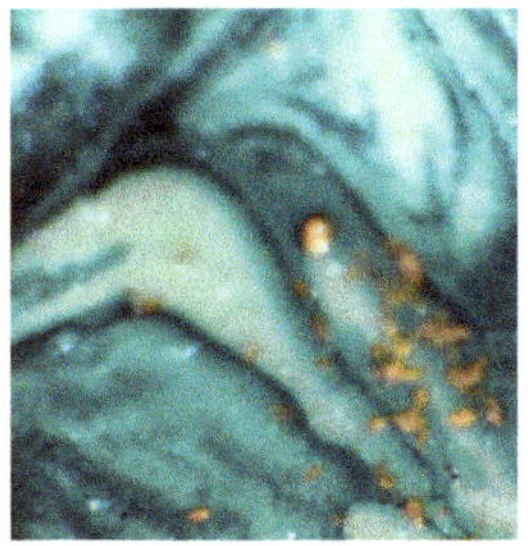

Dirty Pour

For many dice makers, the dirty pour is the perfect method. It's easy to learn and looks incredible – it's also a great way to use up any leftover resin. All you need to do is layer different colours of alcohol ink and even mix-ins into the same cup and pour. This method creates beautiful, rich textures.

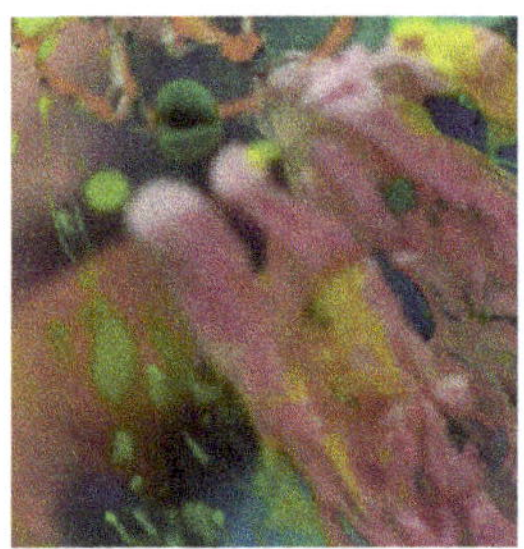

Petri

The petri pour is quite unique. Drip alcohol ink on the top of each dice. Then, add a dense sinker ink, such as "Piñata Blanco Blanco". This creates incredible, otherworldly tendrils. It's easy in theory, but getting it perfect is challenging. You need to get your resin timing right when pouring.

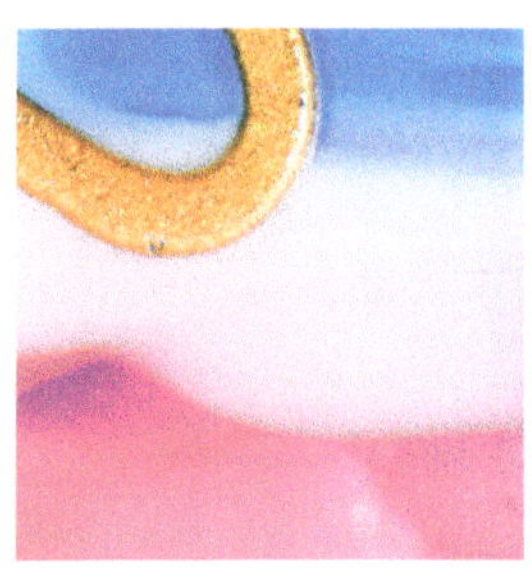

Layering

This method involves layering colours on top of each other (just like the old liquorice all-sorts!). The challenge (as with the Petri method) is that you want to wait until your resin is at the point between "honey" and "too thick to pour". The alternative is to pour your dice in several phases. Let each colour cure before doing the next.

Photo credits [top to bottom]: @critmaker, @chickenwizarddice, @critmaker, @merchandice_au, @devoured.dice, @criticalmissdice. Full photos throughout the book.

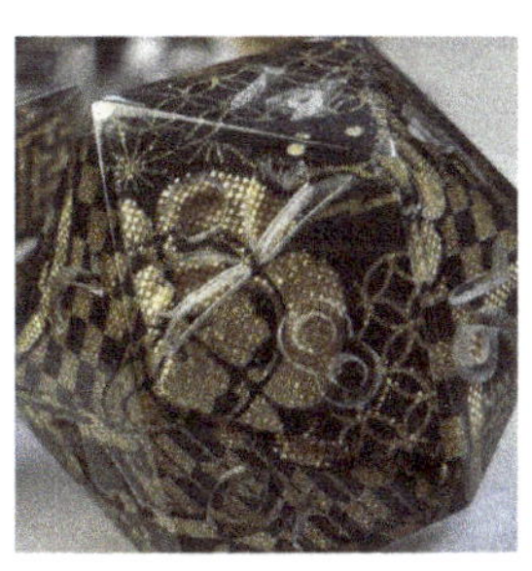

Shell Casting

Sometimes called "inserts" or "blank casting". This one sounds complicated, but isn't. It involves having a secondary casting that's smaller than your primary dice. These are then inserted into your main mould with resin and sealed inside.

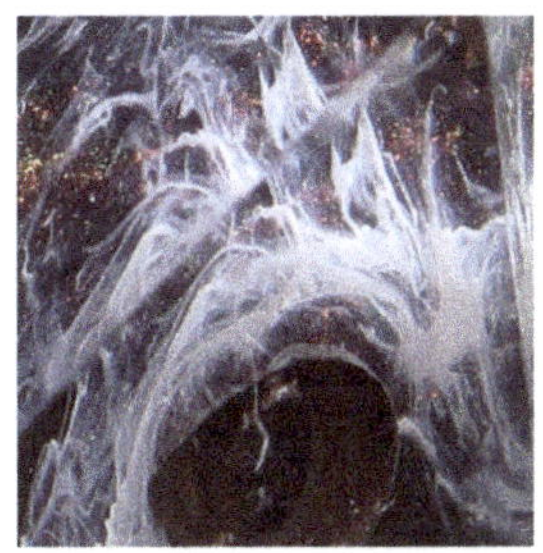

Smoke / Cloud

This involves mixing a dense, secondary colour into the resin with a toothpick or pipette. This creates spectacular cloud and smoke tendrils through your dice. Like other techniques here, the resin must have a honey consistency. This prevents the colours from blending together.

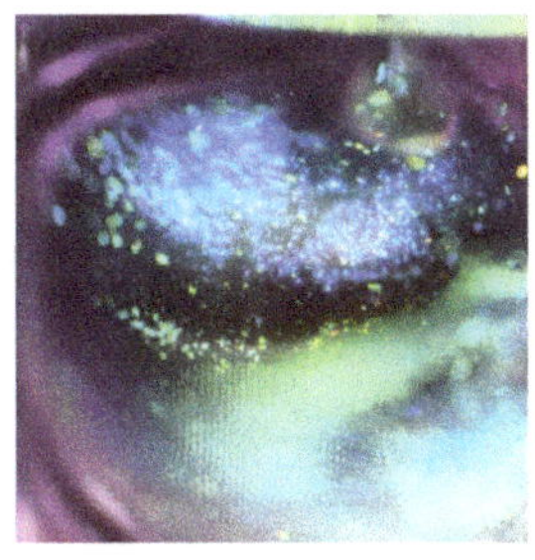

Liquid Core

This is the most in-depth technique we'll cover here. A liquid core dice has a glass sphere inserted into the middle. The sphere is filled with various liquids and mix-ins and sealed with UV resin. The effect is like having a little snow globe in your dice and, it's absolutely spectacular.

THOUGH THERE ARE MANY MORE TECHNIQUES OUT THERE, THESE ARE THE MAIN ONES, AND MASTERING THEM ALL WILL MAKE YOU THE ULTIMATE CRITMAKER!

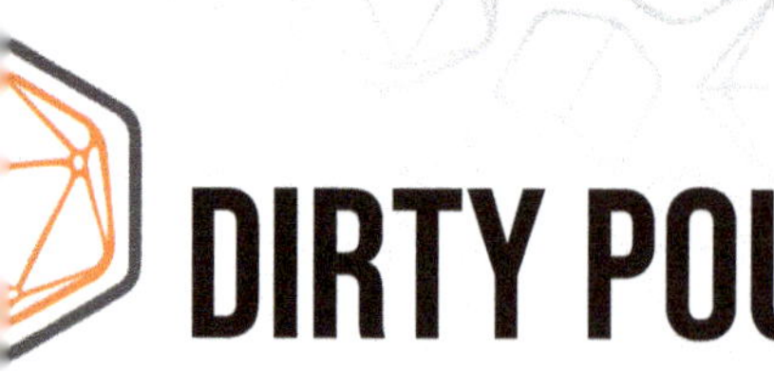

DIRTY POUR

LEVEL: (1) 2 3 4

PPE: 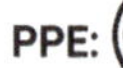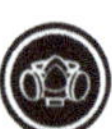

WHAT YOU'LL NEED
- Mixed resin
- Dice mould
- Mica powder or resin pigment
- An assortment of alcohol inks
- A toothpick

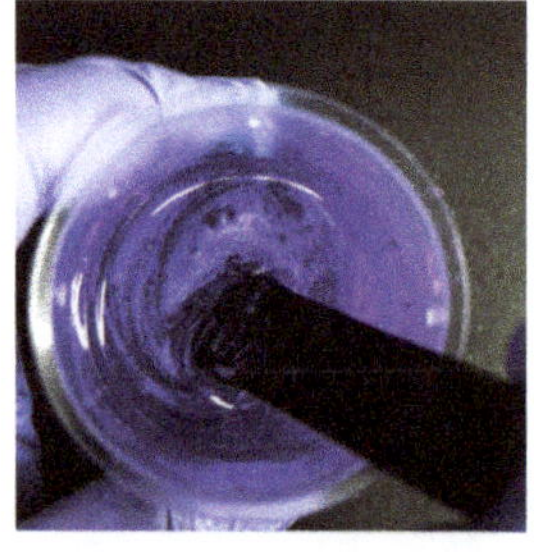

1 Add your mica powder or resin pigment to your mixed resin until it reaches the desired colour.

2 Start adding some drops of alcohol ink. The first colour you add here will be the most prominent! Don't stir it, let it sit.

3 Add a drop or two of another colour on top of this! Get creative, but don't overdo it!

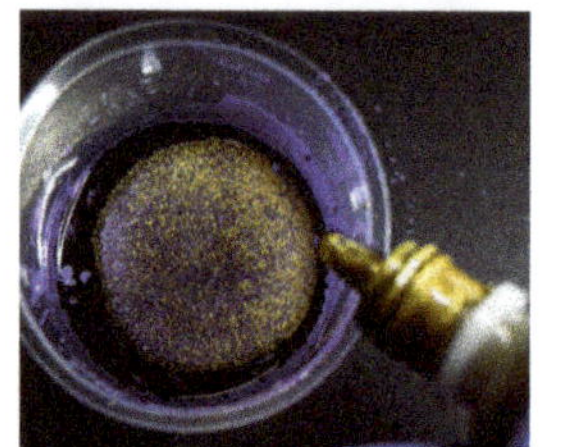

4 Give the cup a gentle swish around, or use a toothpick to make patterns and swirls on the surface.

5 Slowly pour it into your mould in a circular or swirling motion to add interest and texture.

6 From here, it's the same as the basic pour; apply a small amount of leftover resin to the lid and squish it down.

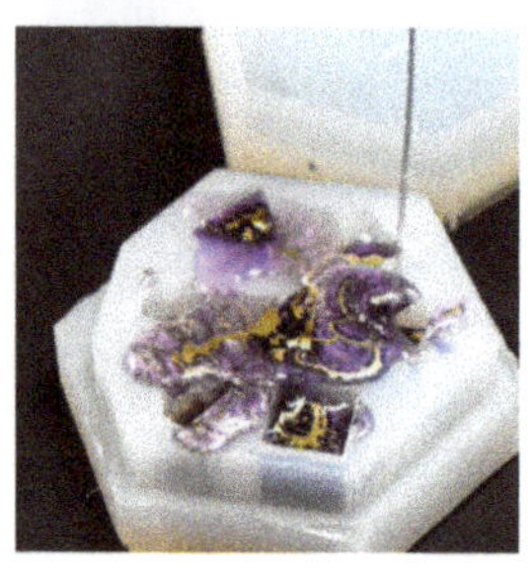

Note: There are also specialised "dirty pour cups" with multiple sections for different colours! Give them a go and see which you prefer.

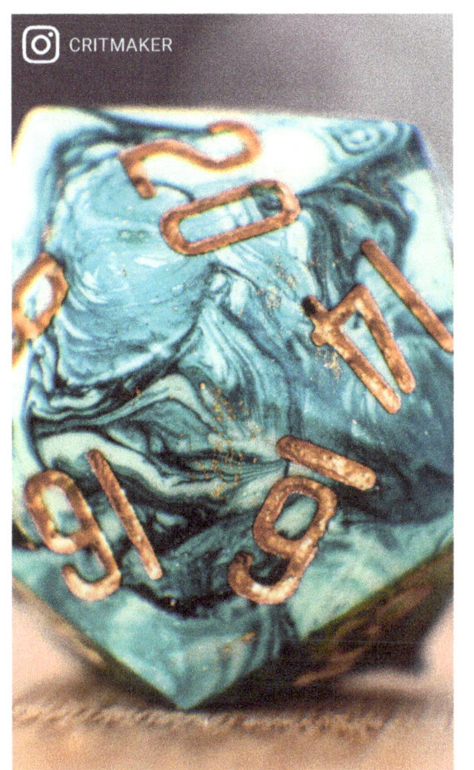

CRITMAKER

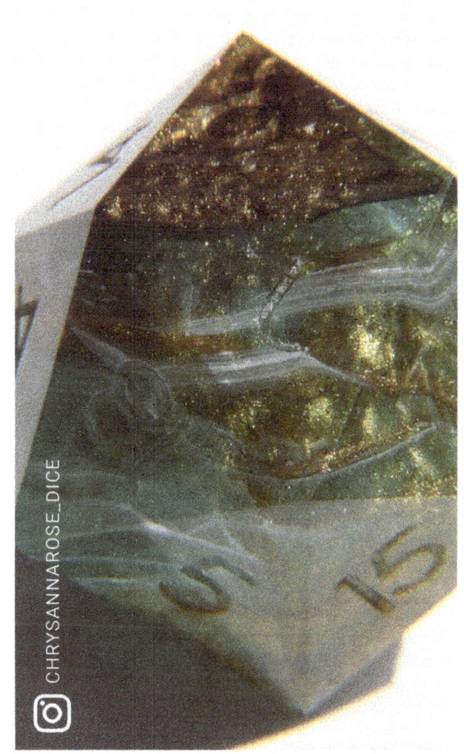

CHRYSANNAROSE_DICE

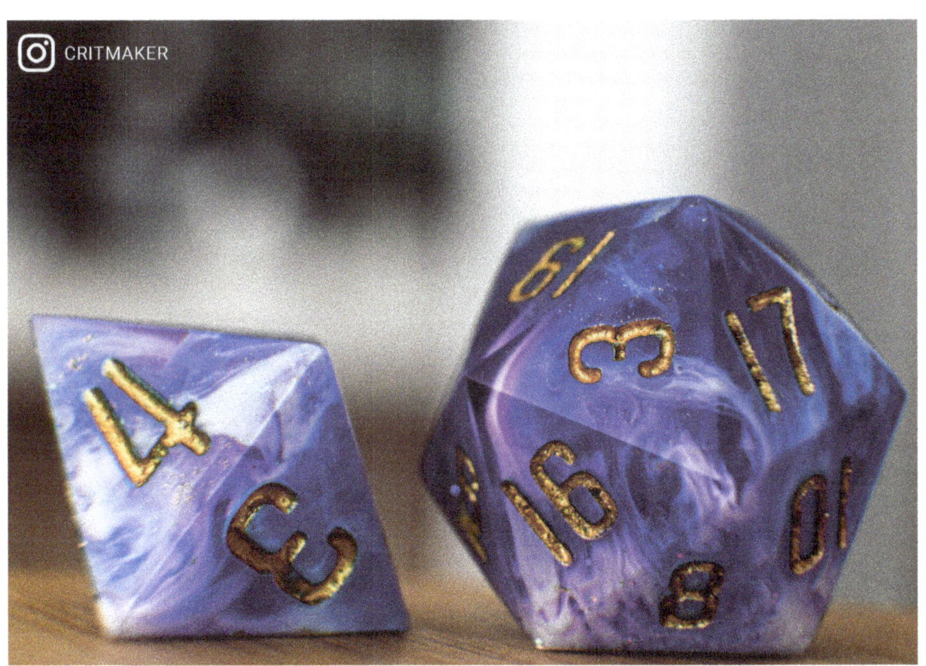

CRITMAKER

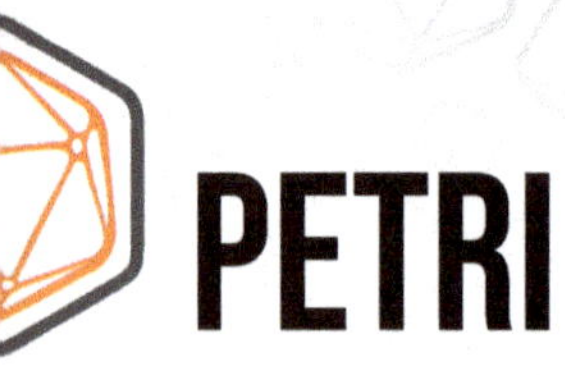

PETRI

LEVEL: 1 (2) 3 4   **PPE:**  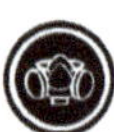 

WHAT YOU'LL NEED

- Mixed resin
- Dice mould
- An assortment of alcohol inks
- Piñata Blanco Blanco

The key to petri is knowing your resin and the time it takes for the ink to seep into it. If you find the ink just gathers at the bottom, you'll need to wait longer for your resin to thicken. If it just sits on top, you need to wait less time!

For most Petri dice, it's often best to use clear resin without any additional mix-ins apart from alcohol inks, that way you can really see the tendrils!

1 Fill the dice about halfway with clear resin. Place one to two drops of your primary ink colour into each dice, spacing them out. You can add a secondary colour on top if you'd like.

2 Now, add one to two drops of "Piñata Blanco Blanco" (our sinker) on top of the drops you just placed. Wait a few minutes for the ink to sink down into the resin. You can also colour the white ink to get some amazing colours!

3 To help these cure faster, we want to create a circle of resin around each dice cavity. Then, fill it up following the inside of the circle. If you do this right, the resin will slide down the sides, trapping the alcohol inside.

4 Fill each dice to the top – some alcohol ink will rise to the surface; this is okay! Wait a few minutes for any bubbles, and pop them with your long neck lighter. Be mindful that the top is now covered in alcohol, so don't spend too long in one spot!

Note: If you don't have a sinker, you can add mica or pigment to translucent alcohol ink and use that instead (it's sometimes called *"minking"*).

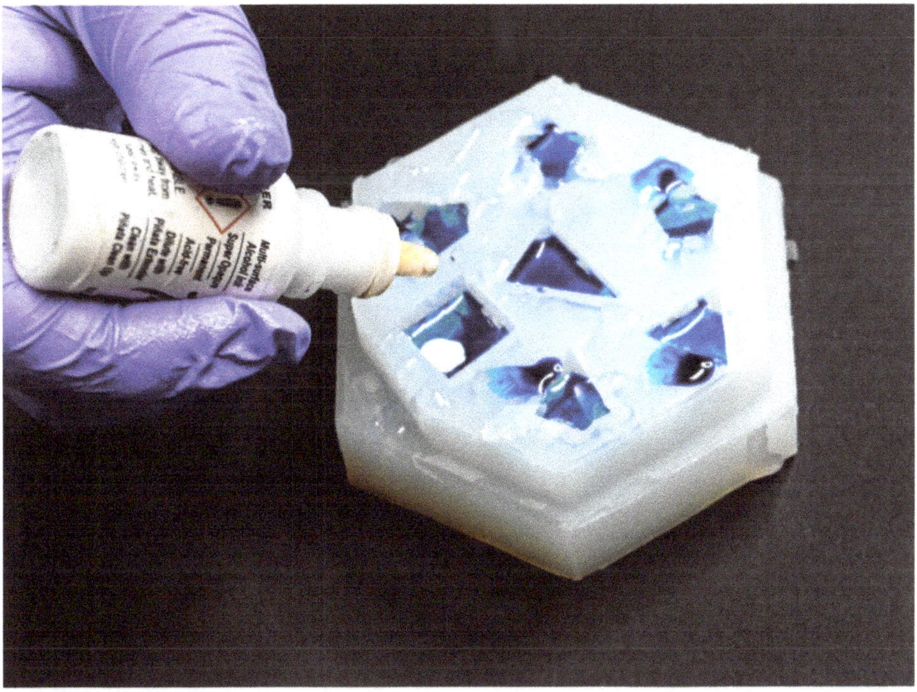

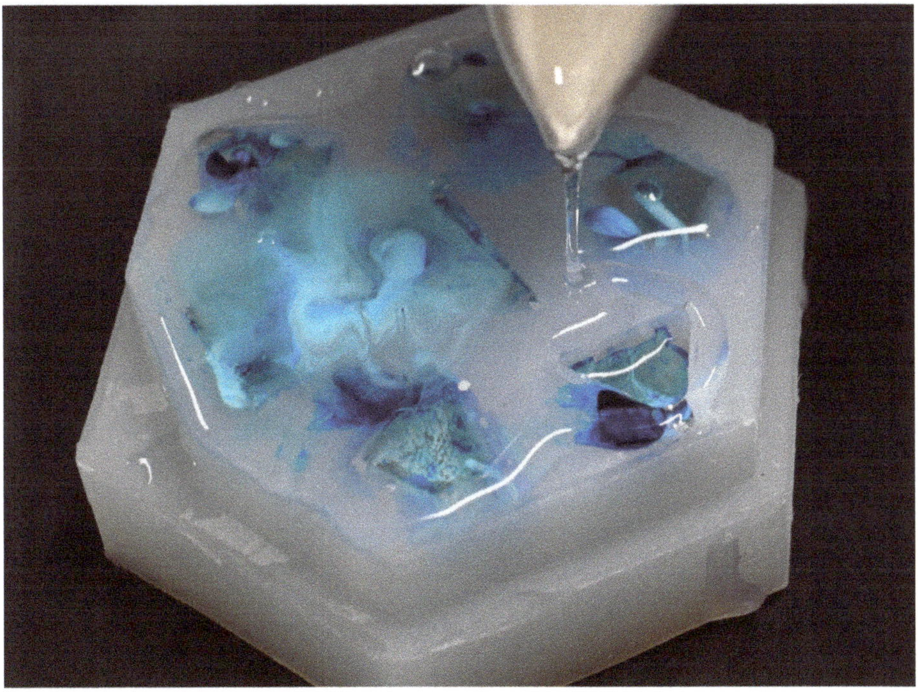

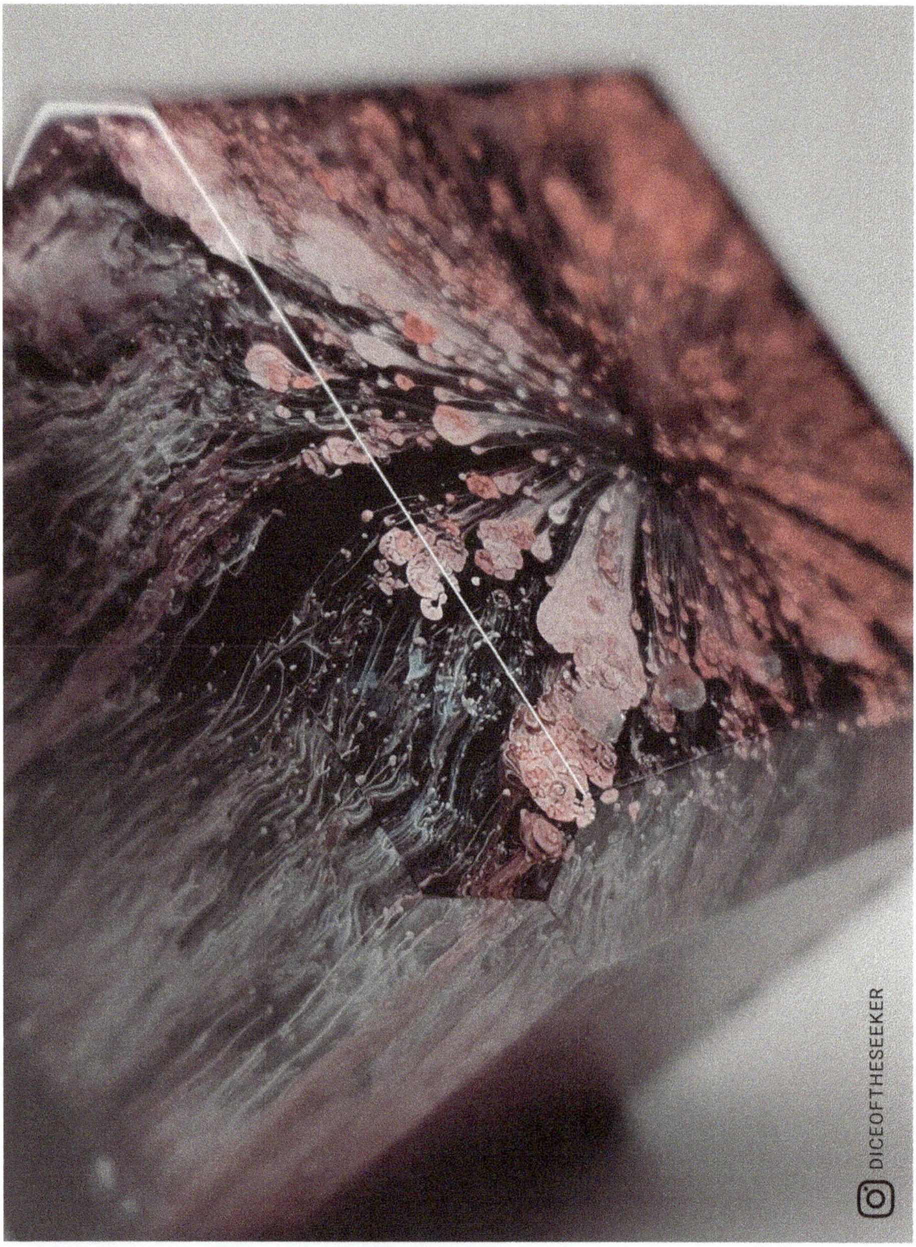

If you've followed this guide, we'd love to see the result! Come join us in our dice-making community on Discord.
(Scan QR code or bit.ly/critmaker).

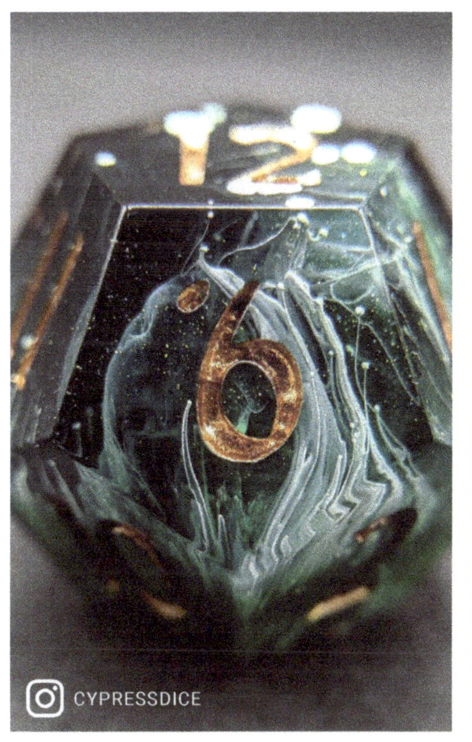

CYPRESSDICE

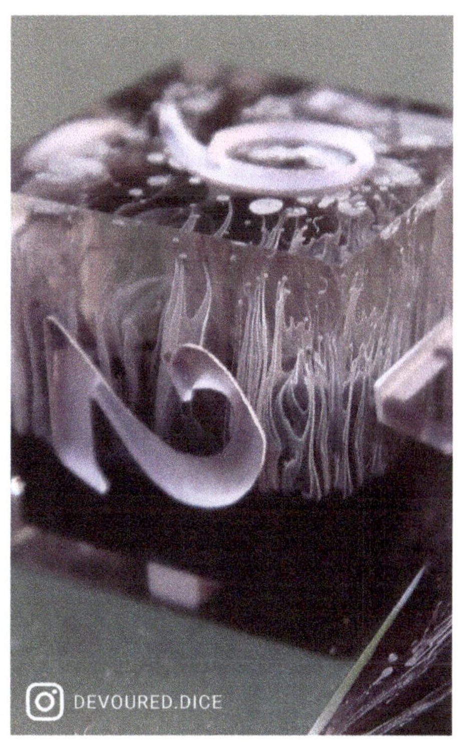

DEVOURED.DICE

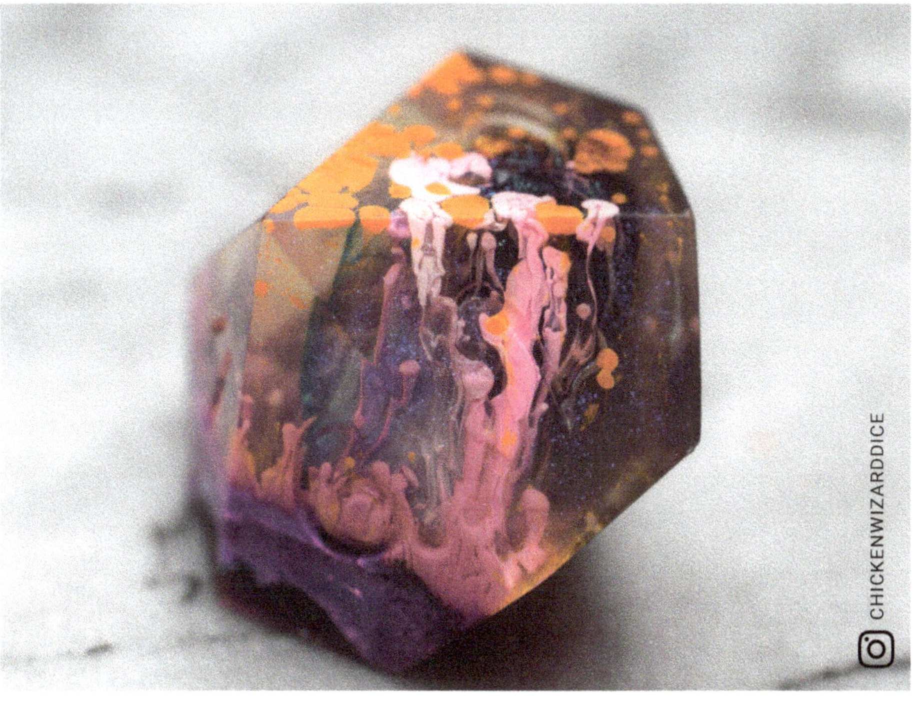

CHICKENWIZARDDICE

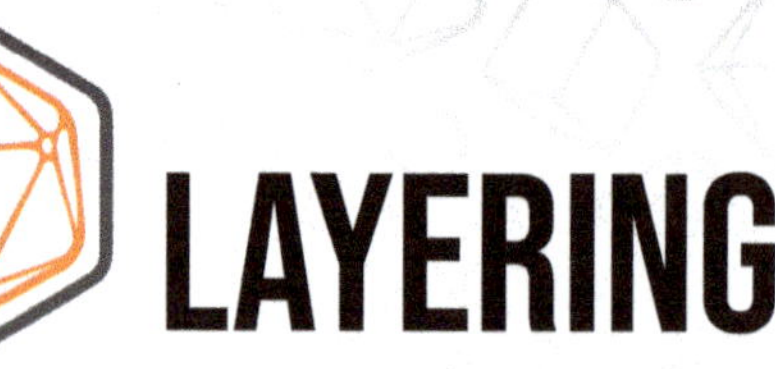

LAYERING

LEVEL: 1 **2** 3 4

PPE: 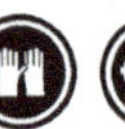 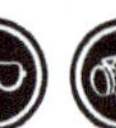 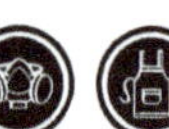

WHAT YOU'LL NEED
- Mixed resin
- Paper cups
- Stirring sticks
- Mix-ins

Layered dice can look like liquorice all-sorts, flags, gradients, or brown sludge. It all depends on the time spent getting it right!

There are three ways to nail layered dice.

Multiple cures – for the most vivid effects you pour one layer of resin and let it set. Then you pour another on top, and so on. Think about a trifle or layered dessert. This approach, while time-consuming, will yield the best possible layer separations. You'll need to experiment on how long you must wait. I'd recommend waiting 8-12 hours as this should give the resin time to reach the gel stage before pouring the next layer.

Late-pouring – this involves understanding the working time (or pot life) of your resin. Then, you wait for the latest possible moment before adding it to the previous layer. This method isn't perfect. But, you'll get beautiful gradients and wave-like structures throughout your dice.

Saturation – possibly the easiest method is to simply use a high saturation resin pigment. The extra weight of the pigment helps the layers to sit on top of each other. You won't get perfect separation (like the watermelon dice to the right) but you will get some beautiful gradients!

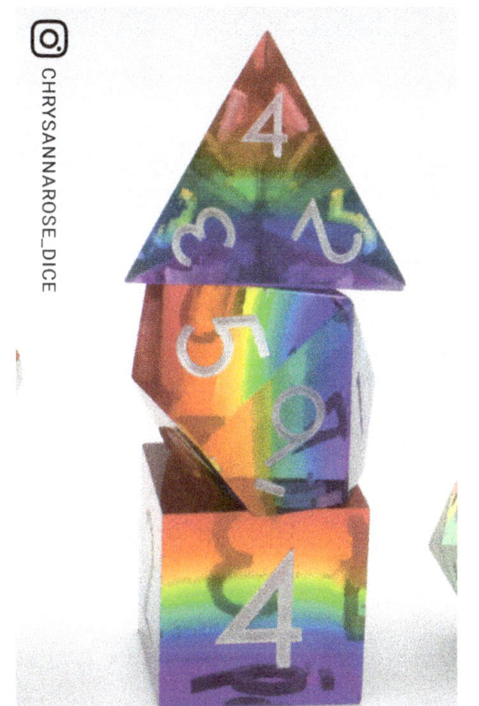

CHRYSANNAROSE_DICE

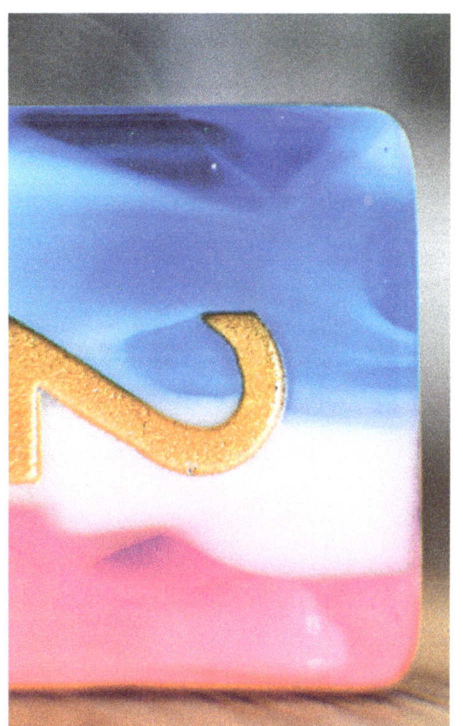

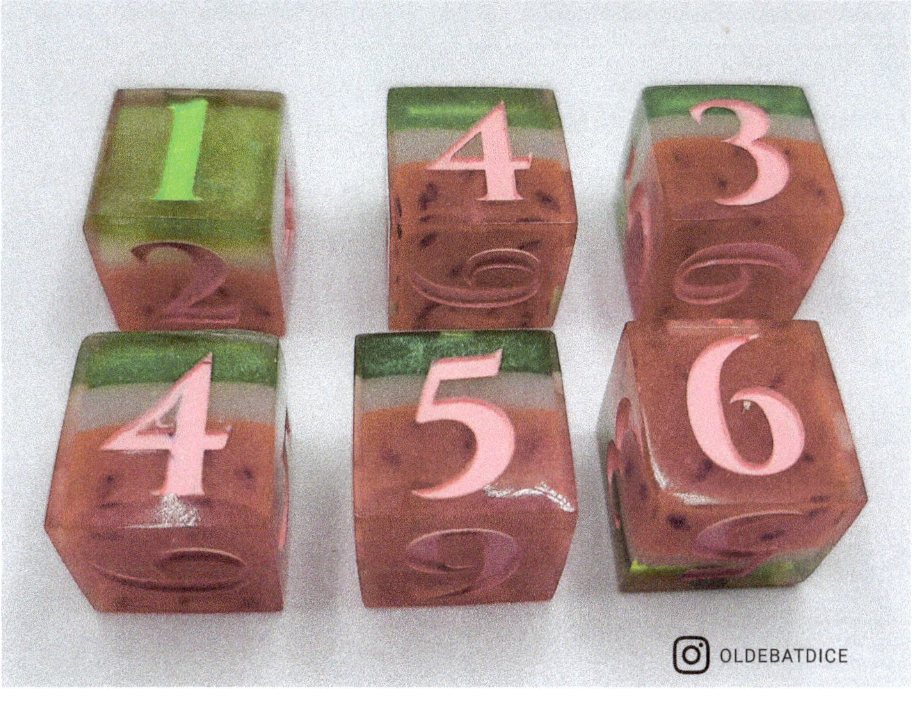

OLDEBATDICE

SHELL CASTING

PPE:  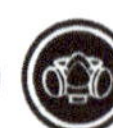 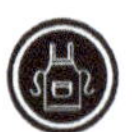

WHAT YOU'LL NEED

- Dice Mould
- Blank Mould (designed for your dice)
- Mixed resin
- Stirring sticks
- Your imagination!

To get started with this technique, you'll need _two_ separate moulds. One mould is full size and has the numbers. The other is slightly smaller and has *no numbers*. These "blanks" are specially made from the same original masters with a slight size offset. You can't just use any blank mould – it must be custom-designed based on the original!

Generally, if the depth of the numbers is, e.g. 0.9mm, then the blank dice are offset on all faces by 0.9mm too. That means they will fit snugly behind the numbers in your mould without moving around.

One of the main benefits of casting with blanks is that it doesn't matter if there are voids or uneven surfaces on them as they'll be filled in the second casting. Also, due to the nature of resin, you don't really need to polish them beyond a matte finish.

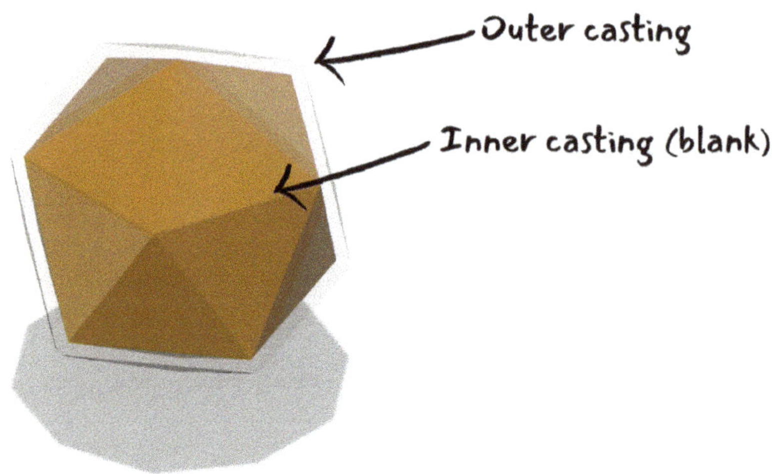

Here are just a few possible uses for blanks:

 Casting uneven objects like coffee beans or dried insects.

Applying washi tape or nail stickers.

Sticking book pages or comics to the faces.

Water marbling or hydro dipping.

Add small items such as skulls or bones you don't want to sink to the bottom of your dice.

Increasing the durability of petri dice by encasing them in solid resin.

Making beautiful "geode" style designs by physically cutting the blank and applying glitter, mylar flakes and even crystals.

> DreamyDice has a great tutorial on this!
> (*Scan QR code or* bit.ly/geode-dice).

Creating all these different types of blanks is out of the scope of this guide. But, the general idea is to fill your blank the way you would normally, including adding any mix-ins or objects. Then you squish it down and wait for it to cure.

Once you have a cured blank, you add a small amount of resin into the shell mould and squeeze the blank inside. It should be a nice, snug fit.

Top it off with resin like always and then squish and cure! That's it!

Casting with blanks is fun and it yields some of the most *incredible* dice art.

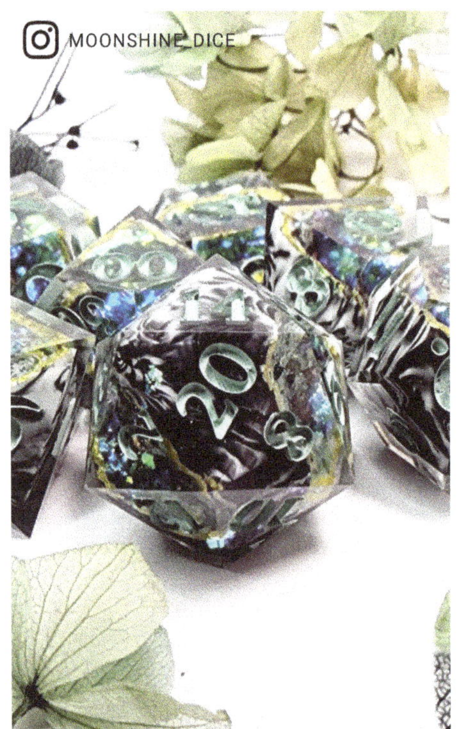

MOONSHINE_DICE

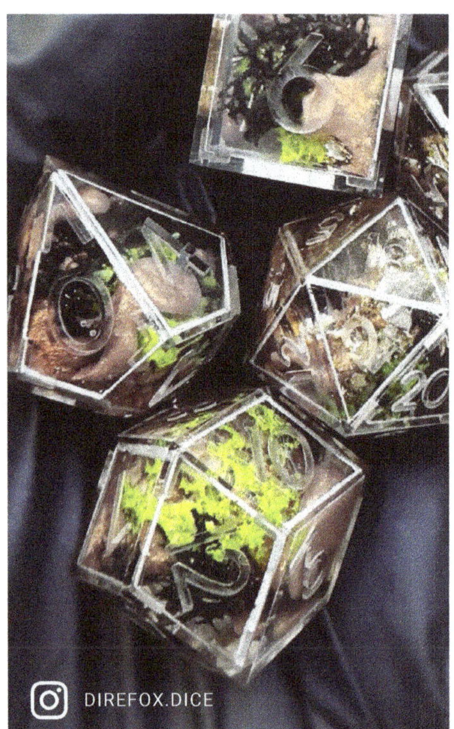

DIREFOX.DICE

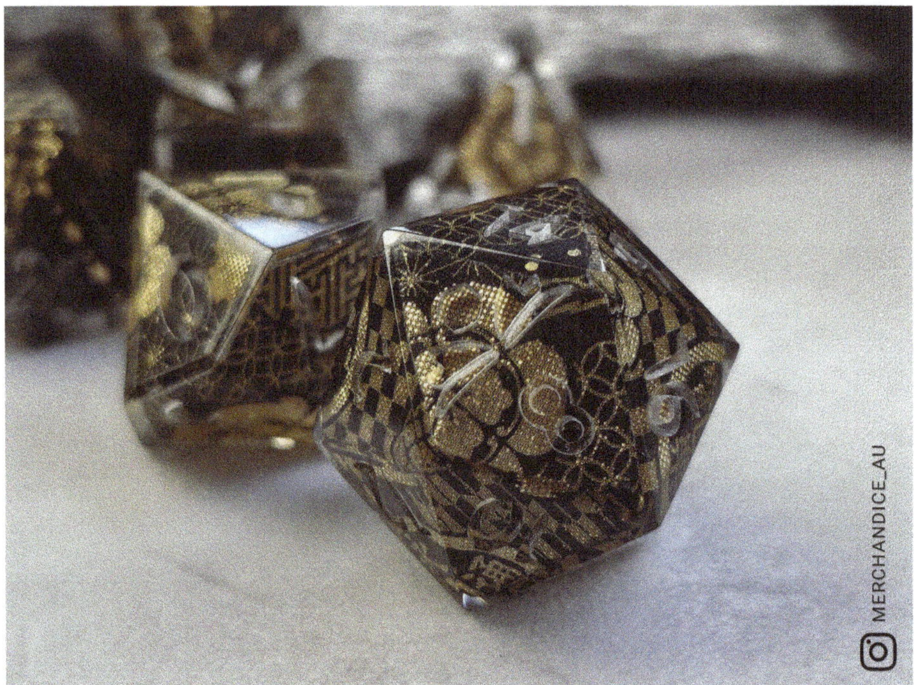

MOONSHINE_DICE
MERCHANDICE_AU

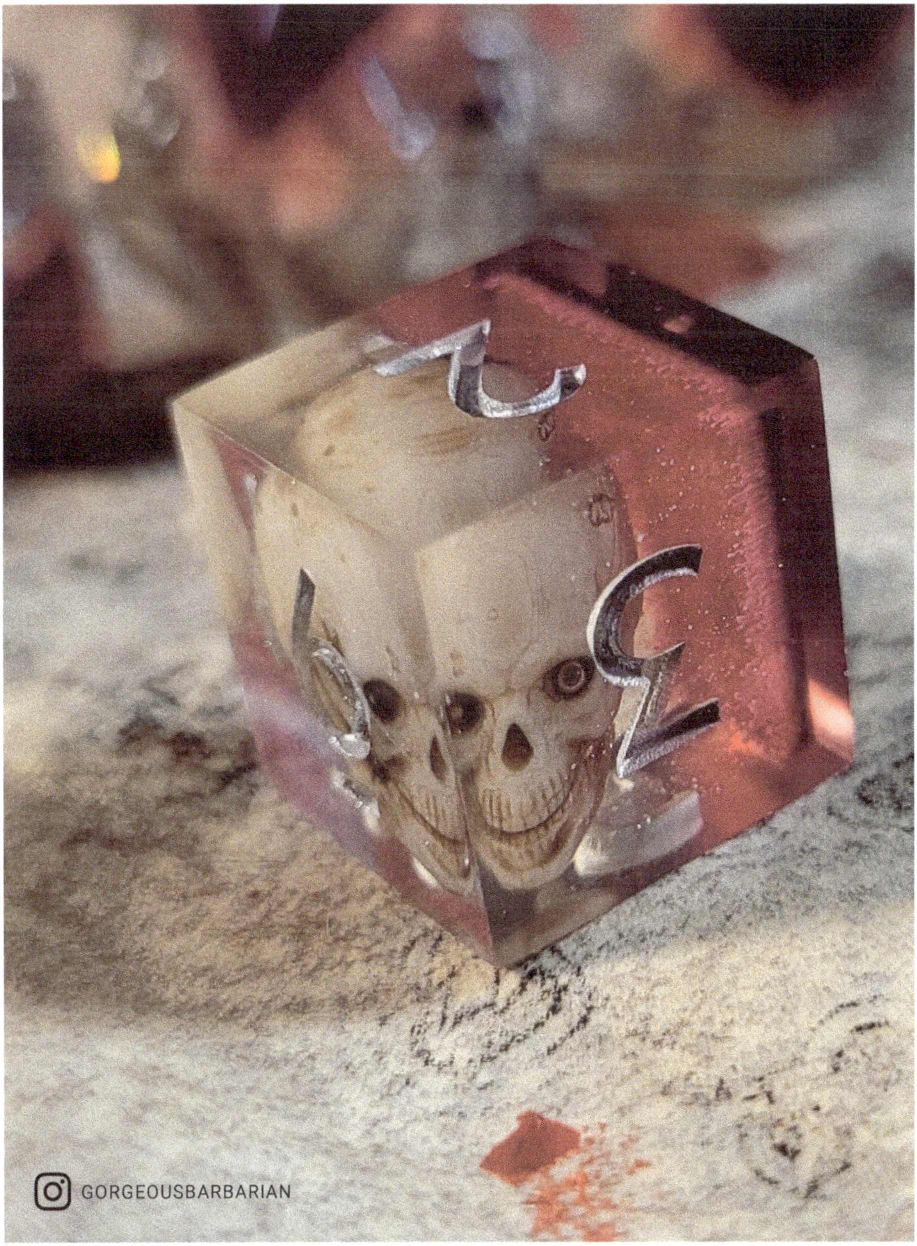

If you've followed this guide, we'd love to see the result! Come join us in our dice-making community on Discord.
(Scan QR code or bit.ly/critmaker).

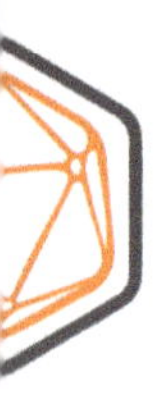

SMOKE/CLOUDS

LEVEL: 1 (2) 3 4

PPE:   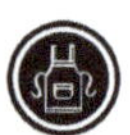

WHAT YOU'LL NEED

- Mixed resin
- Dice mould
- Mica powder or resin pigment
- White alcohol ink or pigment
- A toothpick, pipette or syringe

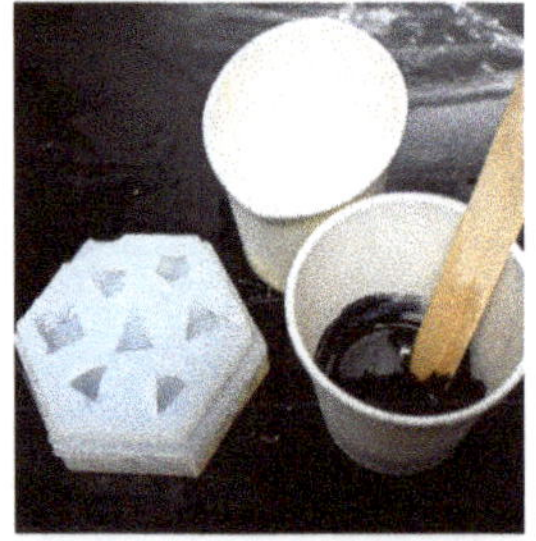

1 For this technique, make sure your resin is at a honey consistency so you don't mix the colours.

2 Fill your mould about $^1/_2$ to $^3/_4$ of the way with your main colour.

3 For subtle clouds, mix some of your resin in a separate cup with pigment or alcohol ink and poke it into your mould with a toothpick or pipette. Swirl it around to create interest.

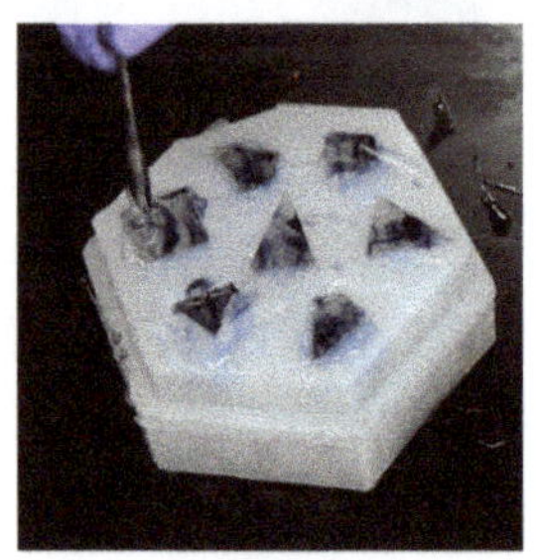

For a more intense cloud effect (as shown in the photos), you can drip resin or pigment directly onto the top of your dice, let it start to sink in (similar to petri) before using a toothpick to push the ink down into the mould.

4 If there's still room left in the mould, top it up with any remaining resin from your primary colour.

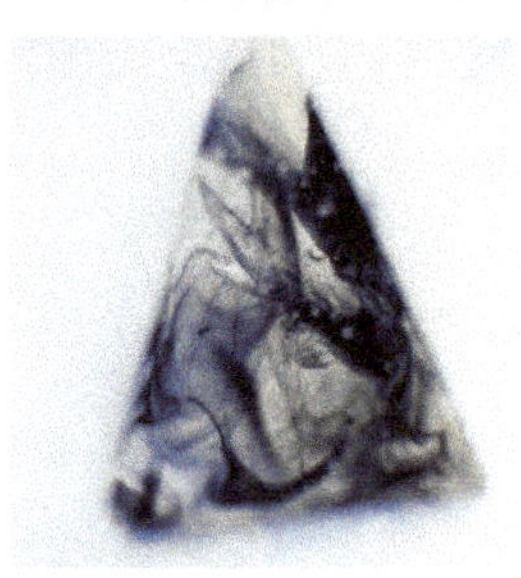

Like many styles, the consistency of your resin will be key to getting beautiful separation and not just mixing the colours together!

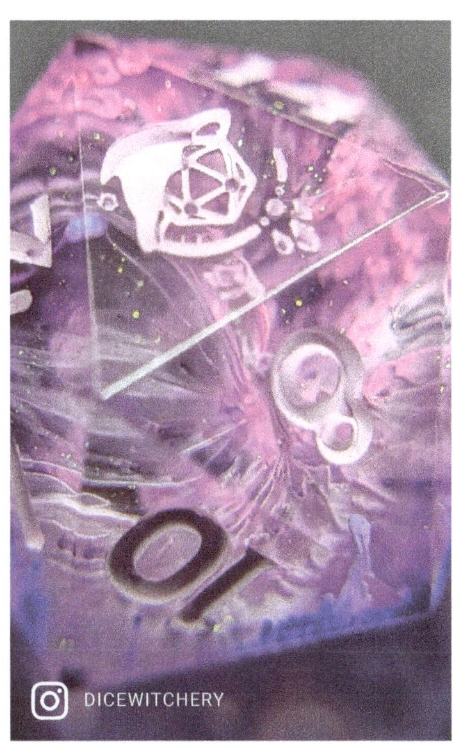

DICEWITCHERY

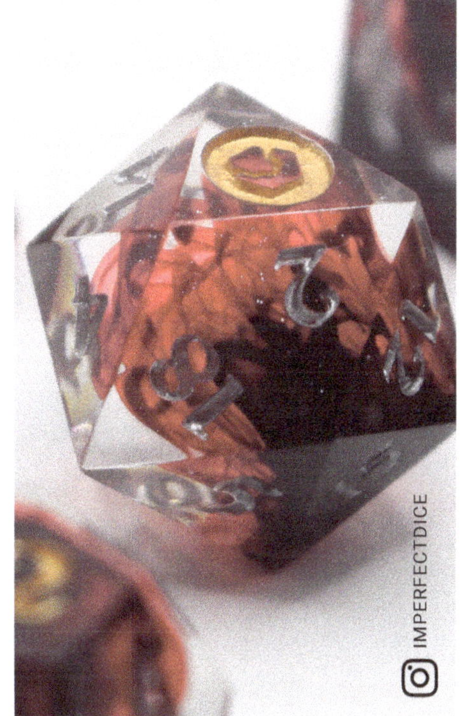

IMPERFECTDICE

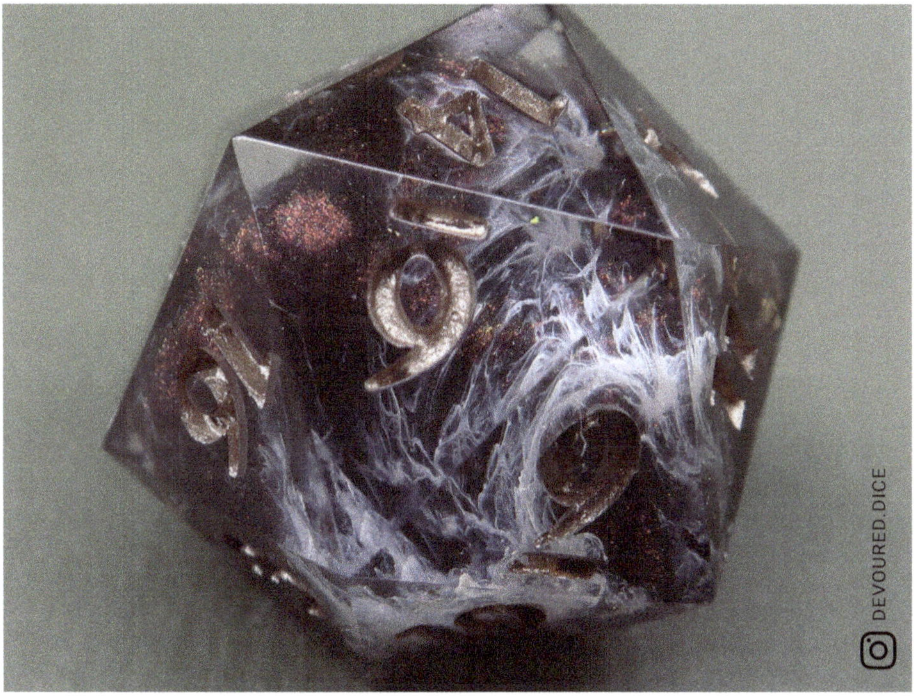

DEVOURED.DICE

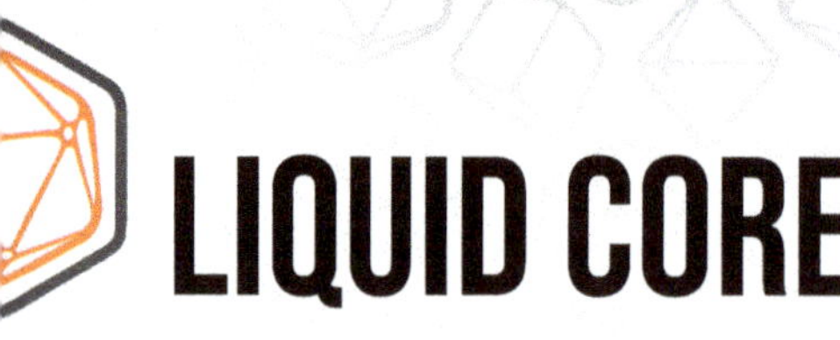

LIQUID CORE

LEVEL: 1 **2** 3 4

PPE: 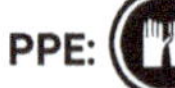   

WHAT YOU'LL NEED

- Mixed resin
- Dice mould
- Mica powder or resin pigment
- White alcohol ink or pigment
- A toothpick, pipette or syringe

The "core" in the name relates to the middle of the dice, which is filled with liquid. Think of little snow globes in your dice!

HOW IS THIS DONE?

The core is a hollow glass sphere with an opening at the top. You fill it with liquid and mix-ins and seal it up with UV resin. The filled cores are placed into your dice moulds and encased in resin. The liquid swirls around when you shake the dice.

You can buy the spheres from Critmaker or another online retailer. They come in a variety of sizes that will fit most standard dice. The sizes you need will depend on your dice – as a general rule, you want them to be around 2mm less than the dimensions of your dice.

LIQUIDS

In our testing, we've found a ratio of 3:1:1 works well as a starting point. This means for 50mL of fluid, 30mL is distilled water, 10mL is glycerine and 10mL is alcohol.

Distilled water will slow evaporation, allowing your glitter/mix-ins to swirl better. Note: demineralised water is not the same as distilled water.

Glycerine is used to help suspend the particles for longer.

99.9% Isopropyl Alcohol keeps things clean. It also helps prevent freezing in winter. We don't have a problem with this in Australia!

Note: you may find some glitters or powders settle too quickly/slowly, clump or even lose colour over time, so it's always best to experiment before selling them! Depending on the purpose, some makers even use more viscous fluids such as baby oil or mineral oil instead.

MAKING LIQUID CORES

1 Stick your cores to your working surface with Blu-Tack or clay. This will prevent them from rolling around while you work.

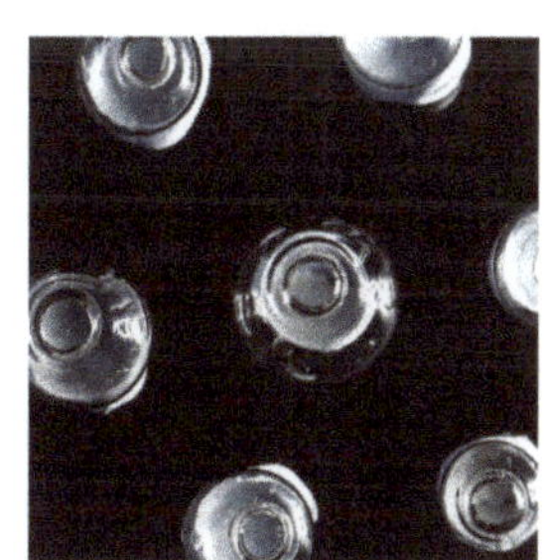

2 Add mica powder or glitter (or both) to your mixture (or directly into the core).

3 Using a pipette or syringe, fill the sphere as close to the top as you can.

4 Get UV resin and run a bead around the outside of the hole and fill it in, ensuring it's completely sealed. While many UV resins won't seep into the liquid, some will. If this happens, you can create a little cap on a piece of silicone with UV resin and then stick that over the hole instead!

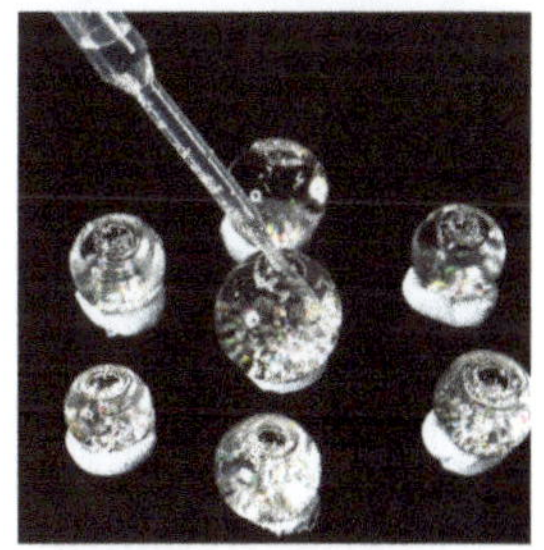

5 Cure the resin with your UV torch – when it's done, check for leaks and give it a test swirl!

6 Now comes the fun part. Half-fill your moulds with epoxy resin and gently insert the filled, sealed spheres into the mould.

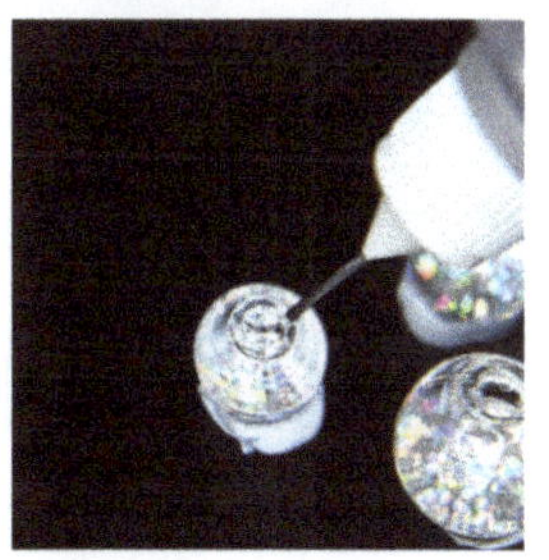

7 Top the dice off as usual until they're domed, and apply a small amount of resin to the lid.

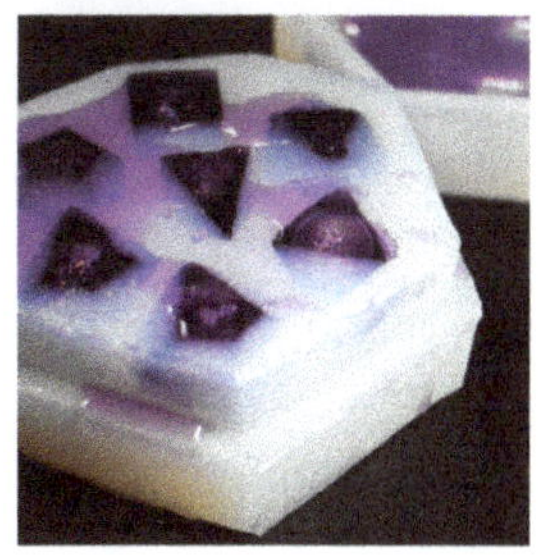

While one of the most in-depth techniques, this yields the most outstanding results. Many people haven't seen liquid core dice in person and are always amazed. As to whether or not they are biased due to the liquid, try "Salt Testing" on page 146.

ARTIST SPOTLIGHT

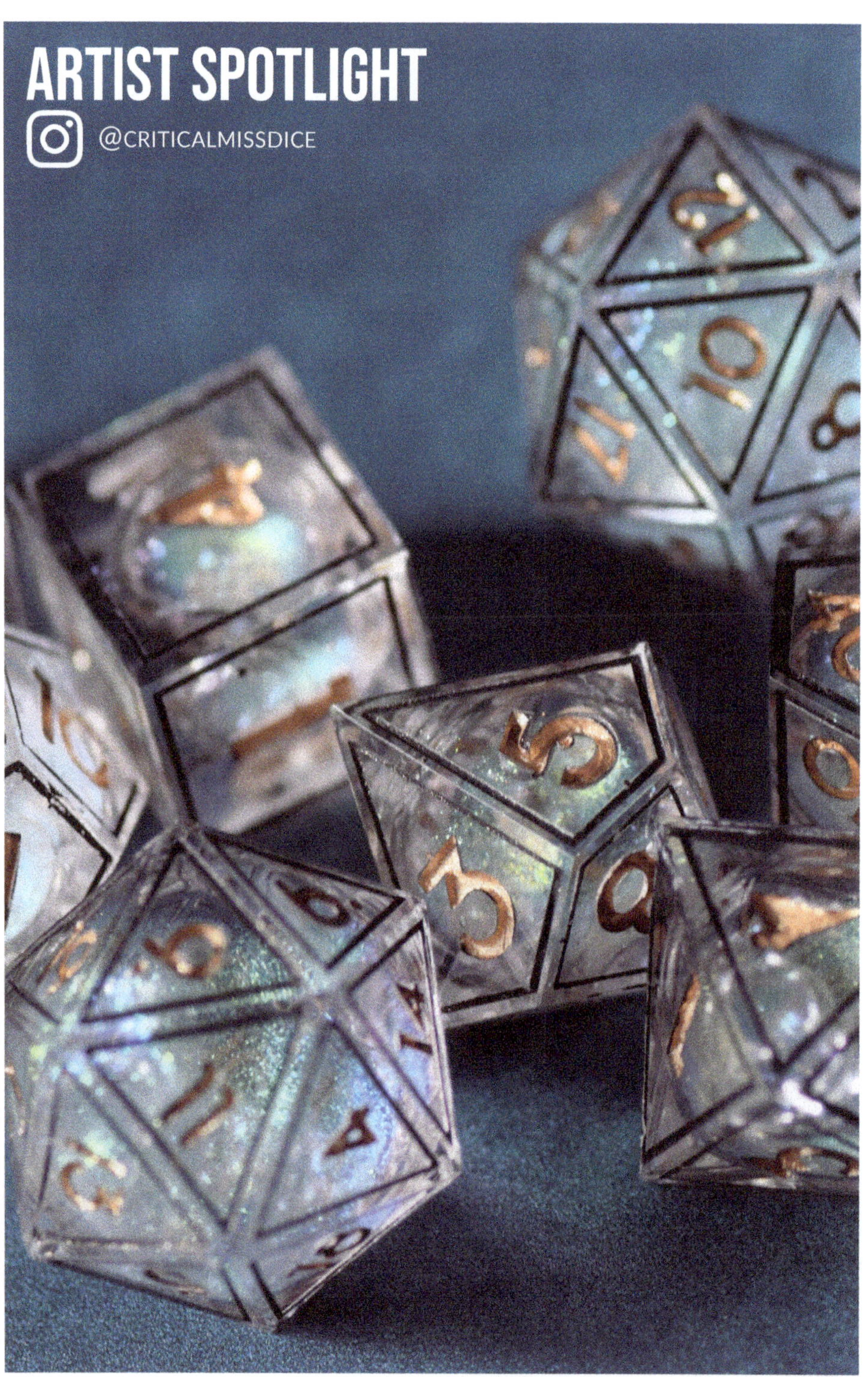

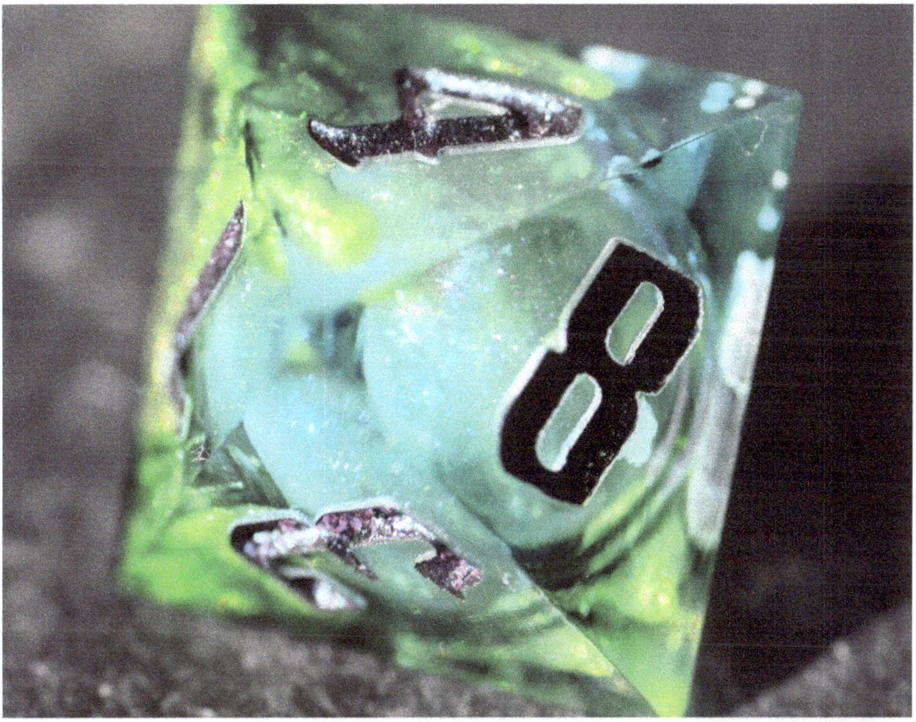

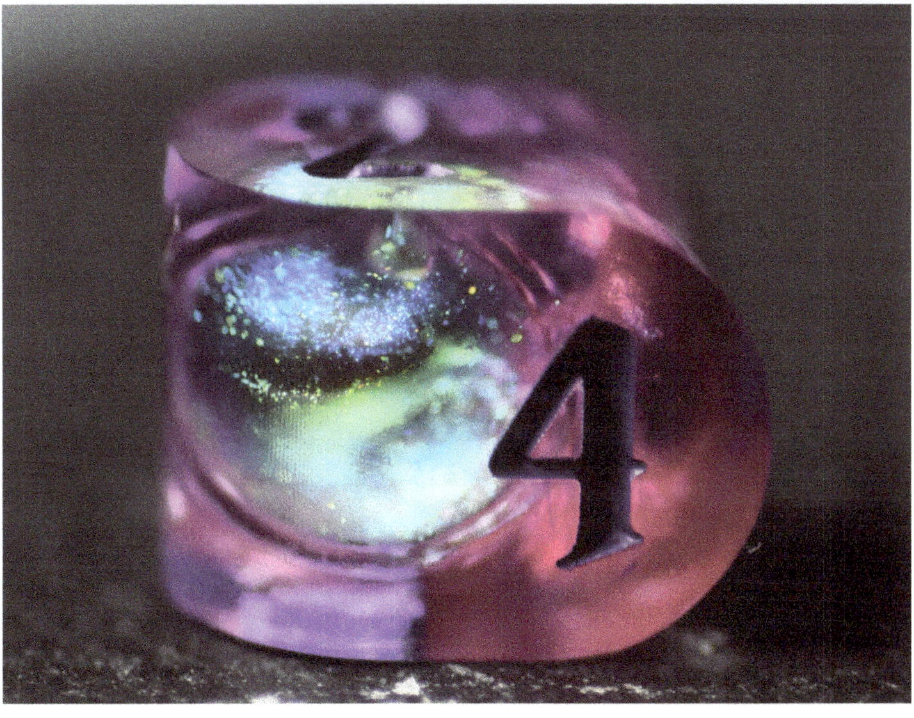

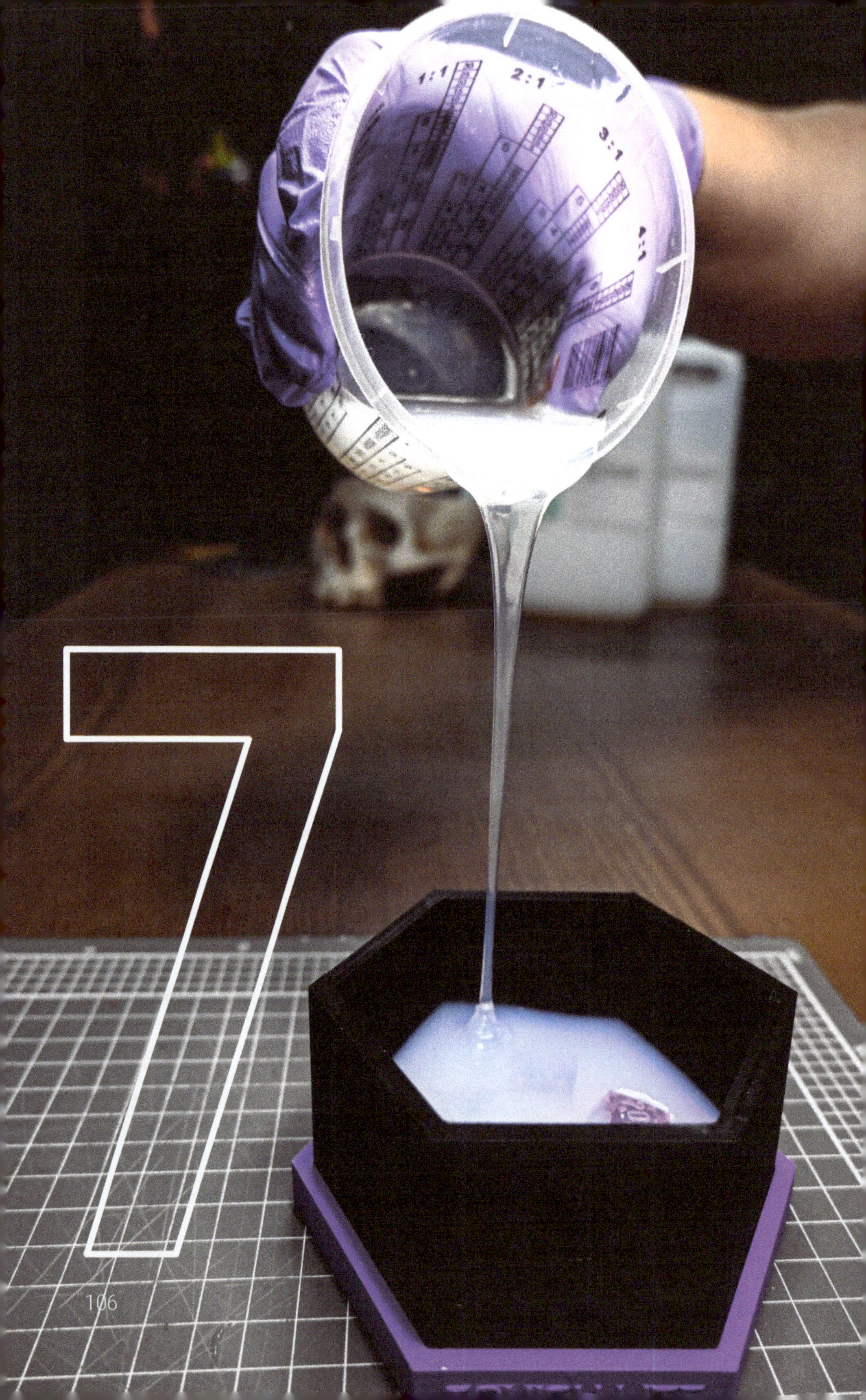

7

SILICONE BASICS

In this chapter, we'll be exploring some of the complexities of working with silicone. How to choose between platinum and tin cure, what to do about cure inhibition and whether or not you should use a vacuum chamber.

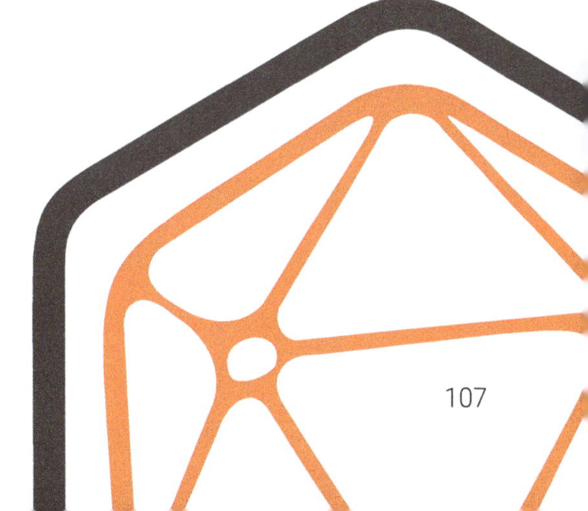

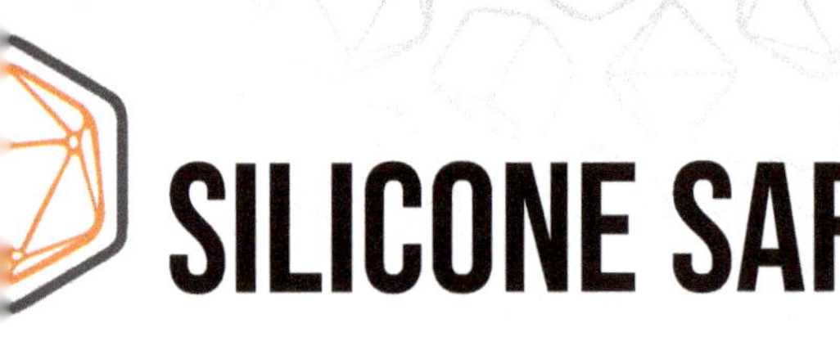

SILICONE SAFETY

LEVEL: 1   2   **③**   4

While cured silicone is generally considered non-toxic, this doesn't refer to its uncured form. Both part A and part B may be hazardous and still be "non-toxic" when cured.

Silicone uses all kinds of different additives and what makes one "safe" does not necessarily apply to the others. It's also important to note that "medical grade", "food grade", etc, generally refers to the cured product, not the uncured liquids.

Not respecting these chemicals can put you and your family at risk.

RECOMMENDED PPE

It's best to wear gloves and safety glasses. Accidents happen, and I'd rather wear gloves and safety glasses than go to the hospital. You wouldn't believe how easy it is to get silicone on your hands and then rub your eyes. I'd also recommend an apron, as uncured silicone will destroy your clothing.

Silicones should only be used in a well-ventilated area.

DO I NEED TO WEAR A RESPIRATOR?

The safety recommendations of your silicone determine whether a respirator is required.

The silicone we use says that a respirator is not required. Yet, it goes on to say that the fumes may cause sinus irritation, asthma, and other effects. It advises you to use a respirator where proper ventilation is unavailable. Since I can neither work outside nor have industrial ventilation, I take that to mean that I should wear a respirator!

It may seem like I'm overstating this (*I am*), but the key to handling any chemical safely is to <u>always</u> read the *Safety Data Sheet (SDS)*.

IMPORTANT TERMS

Cure inhibition
Any contamination (such as sulphur) that prevents the silicone from curing properly.

Cure time
The amount of time it takes for the silicone to harden completely.

Degassing
Removing air bubbles from silicone using a vacuum chamber.

Shore hardness
A measure of how hard/flexible a material is.

Mould release
Any substance that prevents two parts of a mould from sticking together. Dedicated agents like Stoners Mould Release or Petroleum Jelly work great.

Pot life
Like resin, silicone has a pot life or working time.

Registration keys
Also simply called keys, are any deliberate indentation of one side of a two-part mould. When the other side is poured, the silicone fills these indentations. This creates a lock that holds the mould together.

Sprue
A funnel-shaped opening in a mould where resin is poured. After casting, the excess resin formed here is also called a sprue.

Vent
A tiny channel that is moulded or cut into the mould to allow air to escape.

TYPES OF SILICONE

LEVEL: 1   2      4

Silicone is a synthetic polymer that comes in many different forms. You can use it for sealing and lubrication or making perfect moulds that show tiny details. Silicone is a highly adhesive gel or liquid in its most basic state. When catalysed with various compounds, it turns into a solid material. Silicone is chemically resistant, hydrophobic, and *often* completely non-toxic. It's used in everything from aerospace, medicine, children's products to the kitchen.

There are two types of mould-making silicone: **platinum cure** (addition cure) and **tin cure** (condensation cure).

Platinum cure silicone uses platinum as a catalyst. This results in moulds that are more durable and less likely to shrink over time. However, platinum silicone is extremely sensitive to surface contaminants such as sulphur, phosphorus and many solvents and primers[1]. On the other hand, tin cure is less durable and more prone to shrinkage over time. However it offers one distinct advantage: it has very low sensitivity to surface contaminants.

WHY IS SENSITIVITY A PROBLEM?

Sulphur, phosphine & phosphite are common ingredients in printer resins and moulding clays which can be a huge problem when dealing with 3D printed dice masters! When the platinum catalyst in platinum-cure silicone reacts with these components it completely derails the chemical process. The silicone will never set and leaves a sticky mess on your shiny masters. We call this cure inhibition.

WHAT DO WE RECOMMEND?

If this is your first time making a mould, I recommend using a clean, cheap set of mass-produced dice as your masters and a platinum cure silicone. First, the finish should be excellent. Second, you'll have no issues with cure inhibition.

This allows you to get started learning how to make moulds without having to deal with cure inhibition or spending hours sanding and polishing.

1 Silicone and More, "Cure Inhibition or Poisoning of Silicone.", bit.ly/cure-inhibition

CURE INHIBITION

There are a number of ways to deal with the issue of cure inhibition:

1 Use a combination of resin and silicone that does not cause inhibition. This one will take some trial and error to find a combination that works for you. I've tried many of the combinations suggested on Reddit, but could not find a combination that works every time. The least reactive I've used is Siraya Tech Fast Navy Grey.

2 Water curing may be the most effective method for removing the contaminants (depending on your resin). This means post-curing your dice in a clear cup of water for at least 30 minutes. While there have been few studies into why this works, it's believed that the residue of the photo-initiators in the resin dissolve in water when subjected to UV light. This is further backed up by the instructions for Siraya Tech Defiant silicone which recommends "Parts are post-cured by immersion in water for 30 minutes, which eliminates the need for a coating to prevent cure inhibition." Give it a go!

3 Try using a product like Mann InhibitX. This is a barrier coating that you dip the dice into and is supposed to prevent cure inhibition. I've not tried it, but the drawbacks are that it can be quite expensive, may reduce surface details after a few coats and has a limited shelf life.

Jan Mrázek offers a potentially cheap alternative of using a 1% solution of acrylic mixed in acetone along with water curing. *(Scan QR code or* bit.ly/pmma-solution*)*.

4 If you're not in a hurry, let your masters sit for a *couple of weeks*. This allows the surface contaminants to dissipate over time.

5 Fortunately, there is a solution that can save you both time and money. Cast your masters in *tin cure silicone*. This material has very few issues with most resins and you can cast your dice as soon as you've printed them.

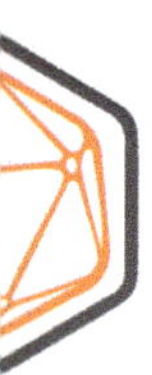

SHORE HARDNESS

LEVEL: 1 2 (3) 4

Shore hardness is a set of three scales that give a common reference point for discussing the hardness of materials.

Shore O – measures very soft rubbers and gels,
Shore A – measures the hardness of flexible / semi-rigid materials
Shore D – measures the hardness of hard rubbers and plastics.

There is deliberate overlap in the scales to be able to give comparisons. E.g. A tyre can be described as 60A, 69O or 16D.

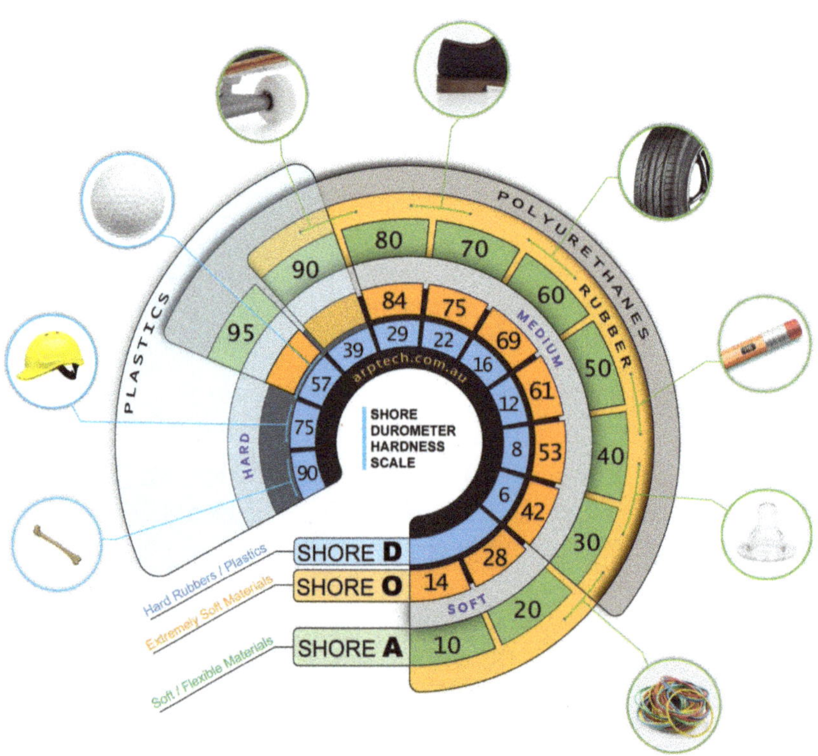

Image courtesy of ArpTech. Used with Permission.

WHY DO I NEED TO KNOW THIS?

When working with silicone, two main questions should be considered. Firstly, how easy will it be to remove dice from the mould and secondly, how long will the mould last?

A higher shore hardness will render beautiful crisp details and last for a long time. But, it might be difficult to demould. This could cause frustration and even repetitive strain injuries when trying to demould.

On the other hand, a lower shore hardness will mean your dice are much easier to demould, but the moulds won't last as long. This is because the softer rubber tears more easily around sharp edges and numbers.

WHAT DO WE RECOMMEND?

For making moulds, we prefer a Shore 20D silicone. It's often associated with rapid-curing silicone and gives the right performance to longevity mix we like. Does that mean it's right for you? Possibly not. The best thing to do is experiment and find out what works best for your moulds.

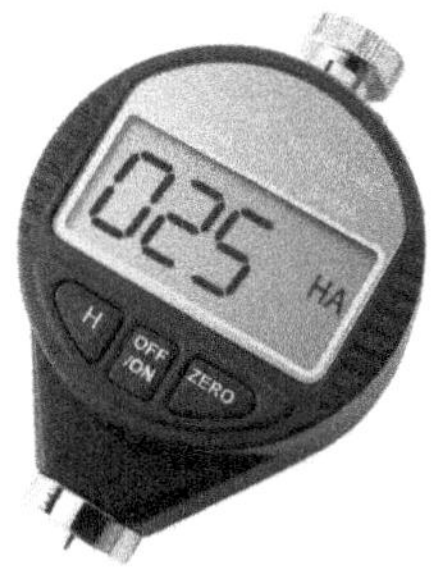

A DUROMETER IS USED TO TEST THE HARDNESS OF RUBBER OR PLASTIC MATERIALS. IT IS PICTURED ON THE LEFT. THE DUROMETER HAS A SPRING-LOADED NEEDLE AT ONE END. IT IS PRESSED ONTO THE MATERIAL. THE RESULT IS DETERMINED WHEN THE NEEDLE STOPS.

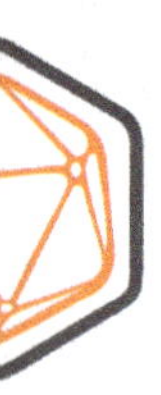

VACUUM VS PRESSURE

LEVEL: 1 2  4

Mixing silicone can cause a lot of bubbles – the material's viscosity makes bubbles difficult to remove and they can get trapped in corners and numbers.

A vacuum chamber is an airtight container that has all the air sucked out of it by a pump. As the air is being extracted, the silicone will bubble up, then settle and most of the bubbles will disappear.

A pressure pot, on the other hand, has air pushed into it, compressing most of the bubbles until they're invisible. It also forces silicone into the finest details.

Some silicones claim to be "bubble-free" or "no vacuum required". But, in our experience, this may not be accurate when casting small items like 18mm dice with tiny numbers. While these small bubbles may be unnoticeable on a larger casting, they'll more than likely wreck your smaller dice moulds.

SO WHICH DO YOU NEED?

If you're wanting perfection, you can't go wrong with both! The vacuum chamber will remove the majority of bubbles, and the pressure pot will finish what's left. The result should be almost perfect moulds every time with no internal or surface bubbling.

If you have to choose, the pressure pot is the best bet. You will ultimately need a pressure pot for resin casting, so you can use one piece of equipment for casting and mould-making! Though it'll remove all the internal bubbles in your mould, you still may be left with some small bubbles on top. These bubbles will only impact how the top of the mould looks, not the quality of the dice you cast.

IF YOU THINK THAT SILICONE IS ONLY GOOD FOR MOULDS, CHECK OUT THESE BEAUTIFUL FOOD-GRADE, SQUISHY, CHONKY SILICONE DICE BY CUMULUS DICE!

CUMULUS_DICE

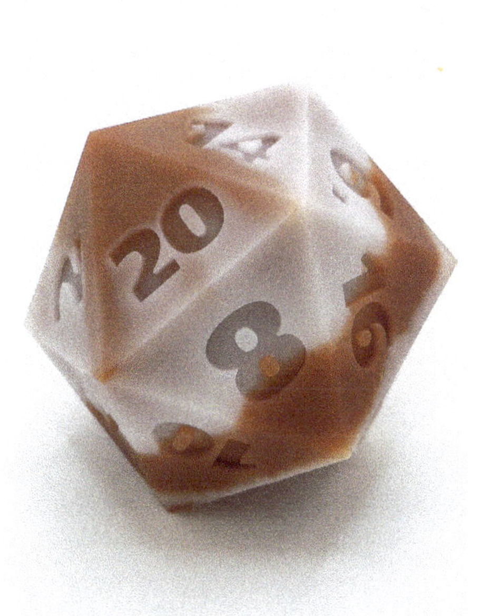

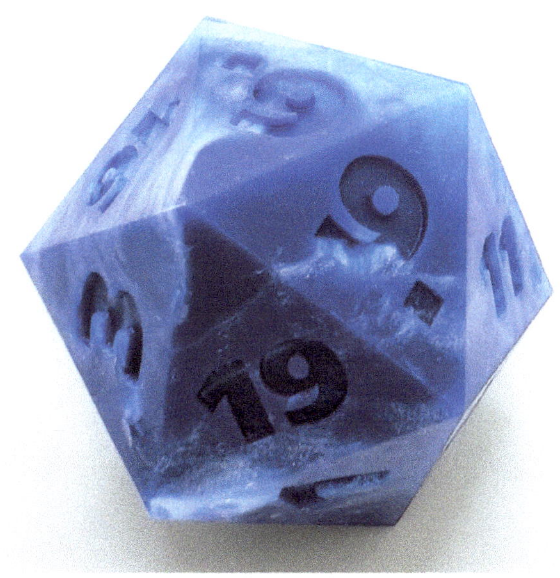

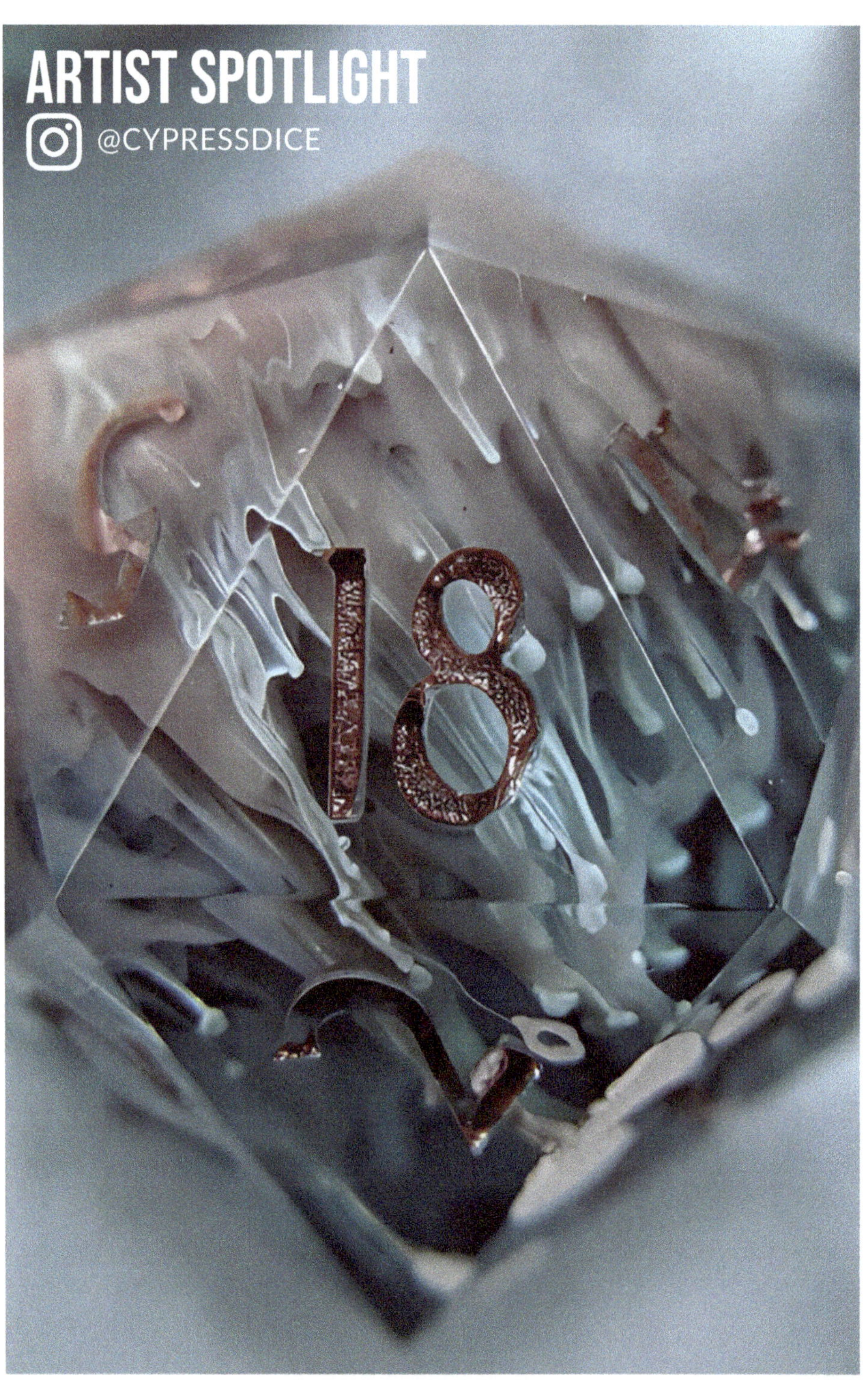

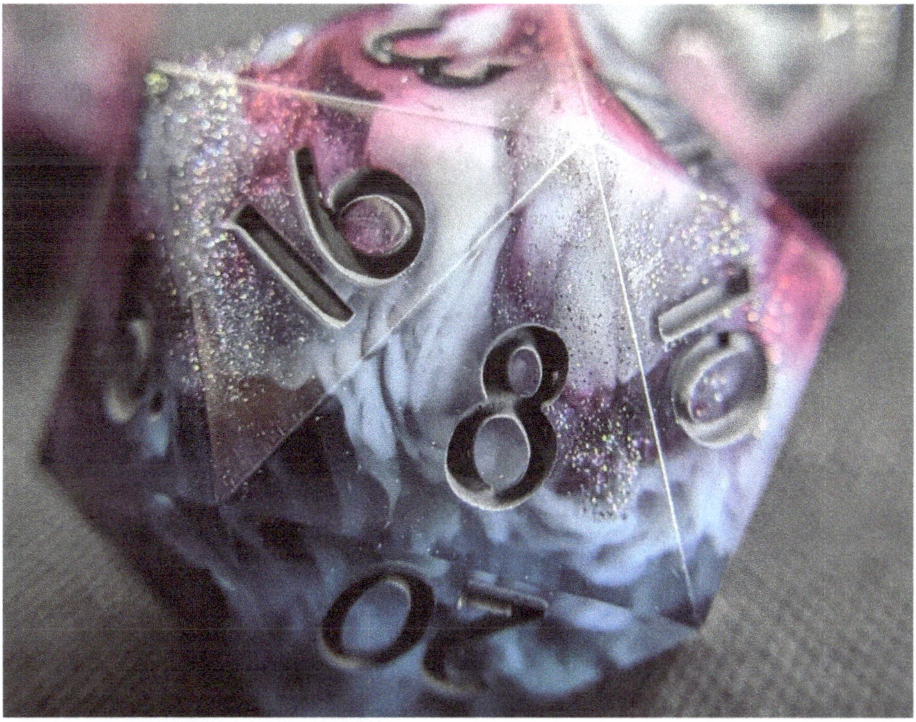

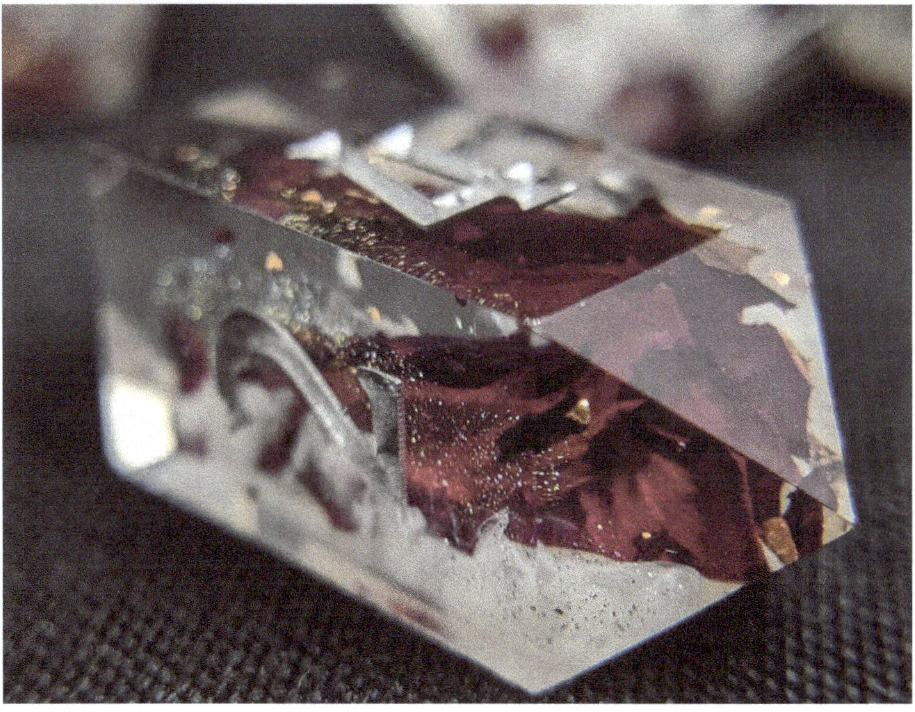

MOULD MAKING

Now that we have an understanding of silicone, this chapter will explore the basics of mould making!

PART EIGHT

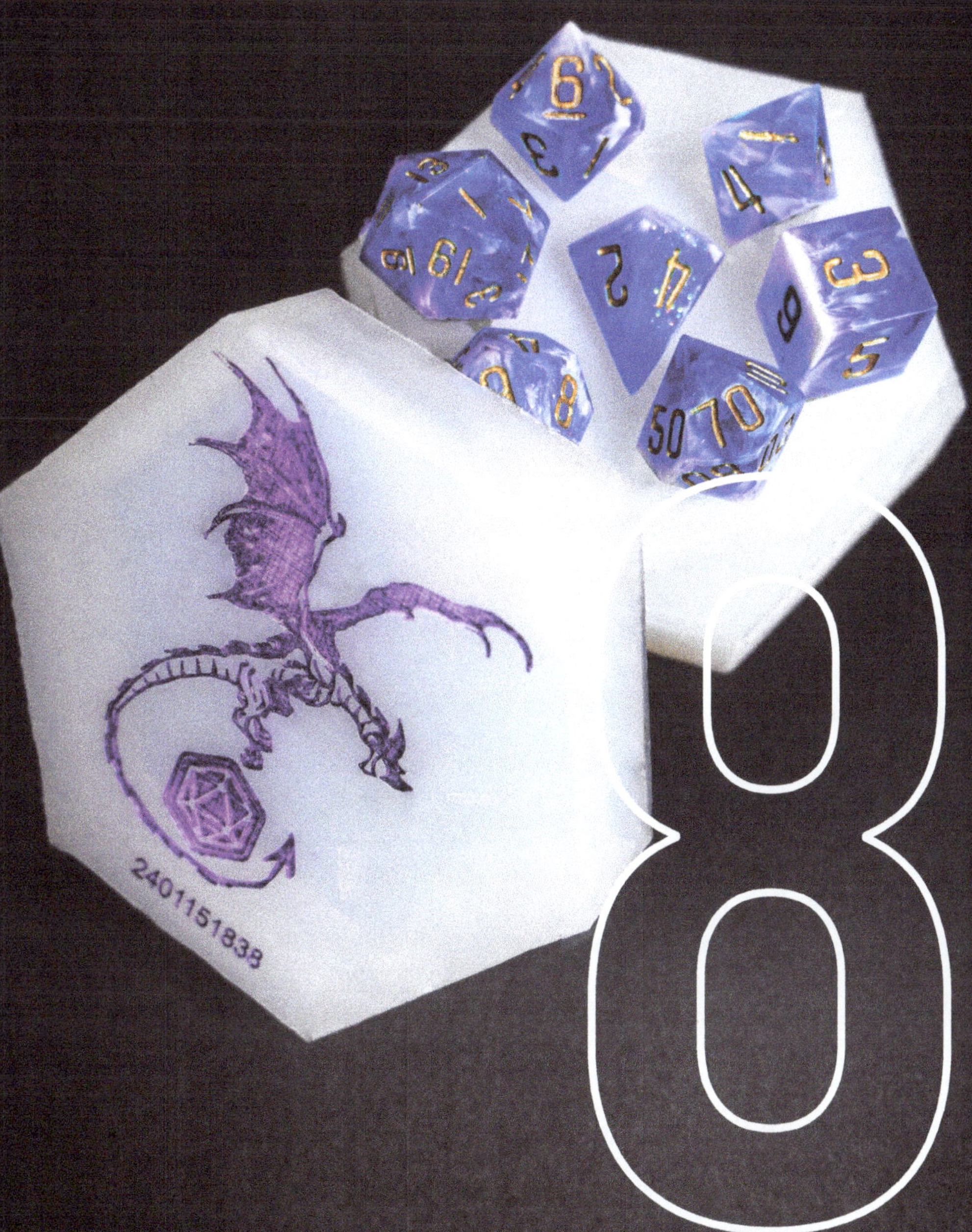

8

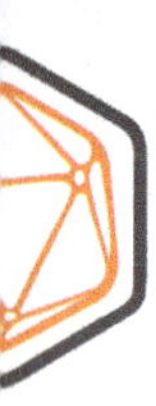

WHICH MOULD?

There are two moulds you'll come across in dice making. The cap mould and the sprue mould.

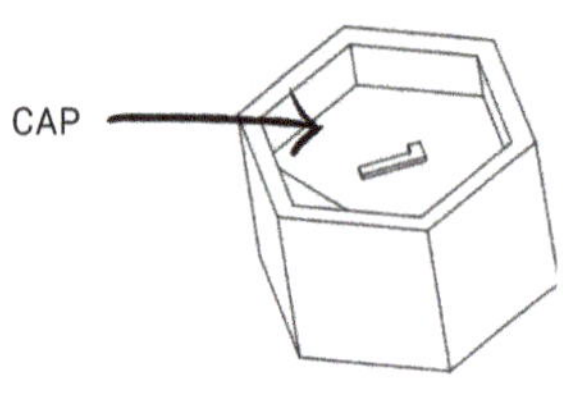

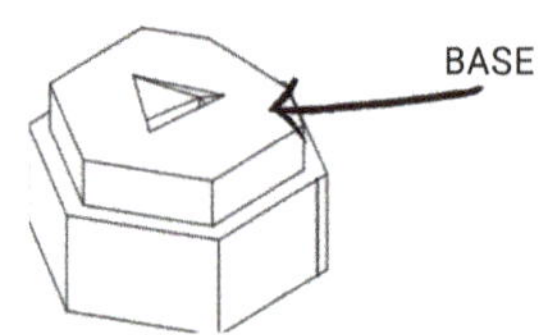

Cap Mould (or Squish Mould) – is a two-part mould where all the faces are moulded into the base except the top which is moulded into the cap. You simply fill it up and "squish" it together and any excess resin leaks out the sides. Its many advantages are an open cavity that's useful for all kinds of pouring techniques, it's easy for beginners to master, it doesn't cause any damage to your masters and there's no cutting required! Disadvantages include a steeper learning curve in terms of dealing with voids and issues if overfilled (see "Preventing Raised Faces" on page 42).

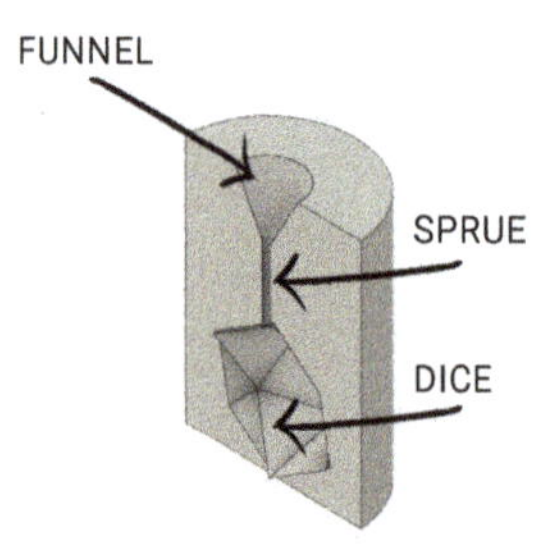

Sprue Mould – A sprue mould is a type of mould used in dice making. It involves attaching a toothpick or wax sprue to the dice, which is then attached to a funnel-shaped object. While many makers drill into their original dice to attach the sprue, it's almost always better to use wax sprues or glue if possible. The funnel is attached to the bottom of a cup or mould frame, and silicone is poured in. After curing, you carefully cut the mould and remove the dice.

The advantage of the sprue mould is that it allows for inserting oddly shaped items without damaging the mould. It can also be useful for those without pressure pots or for casting large dice as the excess resin in the funnel acts as a reservoir.

WE RECOMMEND A CAP MOULD FOR NEW (OR EVEN ADVANCED) DICE MAKERS.

MOULD FRAMES

LEVEL: 1   2   ③   4

A mould frame is anything that holds the silicone and forms the shape of your mould. It needs to be rigid and deep enough to contain the master dice. You can create a mould frame using anything from a section of PVC pipe or a wall made out of Lego bricks. If you're starting out, you can use whatever you have at hand.

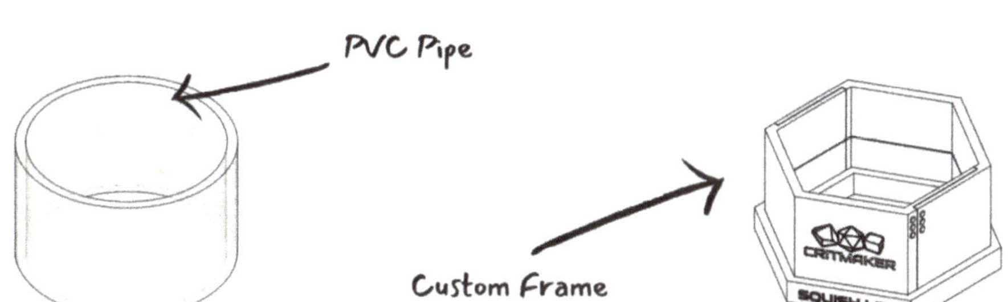

But, as you progress and aim for better consistency, it's advisable to invest in a custom frame.

Silicone is one of the most expensive ingredients in dice-making. The smallest moulds take around 250mL (8.5oz) whereas PVC pipe may use 500mL (17oz) or more. If silicone is cheap, go for whatever size you want, but frames like our SquishLite™ are designed with cost in mind!

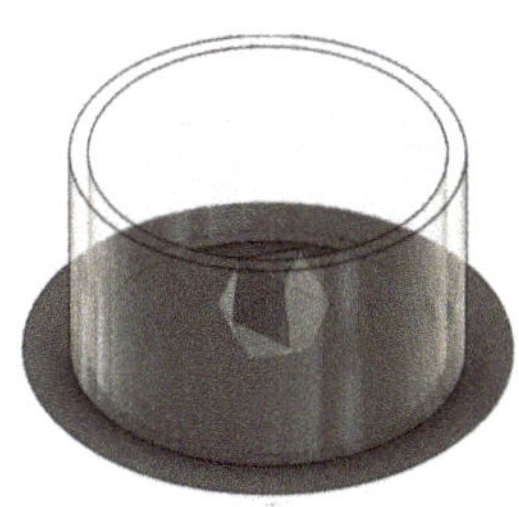

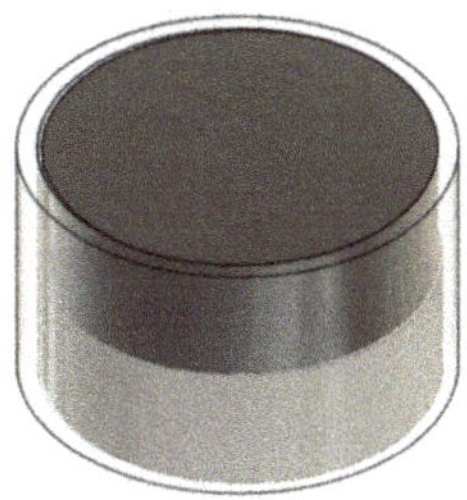

Regardless of the frame, you'll want it high enough to be able to comfortably cast both sides of the mould. We find that around 50-60mm (2 to 2.5 inches) in height works best for a basic set of dice.

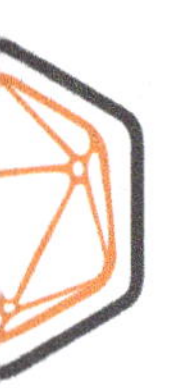

REGISTRATION KEYS

LEVEL: 1 2 (3) 4

Registration keys are anything that can help align the parts of your silicone mould.

Most dice-makers add keys in two ways. They either add objects into the first pour or cut them out before the second.

Consider the following mould. It has a frame, and we've added some random shapes into the mould around our dice.

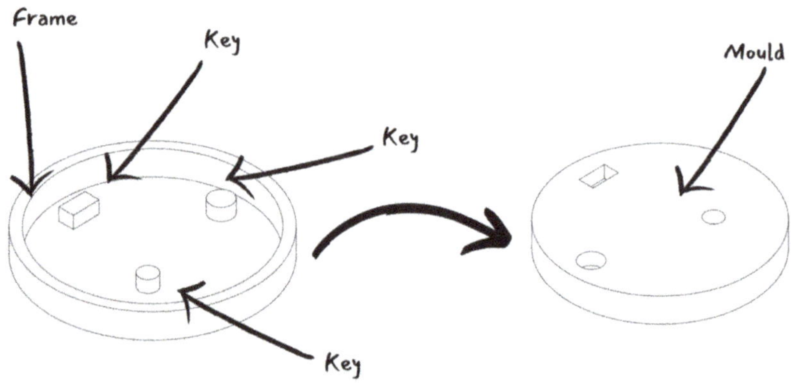

Once we've poured it, we now have these super convenient shapes in our mould that won't allow it to close any other way. This is what keys are for!

ADDING KEYS AFTER THE FIRST POUR

If you don't want to mess around with objects in the base of your mould, you can also cut them into your base after it's cured.

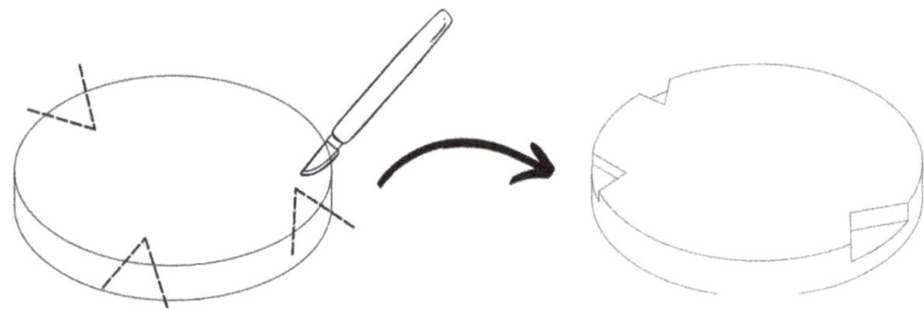

MOULD CONSIDERATIONS

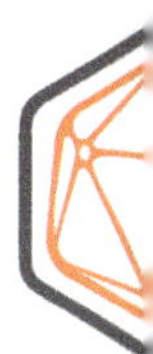

WHICH FACE ON TOP?

Before you get started pouring your mould, you first need to consider which face you want to be on top (the cap).

Many dice makers prefer to use the lowest number (e.g. one), as it's often the easiest to repair in case things go wrong. However, on most dice, the highest face is opposite the lowest! This means you may find that if your mix-ins sink to the bottom, you're going to have a fairly ugly crit face. Some makers prefer to put the crit face on top!

Both options are worth considering, so there's no right or wrong. We generally cast our moulds with the lowest face on top.

CONTACT OR PACKING TAPE?

You'll also need something to put on the base of your mould frame to stick your dice to! This is another one with no right or wrong answer. If you choose packing tape, simply layer it with as little overlap as possible. We prefer to use book-covering vinyl or Cricut Strong Grip Transfer Tape. It's wide enough so there are no seams on your mould, it's sticky enough to keep our dice down and, most importantly, it doesn't leave a sticky residue when we pull it off.

WHICH KEYS?

If you're using PVC, we recommend starting with cutting keys into your mould your first time. With a custom frame, keys may already be included. Either way, it's best to figure it out before your working time starts!

With those three decisions out of the way, let's get on with making our mould!

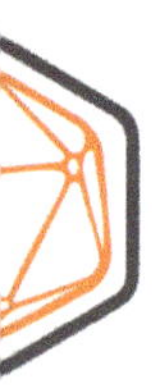

MAKING A CAP MOULD

LEVEL: 1   2   (3)   4   **PPE:**  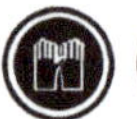  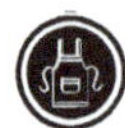

WHAT YOU'LL NEED

- Dice to mould
- Silicone
- A mould frame
- Packing tape or book contact
- Scales

- Measuring cup
- Stirring stick
- Mould release or petroleum jelly
- Objects to use as key (if needed)
- Hot glue gun (optional)

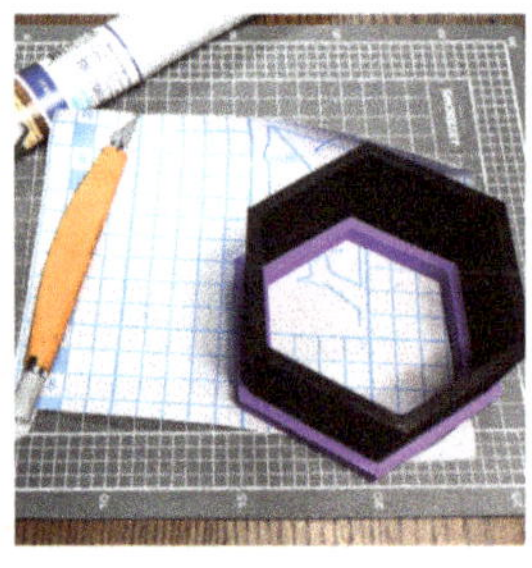

1 Apply contact or packing tape to the underside of the frame (sticky side towards the inside of the frame) and gently place your dice inside, ensuring they are stuck down well. If you're adding keys now, place them in the mould.

2 If you're worried about leaks, you can seal it up with hot glue. We're fairly certain of the bond between our mould frames and the contact vinyl.

3 Mix your silicone as per the supplier's instructions and degas if using a vacuum chamber. Many silicones are a simple 1:1 ratio by volume or weight, but it may differ for your brand.

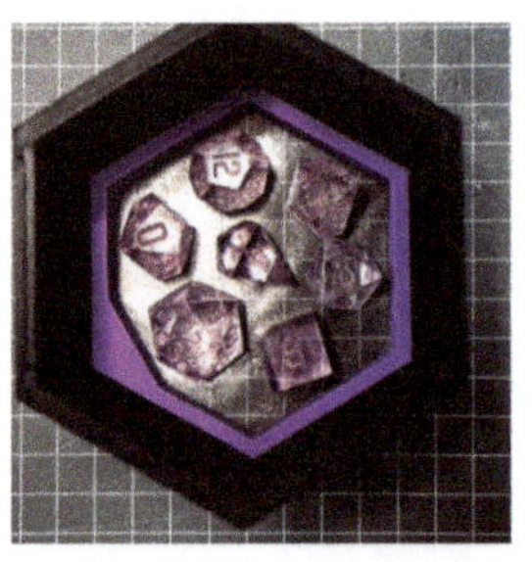

4 It's now time to start pouring silicone over the top of the dice. Try not to start on a face, instead start the stream on the tape and let it flow up around the dice. Pour in a thin, high stream as demonstrated in the photo to the left. You don't need a super-thick base on your mould. Once the dice are covered, we generally fill the mould a further 10mm or about $^3/_8$ inch.

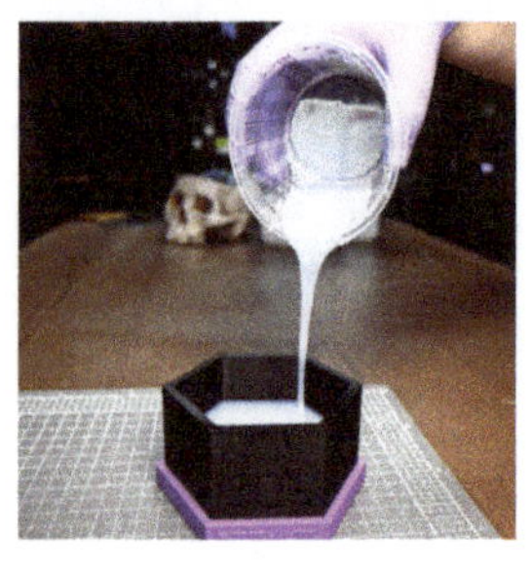

LET YOUR SILICONE FULLY CURE!

5 Once cured, remove the tape from the bottom (gently so as not to disturb the dice or tear the silicone) and remove the mould from the frame. If you are cutting keys, now is the time. Just some triangles are fine, as long as you can tell which way they will go later. Our moulds shown already have keys incorporated into the frame!

NOTE: IF YOU ADDED KEYS TO THE BASE, REMOVE THEM NOW AND CLEAN UP ANY FLASHING THAT MAY PREVENT THE SILICONE FROM GETTING INTO THEM.

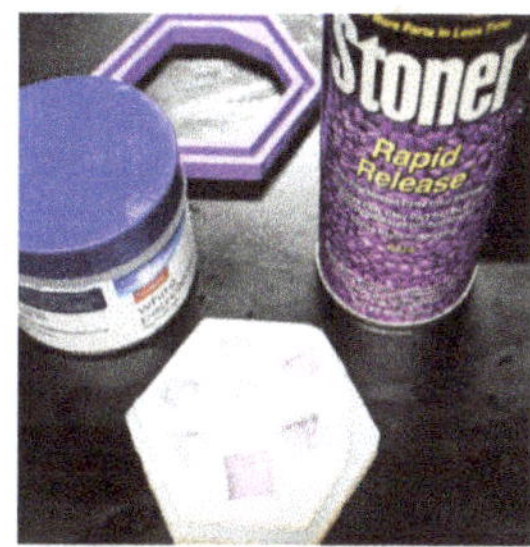

6 It's a good idea to clean up the mould at this point. Remove any flashing (cuticle trimmers are amazing for this) and gently wipe away any silicone that may have crept over the faces. Again, be careful not to disturb your dice (their job isn't done yet!).

7 It's now time to liberally apply mould-release or petroleum jelly to the entire mould. Make sure you get it right into your all your keys and cutouts - any spot you miss will cause the two parts to bind together! If you're using petroleum jelly, apply it with a soft brush (or Q-tip) and avoid the faces entirely. For mould release, just spray it all over, it's a fine mist and the faces will need to be polished anyway.

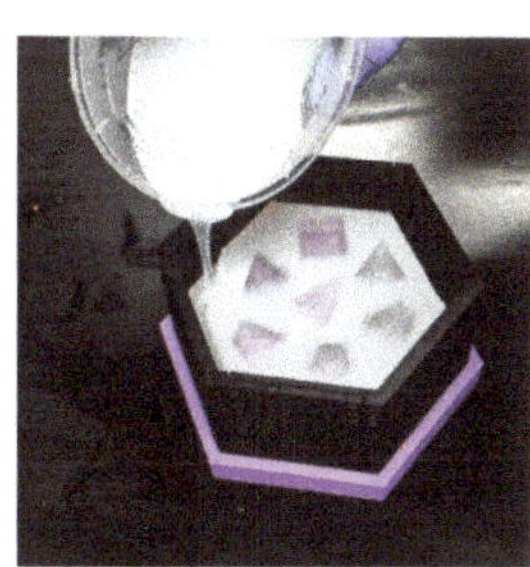

8 Put the mould back in the frame (dice side up) and pour the second layer. Again, this only needs to be about 10mm or about ³⁄₈ inch.

9 If you're using a pressure pot, (we recommend it), set it to 50 PSI and put your mould in for the full cure time.

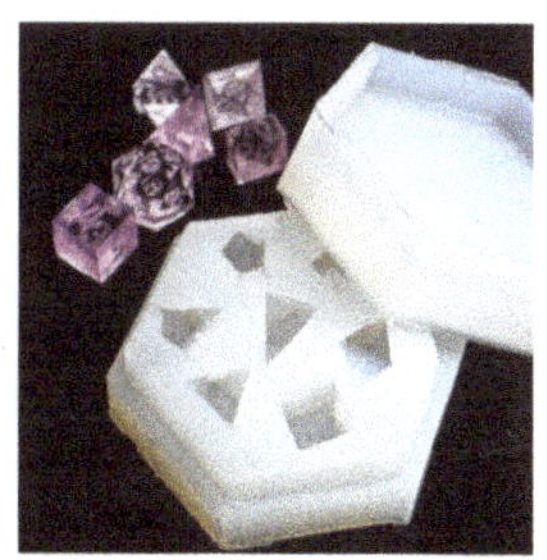

10 Gently pry the two sections apart and remove your masters! You now have your very own mould. If anything has stuck, very gently, pry it apart and slice it away with a sharp knife (try not to touch your masters!)

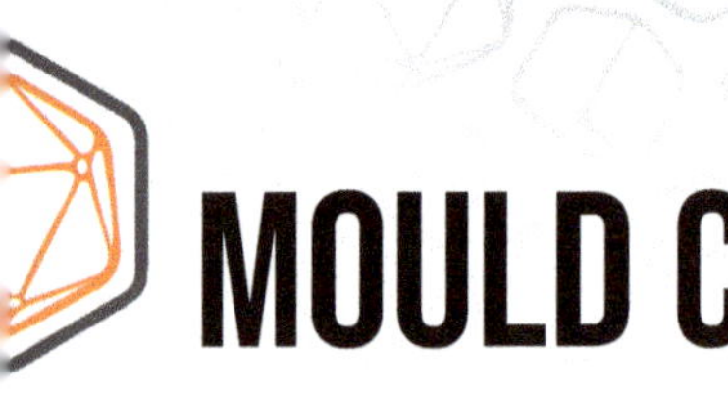

MOULD CARE

Unfortunately, silicone moulds don't last forever. While a good set of high-quality moulds can last for years, every single time you cast from them they are degraded a little more.

Dice moulds have a much shorter life span than standard moulds due to the tiny details and sharp edges which will start to wear after only a handful of castings. Depending on the silicone used, the shore hardness and the complexity of your moulds, you may get a dozen castings out of a mould or a hundred.

Here are some tips for keeping your moulds in pristine condition and even helping to prolong their life.

BE GENTLE

Most dice makers prefer not to use mould release as it takes away some of the shine, which means more sanding. However, mould release will not only increase the life of your moulds, but will make them much easier to demould. The release adds a gentle barrier between the resin and the mould and helps to prevent resin from sticking in the fine details.

Be very careful with sharp objects, whether it be a toothpick creating a smoky effect or extracting your sharp sided dice – take your time and remember those delicate numbers!

CLEANING YOUR MOULDS

The easiest way to clean moulds is with some gentle dish soap and warm (not hot) water. Wipe them out and let them soak to remove any excess resin. Once dried, turn them upside down and let them dry thoroughly before casting again.

Baby wipes are another great alternative. Not only are they extremely soft, but they also contain a very gentle cleanser that helps to remove built-up oils and leftover resin.

 For a deeper clean you can use acetone which removes chemicals and other residues, and just needs a few minutes to air dry. It's best to test this on an older mould before using harsh chemicals on your new shiny ones! It's generally not recommended to use isopropyl alcohol on your moulds as this can degrade some silicones and take the shine off them.

STORE YOUR MOULDS DRY AND FLAT

Did you know that silicone moulds have a library life? This is the amount of time the mould will last without being used. While tin-cure silicone has a relatively short library life of 1–10 years, platinum silicone may last up to 30! Obviously, this depends on many factors such as the chemical components of your silicone, and how gentle you are with them, but it's amazing to think you could still use the same mould in 10 to 30 years time!

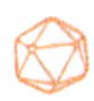 Always keep your moulds in a cool and dry place – the silica in silicone absorbs moisture so it's important to have a fairly constant temperature and to keep them out of the sun.

 You also want to store them perfectly flat to ensure they maintain their correct shape. Moulds that are bent out of shape too long won't go back to their original form.

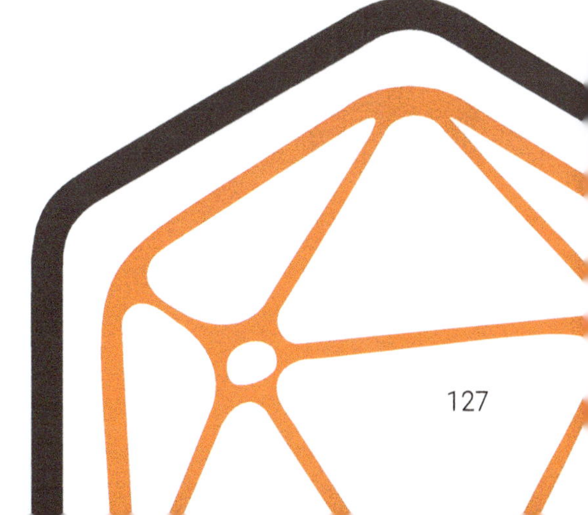

ARTIST SPOTLIGHT

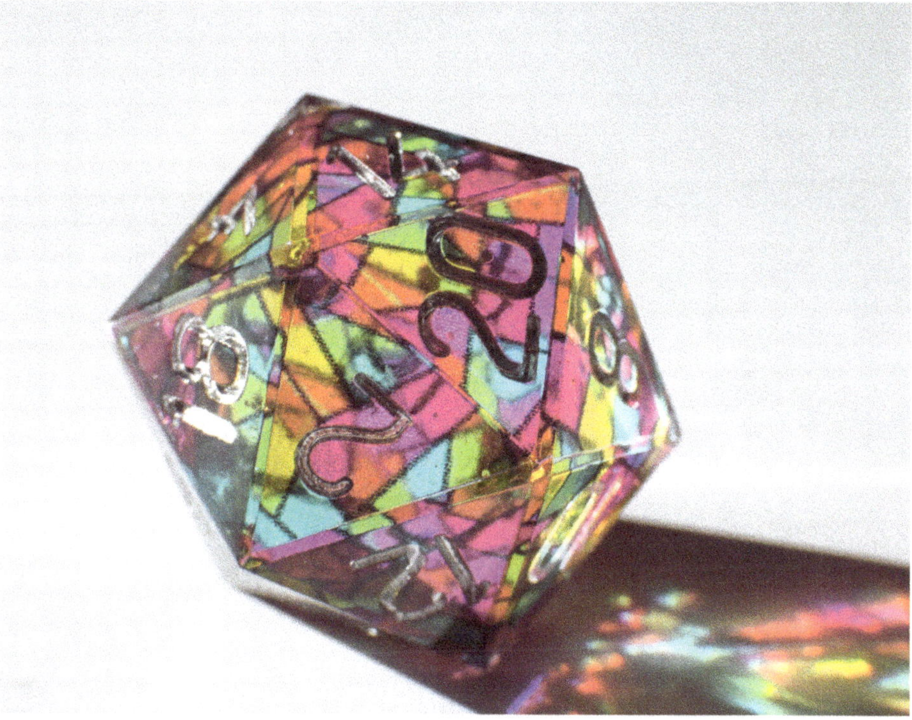

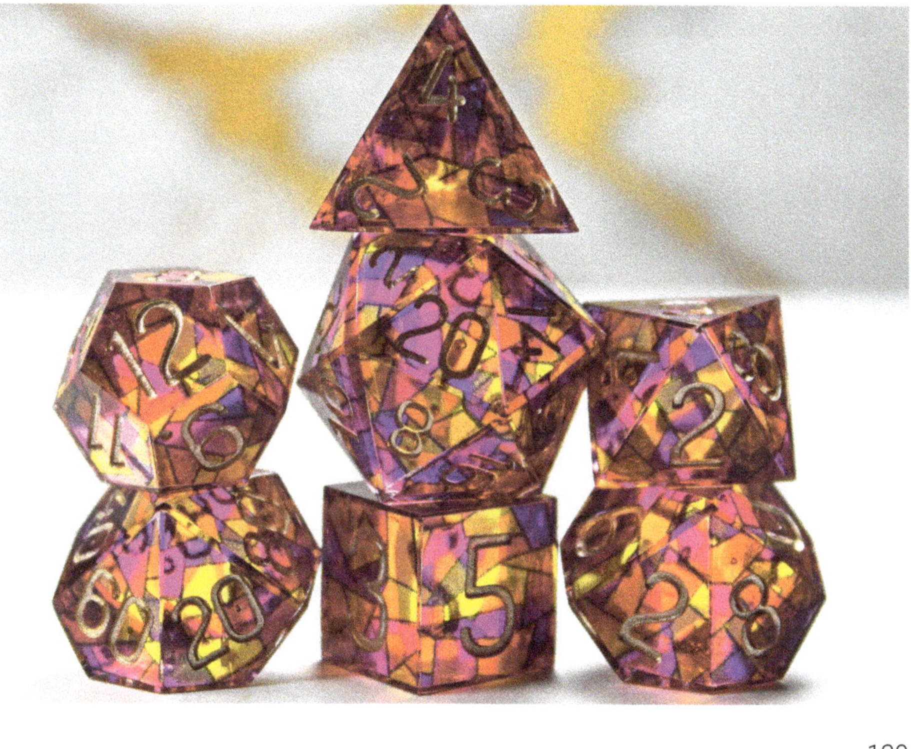

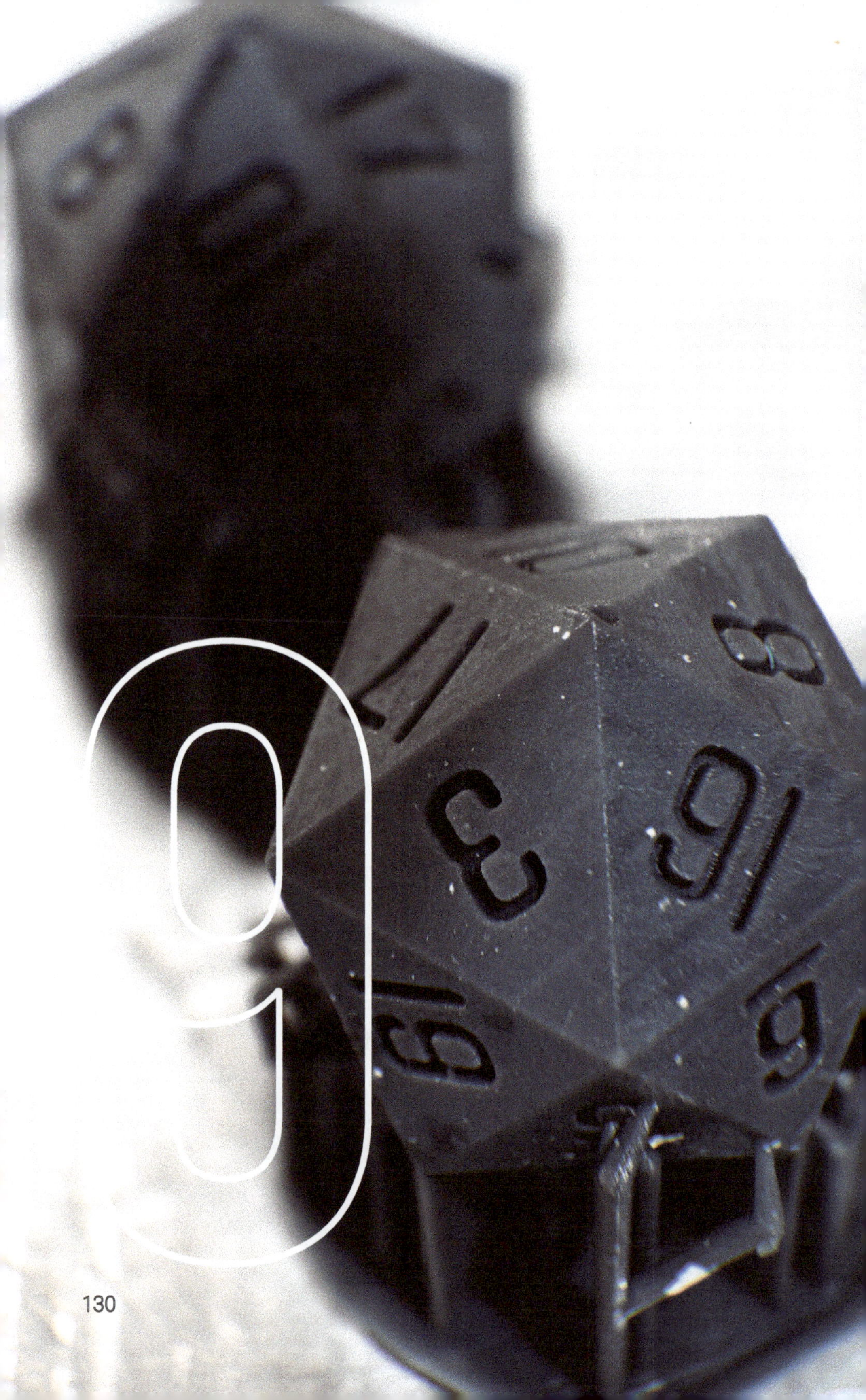

DICE MASTERS

In this chapter we'll explore some of the considerations for designing and printing your very own custom dice masters. This section assumes that you understand the basics of 3D printing and using resin printers.

PART NINE

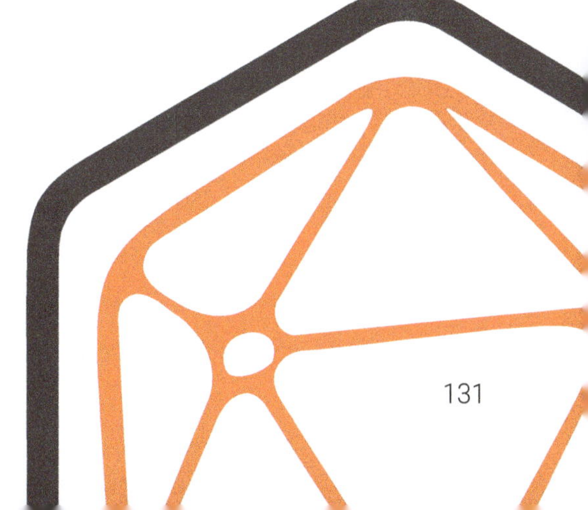

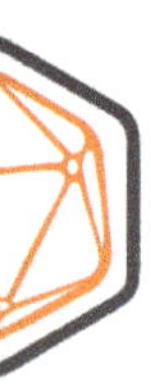

IMPORTANT TERMS

LEVEL:　1　2　3　

Blanks – A dice casting without numbers. It's specially designed to fit inside a master dice mould. Blanks are usually offset on every side by the depth of the numbers so that they fit snugly and stay centred.

FDM – (Fused Deposition Modelling) is a 3D printing technology that builds objects layer by layer by extruding and melting plastic filament through a nozzle.

Masters – A dice master refers to the original or prototype dice used as a template for creating moulds. It serves as the model from which multiple copies or casts are made.

Shrinkage – refers to the reduction in size that occurs during the curing or cooling process of printed resin, leading to slightly smaller dimensions in the final printed object compared to the original digital design.

Slicer – In 3D printing, a slicer is a software tool that takes a digital 3D model and generates layer–by–layer information that the 3D printer needs to produce the object. It "slices" the digital model into layers for the printer to build sequentially.

SLA – (Stereolithography) is a 3D printing technology that uses liquid resin cured by ultraviolet light to create precise and detailed three-dimensional objects.

SLS – (Selective Laser Sintering) is a 3D printing technique that uses a laser to fuse powdered material, typically nylon or other polymers, layer by layer, to create solid objects.

Supports – in 3D printing, supports are temporary structures added to help stabilise and anchor overhanging or complex parts of a printed object. They prevent sagging or collapsing during the printing process.

3D Modelling – the process of creating a digital representation of a three-dimensional object or scene using specialised software.

Typography – the art and technique of arranging and designing text to make it visually appealing and readable.

3D PRINTERS

LEVEL: 1   2   3   **(4)**

3D Printers are great, but not without their frustrations! When it comes to dice, lots of makers will eventually want to make their own custom master dice. While it's possible at home, it can be daunting, and many makers turn to professionals to create their masters for them. There are plenty of great companies out there making professional dice masters.

If you like a challenge, there are two main types of 3D printers presently available for home use.

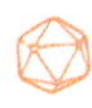 **Fused Deposition Modelling (FDM)** printers use heated plastic to deposit material but cannot print fine enough details (yet) for making dice masters. Popular brands include BambuLabs, Creality, and Prusa.

 **Stereolithography (SLA)** printers use UV resin solidified on a plate by UV-lit LCD or DLP screens, producing perfect details at thin layers. Popular brands include Elegoo and Anycubic. We prefer the Elegoo Saturn and Mars printers for their reliability and ease of use.

While great for printing miniatures, SLA printers are significantly more prone to shrinkage than FDM printers. Not only is it important to properly calibrate your printer (there are plenty of excellent guides online), but you'll also need to calibrate your slicer for resin shrinkage. This is particularly noticeable on the D6, which often prints quite distorted.

 There is a great guide by Jan Mrázek that gives a step-by-step solution to this problem.
(Scan QR code or bit.ly/resin-shrinkage*)*.

While there are currently no consumer-grade Selective Laser Sintering (SLS) printers available, they're worth mentioning as they have great potential in master printing. An SLS printer uses a laser to harden a fine powder into a solid layer. Unlike resin printing, it doesn't require supports or have issues with shrinkage however there are minimum feature sizes which may limit the usefulness.

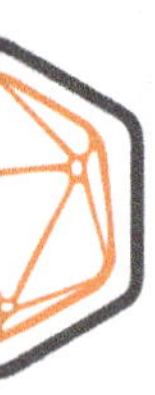

DESIGNING MASTERS

LEVEL: 1   2   3   **(4)**

You don't have to be a 3D modelling expert to design masters – in fact, there are some great free tools available to help that require no modelling experience at all!

DICE MAKING TOOLS

DiceMaker – is a Windows and Linux tool. It has almost all the features you could ever need including bumpers, fin supports and even making blanks with the click of a button. I'd say this app was perfect if they provided Mac version. ankhe.itch.io/dicemaker

DiceGen – is another online, open-source tool that allows you to generate basic dice inside of your web browser. It works on Mac, PC and even tablets. It's easy to use and you can add custom faces and use any font. It's a very simple app with some great features. dicegen.com

Unfortunately at the time of publishing DiceGen seems like it's abandoned. Being open-sourced, it'd be great to see another dice maker pick it up!

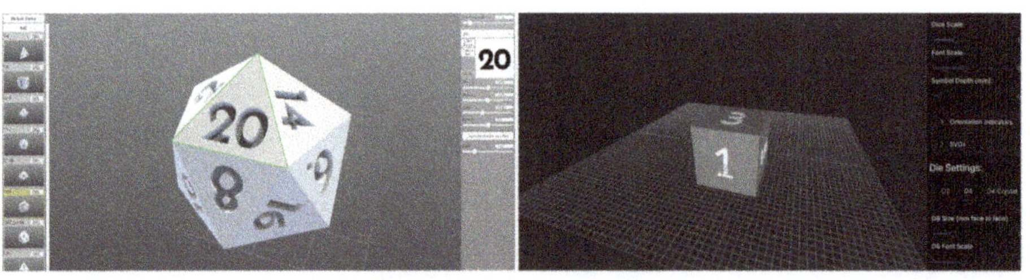

If you're using one of the tools above, you simply choose your fonts, **add logos**, tweak sizes and download the STL files. You can then import these into your 3D slicer and print them. It's worth noting that on both of the above applications, I've had errors due to "non-manifold geometry" while slicing – meaning the models aren't well-formed. This seems to depend on the font used, but we ultimately decided to design our own models using Autodesk Fusion.

DESIGN CONSIDERATIONS

LEVEL: 1 2 3 (4)

Regardless of the tool you use, the same design considerations apply! You can't put any font on your dice and expect it to look good; you must consider your outcome and inspiration.

TYPOGRAPHY

The fonts will dictate the aesthetic of your dice. If you want something scary, use a gothic or horror-themed font like Ironwood or Exocet from Adobe Fonts. They have a whole category! See fonts.adobe.com/fonts/tags/horror

Classic? Go try something from the "clean" category . See fonts.adobe.com/fonts/tags/clean

Experiment with different fonts to make your perfect masters.

Note: There's a lot of debate about what's legal and what's not, stick to open-source or fonts you have *commercial* rights to if you intend selling them. There are hundreds of free fonts offered by Google or Adobe and many more available from sites such as CreativeFabrica (creativefabrica.com) that give commercial rights.

FONT SIZE

It's a sad fact, but as you get older, your eyes get worse! I'm at the point where I appreciate dice with larger numbers far more than artistic ones. Consider your target audience and set your font sizes accordingly. If your dice are designed to be used, also consider that not everyone plays games under studio lights!

ACCESSIBILITY

According to the World Health Organisation, 285 million people are visually impaired. 39 million people are blind and over 246 million have low vision. When considering all those who need glasses to correct some kind of refractive issue, this rises to 2.2 billion! With that in mind, it's important to understand accessibility requirements as a dice-maker. As a general rule, basic fonts work best in high-contrast colours. Consider white on dark colours or dark on light colours. It's not to say that you can't do fancy, swirly fonts, but it's great to keep in mind.

There are even fonts optimised for legibility, such as Atkinson Hyperlegible. See brailleinstitute.org/freefont.

LOGOS

Many dice makers add a logo to the crit faces of their dice as a seal of their brand. It's up to you, but I prefer to keep dice readable, and a twenty is easier to read than a group of elven warriors! If you're going to use a logo, keep it SIMPLE. Resin printers are good at fine details, but you'll get better results from a simple embossed logo.

SHAPES

If you're using a dice generator, you won't have a lot of choices here, but they may give you options for some dice. If you're using a modelling program, you'll want a good set of primitives (geometric shapes without any numbers) these can be downloaded from sites like Thingiverse or purchased from us. Consider modern shapes such as the rhombic D12, the shaved corner D6, jewel-shaped D4s and elongated D10/D100/D8s.

If you want to make your own primitives, you'll need to get a calculator and find some online tutorials for creating each shape (as we did!).

I recommend youtube.com/@thewizardofco

SIZE

There is no correct answer to this; almost every set of dice I own is a different size. Experiment with what works – but consider making the D20 (or primary dice for your game) a little larger – it has smaller faces and, hence, smaller numbers. The best thing to do is base the set off the size of the D6, which is usually 15-16mm face to face.

There's a great article on BrycesDice about this topic – See bit.ly/dice-sizes

NUMBER DEPTH

This comes down to personal preference, but many dice makers find between 0.75mm and 1mm to be good. It depends on the quality of your prints and how much sanding is needed. My earliest dice were 0.75mm and I found after sanding the masters and accounting for minor raised faces, the numbers were just a bit too shallow. Our new masters were printed at 1mm and I think they look great. Note: I had more issues printing at 1.2mm and over due to the larger overhangs.

BLANKS

If you're going to be printing blanks as well as standard masters, you'll want to ensure that they're the correct size. As a general rule of thumb, blanks must be offset equal to the depth of the numbers. For example, if the numbers are 0.9mm, the blank must be offset by 0.9mm on all sides. It is best to leave this to your modelling software rather than trying to do it yourself! The DiceMaker application (see "Designing Masters" on page 134) allows you to create blanks for your moulds with one click.

BUMPERS

These are extra layers over the corners and edges of the dice which you can easily add in the DiceMaker application or a tool like Autodesk Fusion. The benefit of bumpers is that supports can be simpler and, once sanded down, you'll always have perfect edges and corners. They're a great option for less optimised resin printers that may struggle with sharp edges. However, on a quality 3D printer they are usually unnecessary.

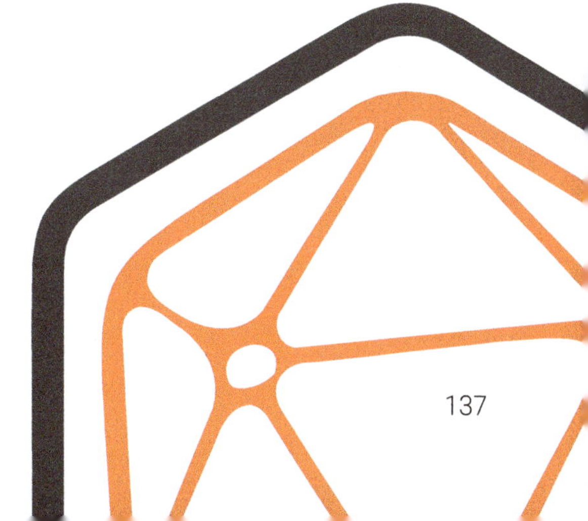

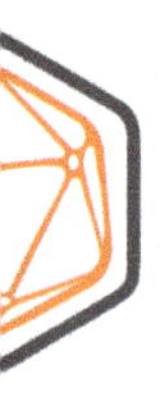

SUPPORTS

MODEL PLACEMENT

For most dice, you want a point facing towards the build plate – this means a single starting point, which is far easier to support in your slicer. For the D6, it's better to face a single edge to the plate as you'll get less distortion.

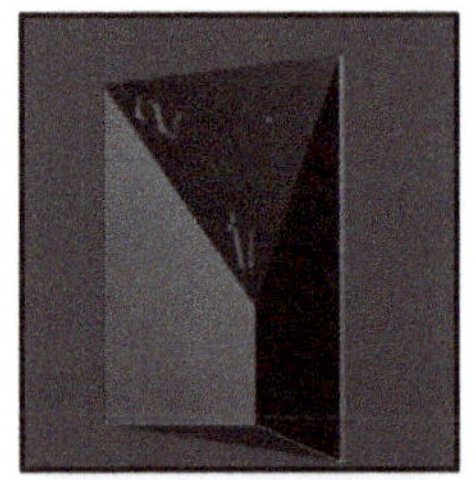

FIN SUPPORTS

Many dice-makers use fin supports on the sharp edges facing the build plate. These are either thin parts modelled into the masters themselves or added in your slicer using extremely close supports.

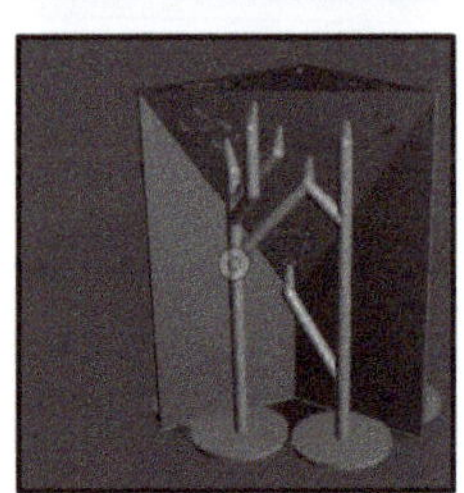

ISLAND SUPPORTS

After the dice are correctly set up with fin supports, you can now do a mixture of auto and manual supports for all the islands. While most slicers have an island detection tool, it's often necessary to look at your models slice by slice and find any areas that aren't connected to the main body and don't have a support directly under them. The example to the left is an island that will likely fail without support.

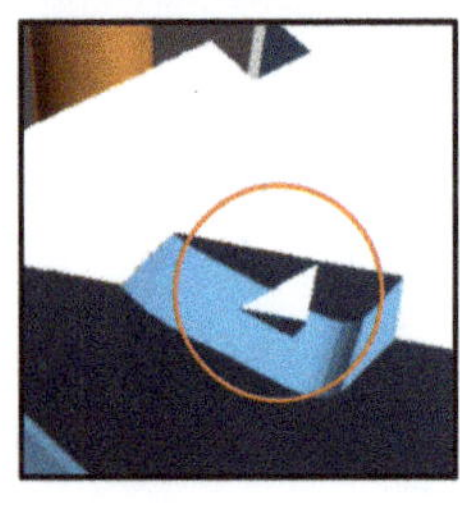

You'll often find these in your downward-facing numbers such as 6, 7, 8 and 9. Though a subtle defect, these number may look like they're sagging after printing.

REMEMBER, THERE ARE NO PRIZES FOR LESS SUPPORTS!

Rybonator has an excellent tutorial on adding fin supports. *(Scan QR code or bit.ly/dice-supports)*.

SANDING AND PREP

LEVEL: 1 2 3 (4)   **PPE:**    

WHAT YOU'LL NEED

- Dice masters
- Polishing Paper
- 800 grit sandpaper

- UV resin & torch
- Magnifying glass with light (optional)

I'm not going to lie; sanding masters takes a LONG TIME. There's a reason some companies sell finished masters for USD$300 or more, and there are very few ways to optimise the process.

1 Start with a high grit sandpaper and remove any bumps left by the supports. You must be precise here, as this paper will take off material quickly.

2 Start with ten revolutions in a circular motion. If it looks good, do ten revolutions on every face of the dice – you need to keep this even. If another side needs more, e.g. 12, do 2 more revolutions on every other face too.

3 Now that you've sanded down any high spots, it's time to get a magnifying glass and identify any low spots. When you find one, apply a tiny amount of the printer or UV resin with a toothpick and cure it with a UV torch. Now sand it again until it's perfectly flat.

4 Now you want to polish the masters, starting with 30 microns (green) and going through to white. After this, it's now time for another inspection under the magnifying glass – chances are, the polishing will highlight the spots you missed earlier. Fill. Re-sand. Re-polish. Re-peat.

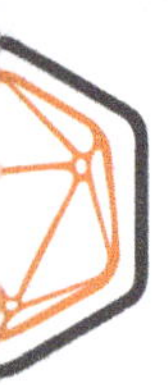

STORING YOUR MASTERS

LEVEL: 1   2   3   

After the countless hours you've spent on your masters, make sure you keep them in a safe place! We recommend storing them in individual bags wrapped in microfibre cloth or cotton wool. You don't want them rubbing against each other.

When you're ready to use them again, simply unwrap them, give them a quick polish and they're good to go!

We recommend cleaning your masters in an ultrasonic cleaner after each moulding to remove any silicone residue or polish.

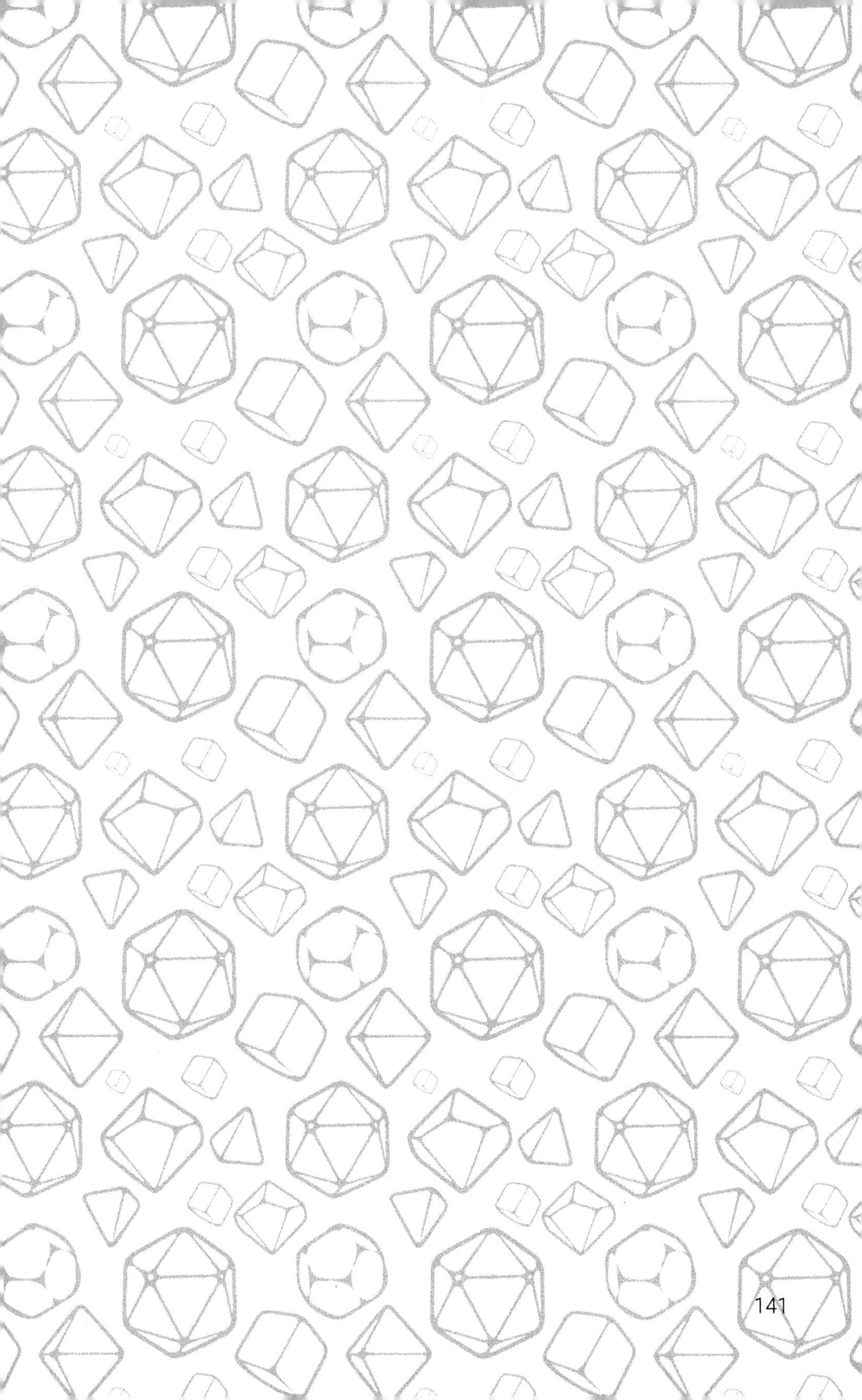

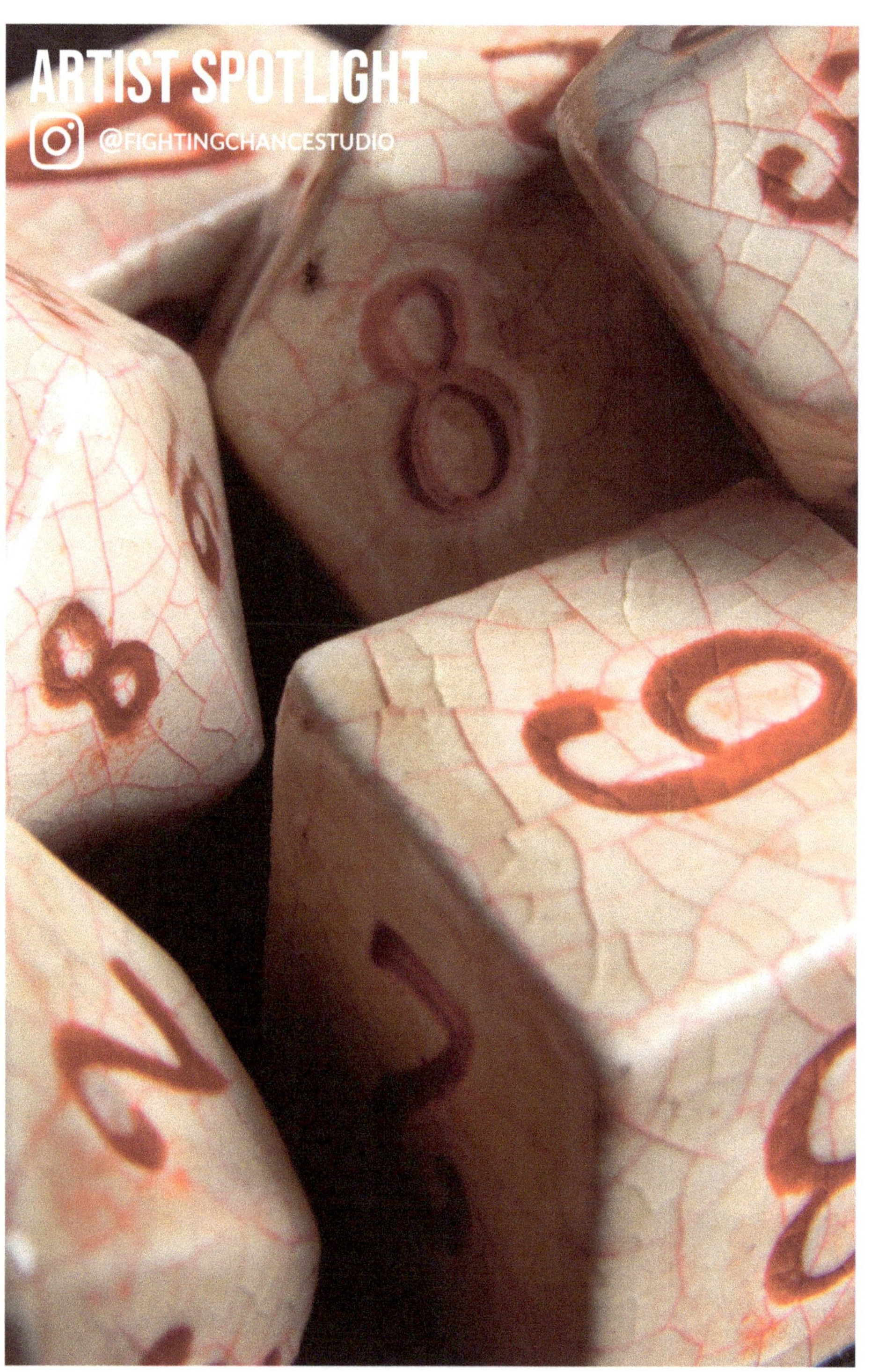

ARTIST SPOTLIGHT
@FIGHTINGCHANCESTUDIO

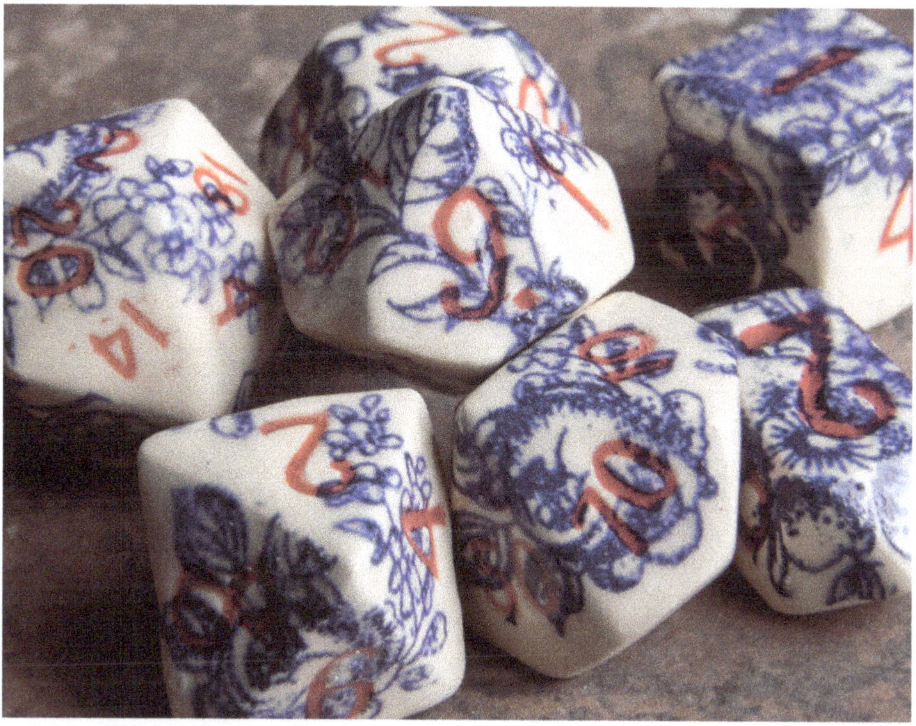

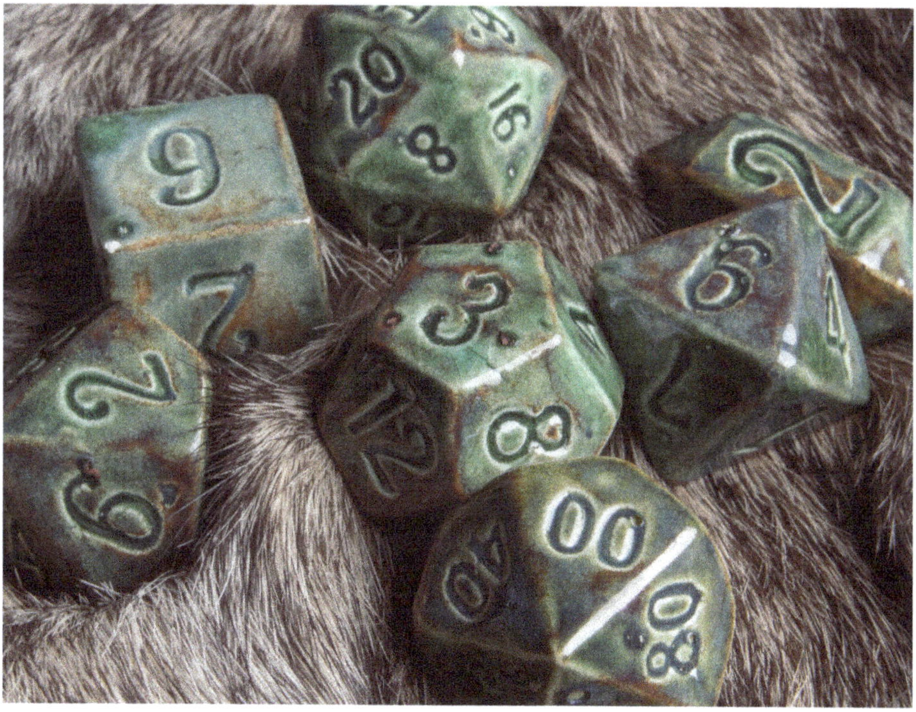

APPENDIX

All the bits and pieces that didn't need a whole section. We'll discuss salt testing, cover some random facts and I'll share a huge list of my favourite resources.

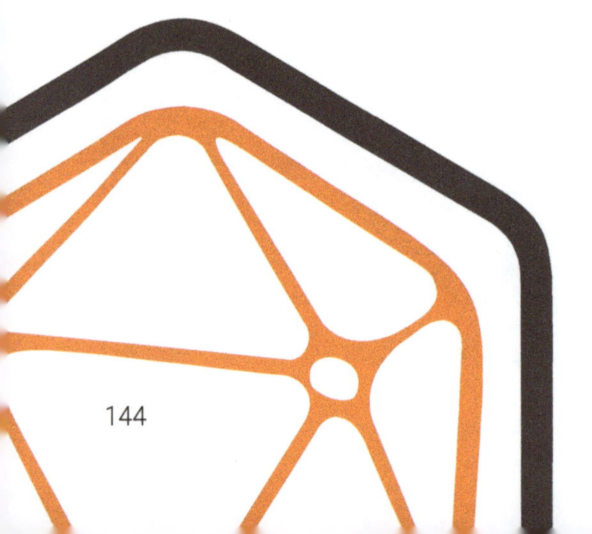

PART TEN

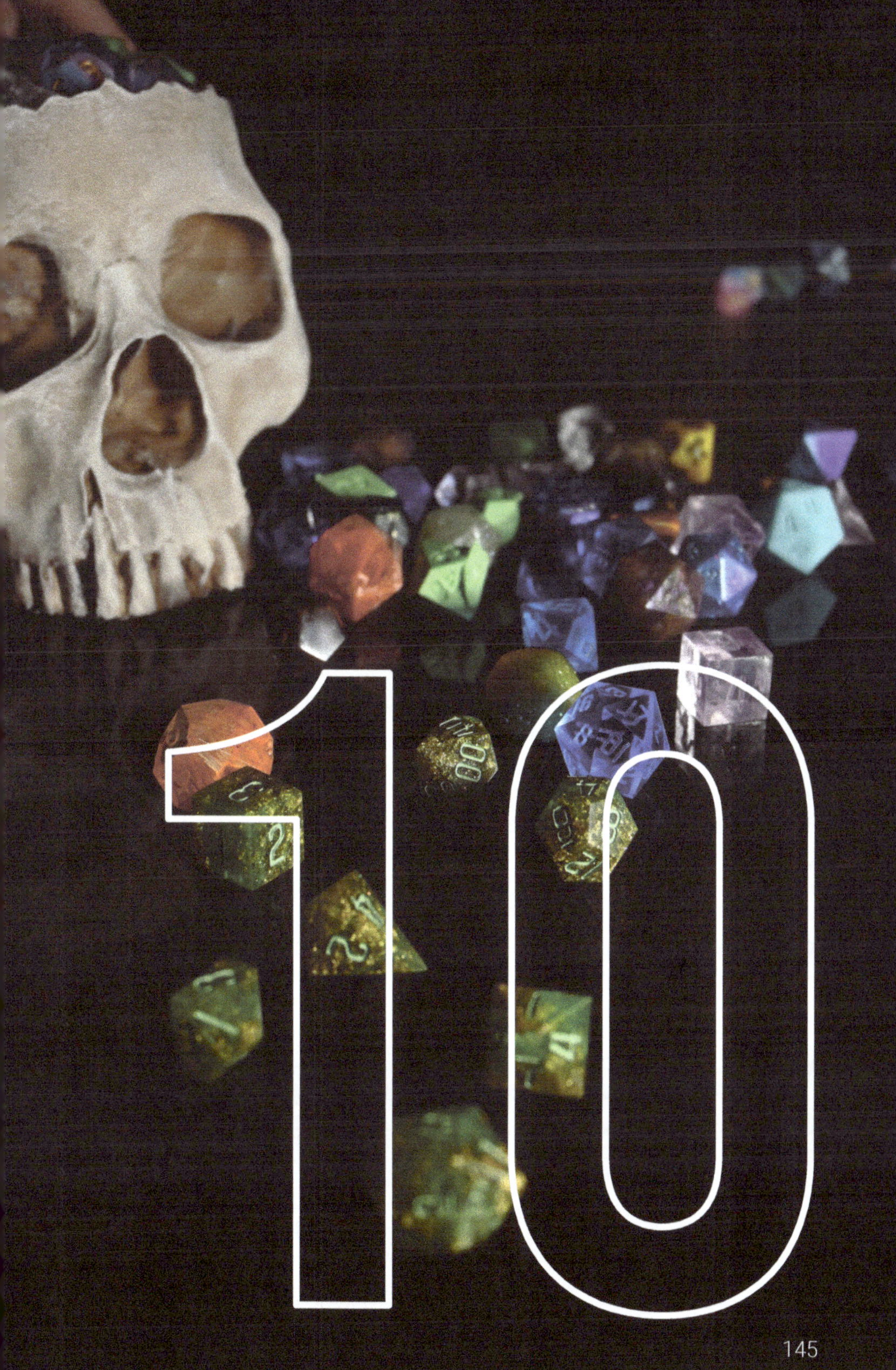

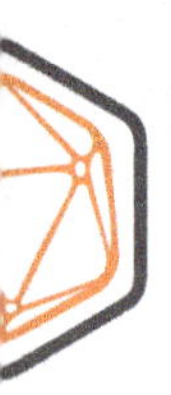

SALT TESTING

LEVEL:  (1)   2   3   4

Ever get the feeling that your dice are just bad? While it's possible your dice are cursed by some dark eldritch power, it's more likely they're incorrectly balanced. While not a perfect method, a saltwater test can help you decide which dice to use and which to lock in the dice jail. Huge shout out to Critical Dice for this guide! See bit.ly/float-test

1   Fill a measuring cup or glass about a third of the way with water and add salt. Lots of salt. You'll want at least six tablespoons.

2   Stir the salt water until no more will dissolve. If it's still crystal clear and dissolved, add some more salt.

3   Place your dice in the water – if it doesn't float, add more salt. Using a pencil or your finger, give the dice a flick so it spins around in the water. When it comes to rest, take note of the number.

4   Repeat the process a dozen or so times with all your dice. The dice should show a different number most times. If it often shows the same number it's possible the dice has a balance issue.

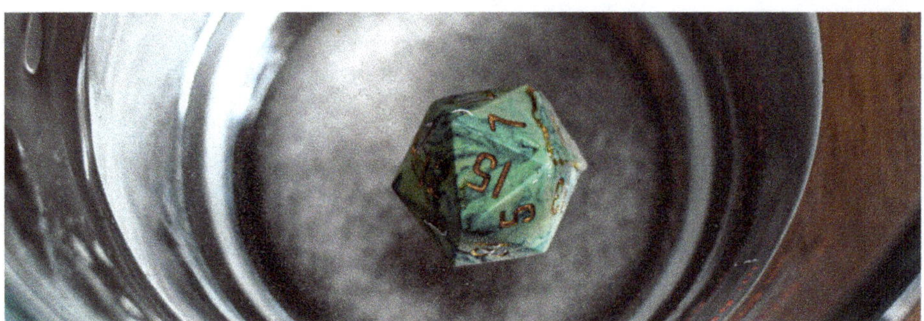

KNOW YOUR DICE

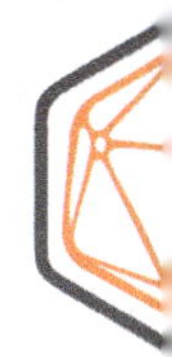

Dice are geometric shapes that when rolled display a random number or outcome from a single upward-facing side. The abbreviated names can be prefixed with a digit indicating the number of dice to roll. E.g. 3D6 refers to rolling THREE six-sided dice.

The most common dice used in tabletop role-playing games are D4, D6, D8, D10, D12, D20 and D100.

D2 – is a two-sided counter, like a coin that has a success and failure face. It has rounded edges, so it cannot be considered a polyhedron. Instead, it falls into the category of a curvilinear geometric shape known as a cylinder.

D4 – a four-sided die, known as a tetrahedron. The most common shape is a pyramid. But, there are many variations. For example, there are shard or jewel styles. These have more than four faces, but can only land on a primary face.

D6 – is the most familiar form of die, and it is a six-sided cuboid dice with either pips or numbers representing the faces.

D8 – is an eight-sided die, known as an octahedron.

D10 – is a ten-sided die often used with a percentile die to give a number out of 100. The shape used in most role-playing games is a pentagonal trapezohedron. The 10th face is a 0.

D12 – is a twelve-sided die, known as a dodecahedron.

D20 – is a twenty-sided die, which is the most common dice used in role-playing games, such as Dungeons and Dragons. It's known as an icosahedron.

D100 – This one doesn't usually follow the standard naming convention. More often than not, a D100 is a ten-sided dice, referred to as a percentile dice with faces 10, 20, 30, etc. When used with a D10, the percentile can give a number out of 100. For example, 30 + 7 = 37.

An actual 100-sided shape is called a hectogon or hecatontagon.

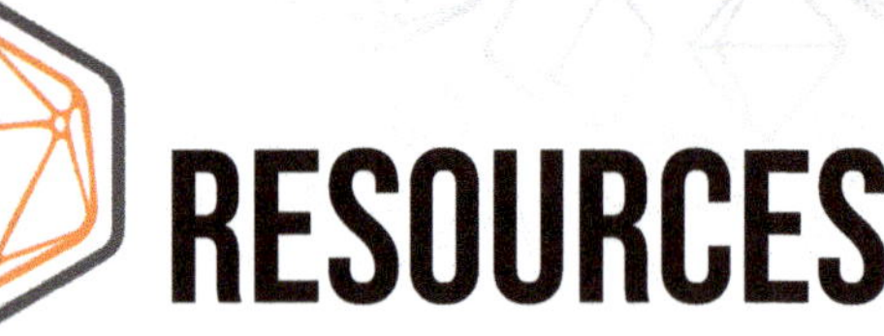

RESOURCES

YOUTUBE INSPIRATION

There are dozens of great content creators out there; here are a few of my personal favourites and ones I've followed for a long time!

Dice Druid
Dice Druid does incredible dice-pouring tutorials and runs one of the only brick-and-mortar dice stores!
youtube.com/@DruidDice

Dreamy Dice
Does fabulous tutorials and is an expert in geode dice designs. Every single video is better than the last, and I get excited when I see a new one online.
youtube.com/@dreamy_dice

Evan and Katelyn
Some of the best and most contagious makers on YouTube. You can't help but love their enthusiasm and make, fail, make approach! Great resin videos. One of my favourite channels.
youtube.com/@EvanAndKatelyn

Faux Hammer
With a solid mix of miniature painting tutorials and printer and resin reviews. A great resource for miniature lovers and dice printers alike!
youtube.com/@FauxHammer

Rybonator
This guy makes the best dice making videos. He's the O.G. that all dice makers refer to online. Start at his early videos and keep going to understand how dice making has evolved.
youtube.com/@Rybonator

Robert Tolone
Robert is an expert on silicone moulds and resin casting. My wife and I love his calm manner and approach to things – he's a bit like the Bob Ross of resin casting!
youtube.com/@RobertTolone

SmoothOn
Not only do SmoothOn make fantastic silicone, but they also make great mould-making videos!
youtube.com/@smooth-on

The Crafts Man
Go for the resin tips, stay for the feels! TheCraftsMan is a staple in the maker scene making beautiful handmade toys, animations, music and pretty much anything!
youtube.com/@TheCrafsMan

VogMan
Biff! Pow! Zap! VogMan reviews resin printers, makes awesome videos on lost-wax casting and moulding, and

does some great tutorials on 3D modelling, too.
youtube.com/@vogman

REDDIT

Dice Making

This subreddit is a wealth of info and a great help in times of frustration!
reddit.com/r/DiceMaking

Dice Porn

Don't let the name fool you; this subreddit is 100% SFW (Suitable For Work) – beautiful dice inspired by talented makers and collectors.
reddit.com/r/DicePorn

Resin Casting

Another great resource on Reddit – don't ask about dice, or they'll send you to DiceMaking!
reddit.com/r/ResinCasting

SOFTWARE

Autodesk Fusion

I have a soft spot for this modelling software, even if cheaper ones are available! All our products are designed with this.
autodesk.com/products/fusion-360

Blender

Probably the best fully featured 3D modelling tool ever made. Did we mention it's free?
blender.org

DiceGen

An online, open-source dice generator – select your font, add any SVG files for logos, and download them to STL. Great app – but seems to be abandoned.
dicegen.com

DiceMaker

This is a Windows application for generating dice masters. It has many great features, though it would be good to see a Mac version!
ankhe.itch.io/dicemaker

Tinkercad

This free 3D editor by Autodesk is very popular with the dice community and modellers alike. Not as full featured as Fusion or Blender, but has a much easier learning curve.
tinkercad.com

MISC

Awesome Dice

The best timeline of dice throughout history I've seen is at awesomedice.com/blogs/news/history-of-dice

Dice Collector

Kevin Cook holds the Guinness world record for over 11,097 dice collected since 1977. This book is in his collection too!

dicecollector.com

Veronique Greenwood

Excellent article on the shape of ancient dice and how beliefs have shifted from fate to chance.

bit.ly/fate-to-chance

PRODUCTS WE USE

Barnes

Australian store for all things casting and moulding.

barnes.com.au

JustResin Pigment

Beautiful pigment powders and pastes.

.justresin.store

Mont Marte Acrylic Paints

They are super thick paints with great, dense colours.

montmarte.com/collections/acrylic

Pearl Ex Powdered Pigments

They have vibrant colours and come in great selection packs to get you started.

jacquardproducts.com/pearl-ex

Piñata Inks

Rich, vibrant inks and their Blanco Blanco white is indispensable!

jacquardproducts.com/pinata-alcohol-ink

Ranger Ink

Another great supplier of quality alcohol inks.

rangerink.com

DICE MAKERS WE LOVE

Archival Dice

Makes beautiful sharp edged dice out of polymer clay.

instagram.com/archivaldice/

Arty Laboratory

Some of the most beautiful floral dice I've seen.

instagram.com/artylaboratory

Chicken Wizard Dice

Probably makes the most incredible petri dice ever.

instagram.com/chickenwizarddice

Chorts Horde

Chort Horde may well make some of the most spectacular dice I've ever seen. Enough said. Check them out.

instagram.com/chortshoard

Clerics Components

Expertly made masters and inclusions.

instagram.com/clericscomponents

Color Spray Creations

Some of the most beautiful dirty pour dice and inserts I've seen.

instagram.com/colorspraycreations

Critical Miss Dice

Not only do they make incredible liquid core, but they may also well be the world's foremost expert on the topic!

instagram.com/criticalmissdice

Cult Dice

Dark, underworld themes and incredible dice shapes. One of my favourite dice artists.

instagram.com/cultdice

Cumulus Dice

Beautiful, squishy, silicone dice!

instagram.com/cumulus_dice

Cypress Dice

Talented maker of gorgeous petri dice and swirling portals.

instagram.com/cypressdice

Delvewood Dice

Makes beautiful wood, resin and mixed-media dice.

instagram.com/delvewood

Devoured Dice

Aussie dice smith specialising in smoky dice. So smoky and so incredible.

instagram.com/devoured.dice

The Dice Djinn

Amazing washi tape dice and unique shell casts.

instagram.com/thedicedjinn

Dice of the Seeker

Talented UK artist making unique creations out of resin and jesmonite.

instagram.com/diceoftheseeker

Dice Witchery

Gorgeous inclusions and geodes.

instagram.com/dicewitchery

Direfox Dice

Incredibly talented Australian artist. From prehistoric fossil dice to eldritch tendrils.

instagram.com/direfox.dice

Dracolis_

I'm in love with the black-hole dice and the shimmering portals. Don't forget the underscore at the end!

instagram.com/dracosolis_

Fateseeker Dice

Incredible otherworldly colours, clean lines and exceptional photographs will always light up your feed!

instagram.com/fateseekerdice

Fighting Chance Studio

More than just ceramic dice, these ceramic art pieces are family heirlooms.

instagram.com/fightingchancestudio

Gorgeous Barbarian

Lithuanian maker specialising in handmade artifacts, terrain and dice.

instagram.com/gorgeousbarbarian

Hedron Rockworks

Hand-made, hand-carved gemstone dice. Absolutely breathtaking!

instagram.com/hedron.rockworks

Hexed RPG
Incredible swirls of magic and arcane energy with gorgeous clean numbering.
instagram.com/hexed.rpg

Infernal Foundry
Amazing necromancer and hellfire style dice! This is one maker to keep your eye on.
instagram.com/infernalfoundry/

Jodie's Dice Farm
Specialises in eco-friendly Jesmonite dice with goth vibes.
instagram.com/jodiesdicefarm

Level Up Dice
People line up for ages to buy these dice at conventions. And the reason is that they're gorgeous. So many amazing semi-precious stones!
instagram.com/levelupdice

Maluridae Dice
Simple, clean, sparkly and perfect dice. I've seen these in person many times and they are amazing.
instagram.com/maluridae.dice

MerchanDice
Talented Melbourne dice and mould maker and 3D printer.
linktr.ee/MerchanDICEau

Moonshine Dice
Australian dice maker doing incredible inserts, geodes and floral dice sets.
instagram.com/moonshine_dice

The Reliable Rogue
Almost everything they do is amazing. The flames, writing, and potion bottles are divine!
instagram.com/thereliablerogue

R.G. Dice Boutique
Classical artist and painter, these stained glass dice are one of a kind works of art.
instagram.com/rg_diceboutique

Salty Stormtrooper
Awesome dice designer, artist, and leather worker. Amazing, intricate dice masters.
instagram.com/_dam_art

The Shifty Charlatan
Gorgeous colours, shapes and liquid core dice.
instagram.com/shiftycharlatansdice

Transmutation Dice
I had no idea how much I LOVED stained glass dice until I saw this maker.
instagram.com/transmutationdice

Yaniir
Talented designer, artist, jewellery-maker, and "Enchanter of Polyhedral Phylacteries". Don't forget the underscores – "_yaniir_".
instagram.com/_yaniir_/

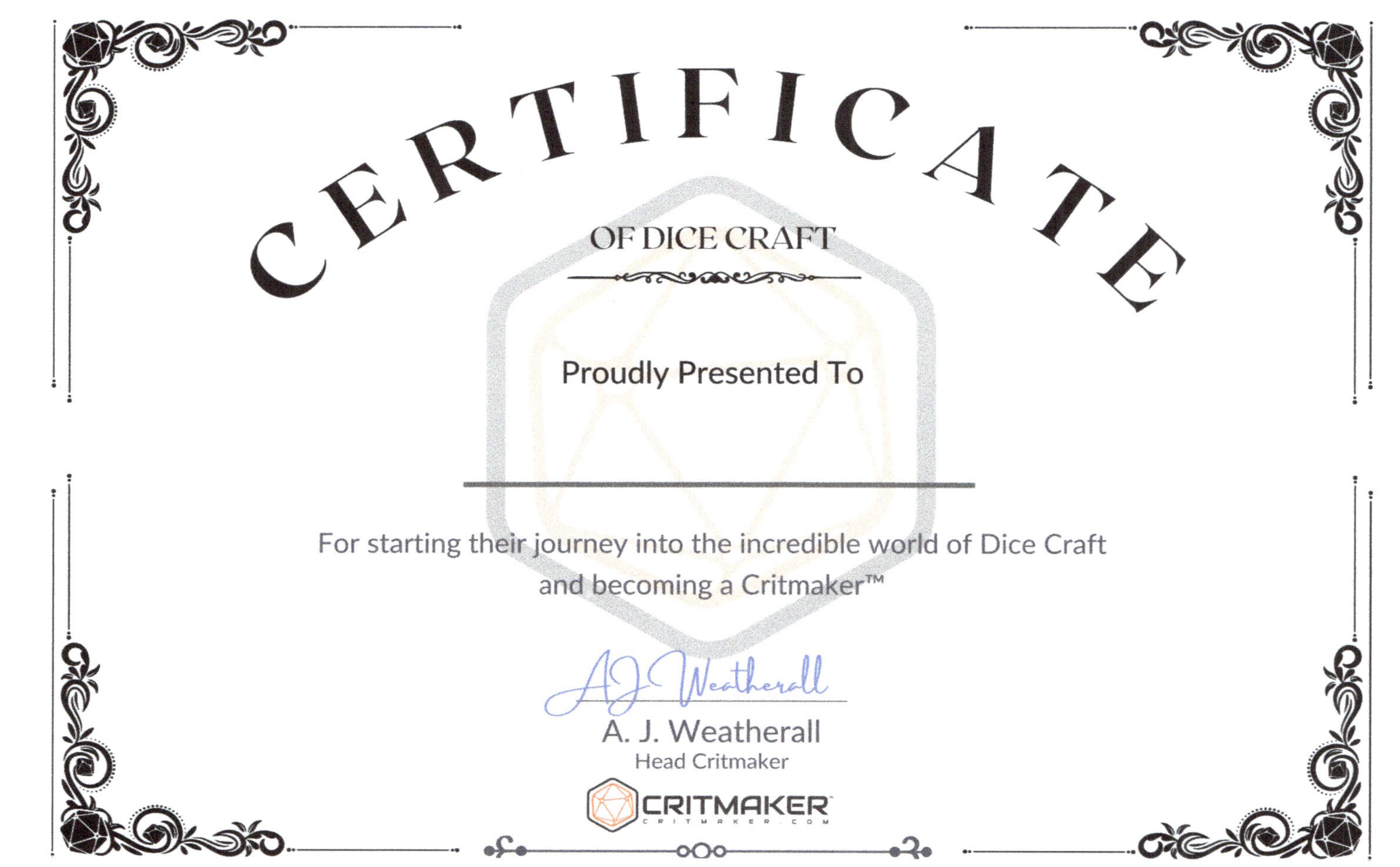

CERTIFICATE
OF DICE CRAFT
Proudly Presented To
For starting their journey into the incredible world of Dice Craft
and becoming a Critmaker™
A. J. Weatherall
Head Critmaker
CRITMAKER
CRITMAKER.COM

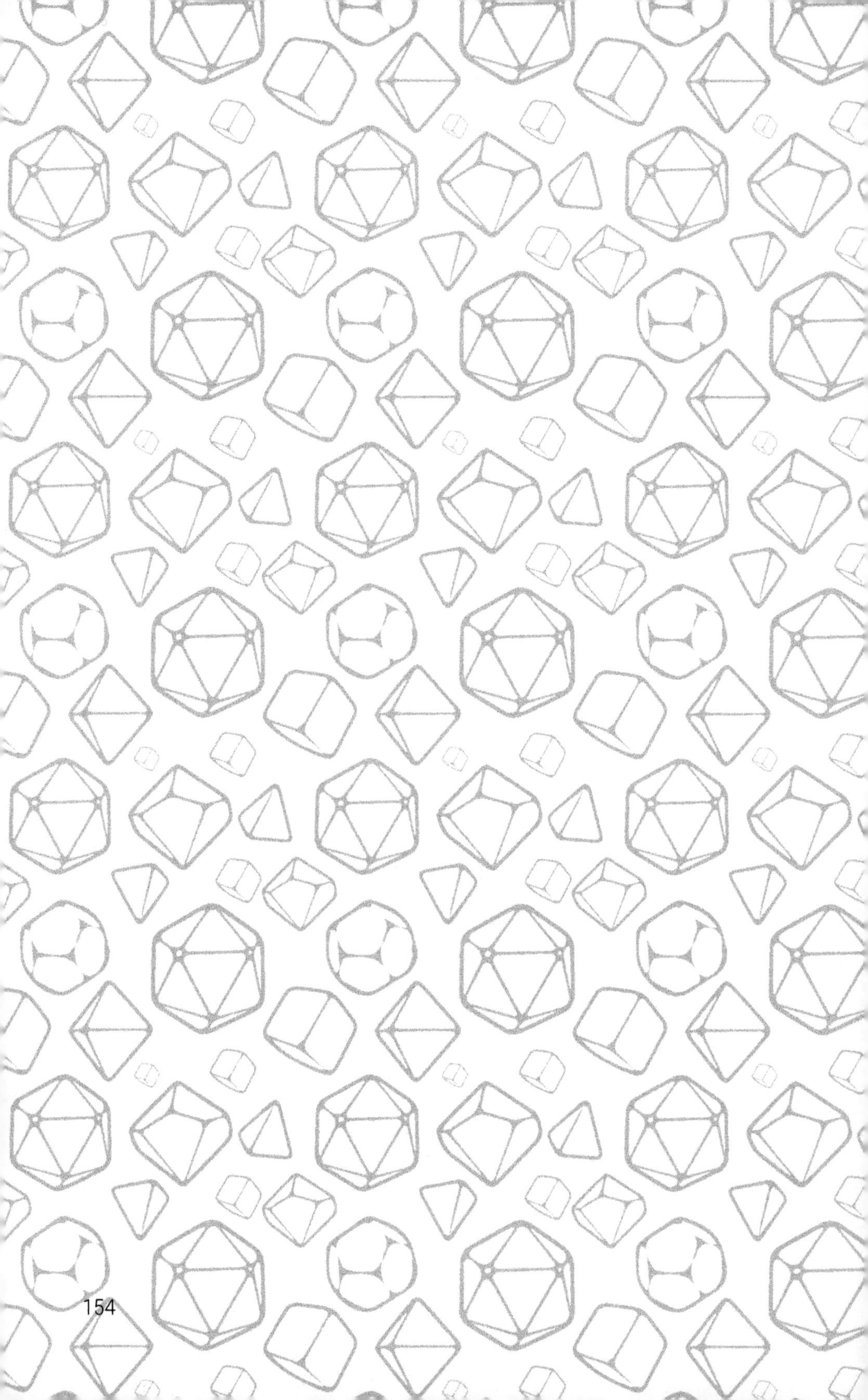

ACKNOWLEDGEMENT

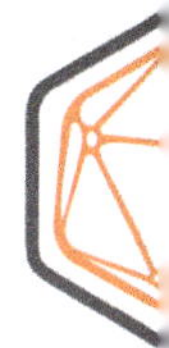

First and foremost, I'd like to publicly appreciate my ever-patient wife, Zoe, who puts up with a kid-ult like me and never bats an eyelid when I discover a new hobby.

To our dear friends and fellow geeks, Tim and Meagan, this book never would have happened without the invitation to join your D&D game. Our fellow adventurers, David and Kasia for being the best party anyone could want and being the sounding board for many of my crazy ideas!

This book wouldn't be the collaborative effort it was without the incredible dice makers who volunteered their images and time to review this book and offer advice. This final version of the guide is so much richer because of your input. So a big thank you (in alphabetical order) to Ailie, Cameron, Christina, Claire, George, Georgina, Jade, Madison, Nichelle, Tim, Urtė and Zoe. You know who you are!

To Rybonator, without your incredible videos, I never would have known what was possible. I'd also like to offer a big thank you to the artisans and makers of the r/DiceMaking community on Reddit and Instagram filling my feeds with beautiful images and great tutorials.

And to you for reading this guide; you have made my dream come true – I hope you got something out of it. Please consider leaving a positive review; we rely on it as an independent author and publisher!

We'd also love to see your creations on our Discord and Instagram page.

MORE FROM CRITMAKER

More than just a companion to the Critmaker™ Guide to Dice Craft, this journal is a tool to help you become a better dice maker.

Each page will help you to uncover your inspiration, visualise your creations and record details of the method you used. After every 10th design, there's a place to reflect on your progress and ask yourself what you've learned and what you can improve on for future designs.

Not only does the journal help you to record your journey and reference your designs later, but it's also a practical way to measure your progress as a Critmaker™.

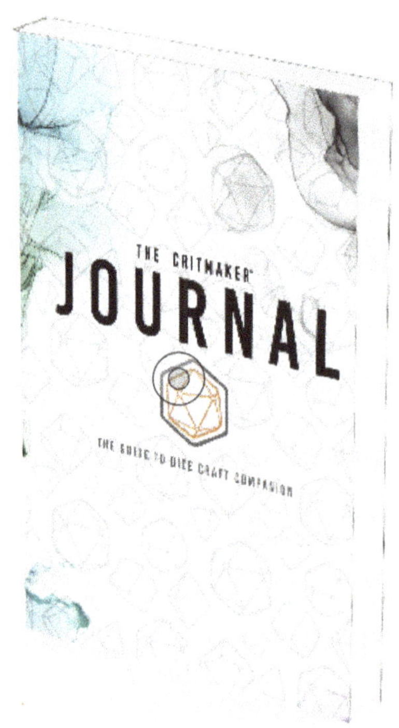

GRAB THE CRITMAKER JOURNAL FROM AMAZON OR CRITMAKER.COM

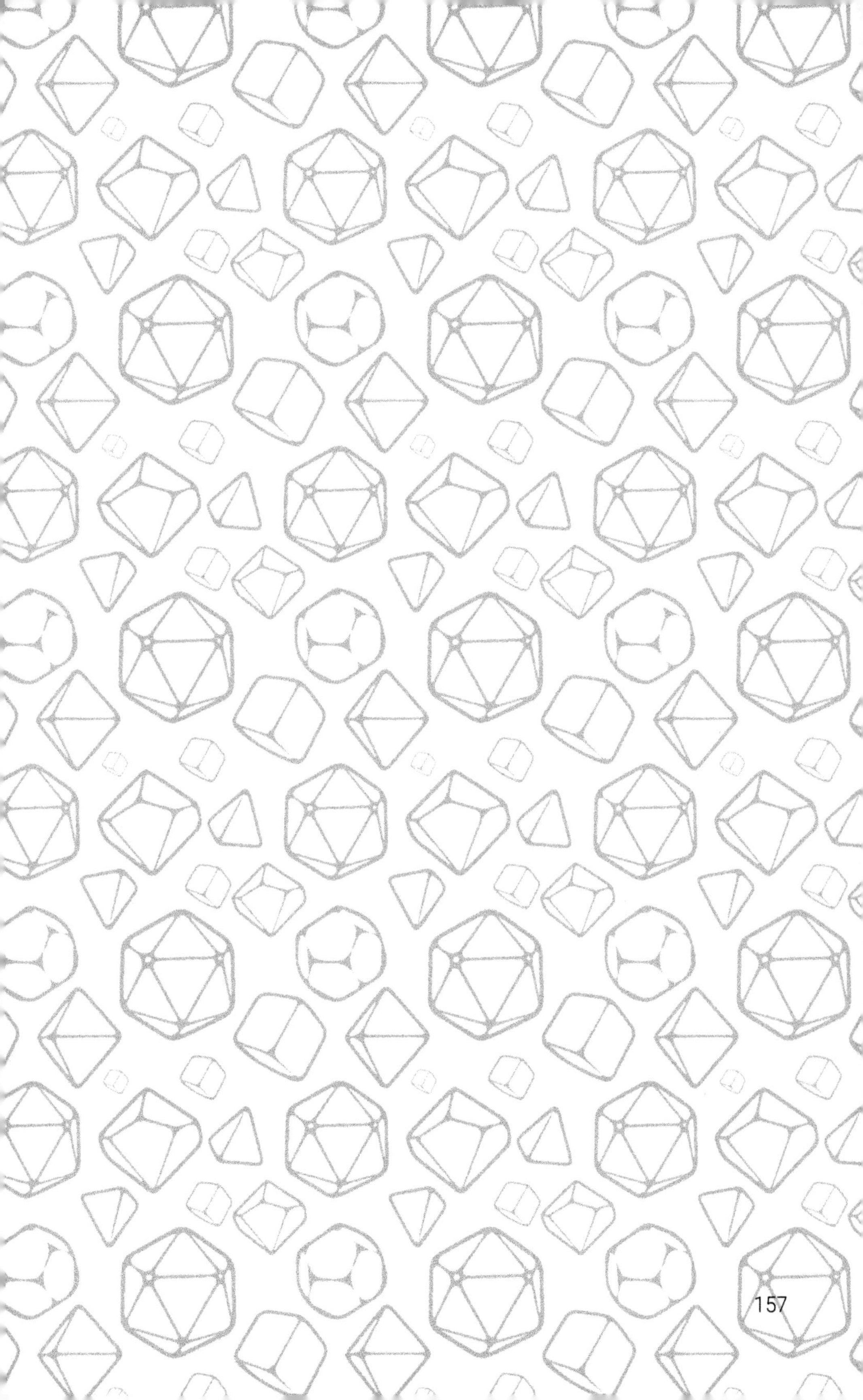

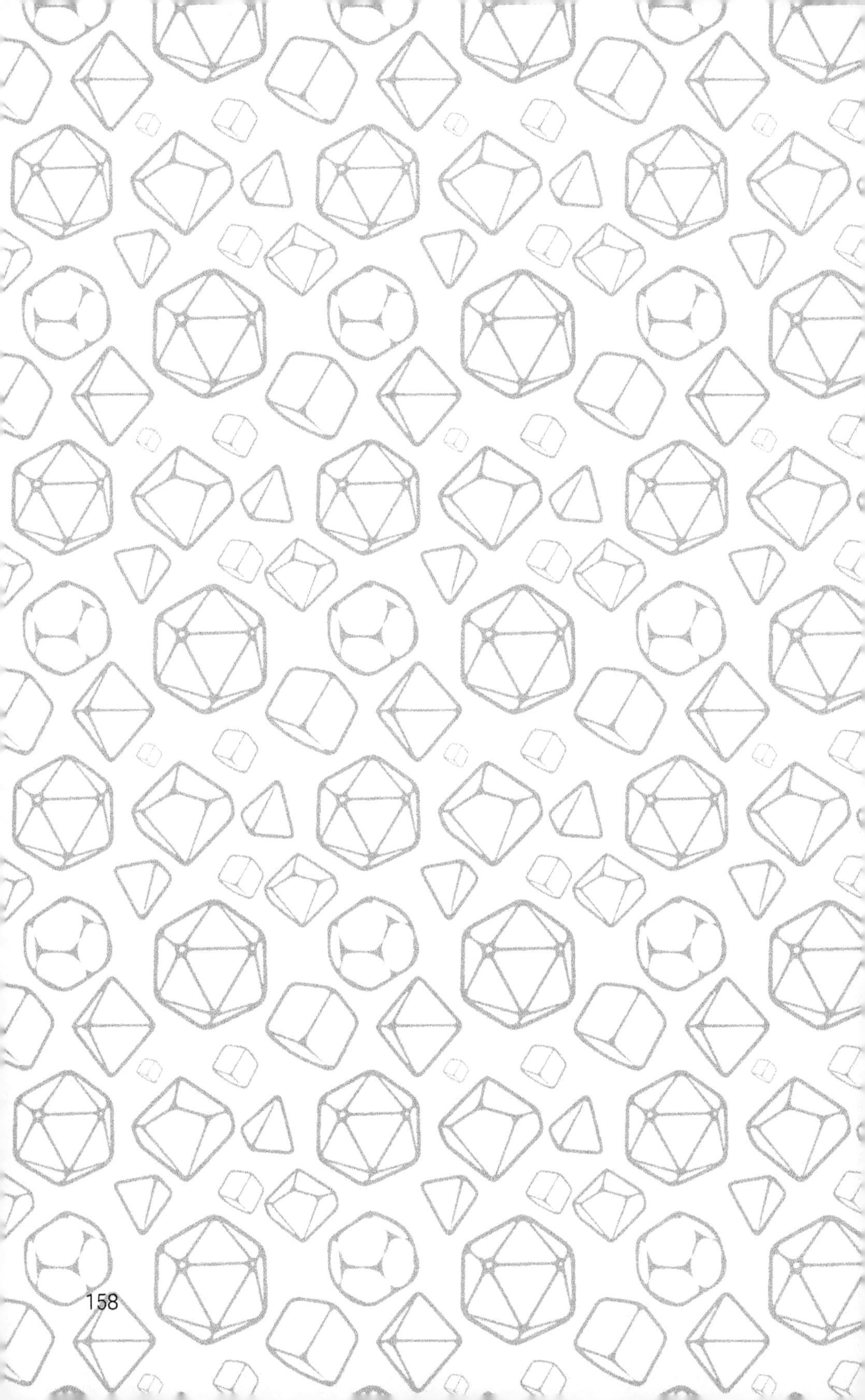